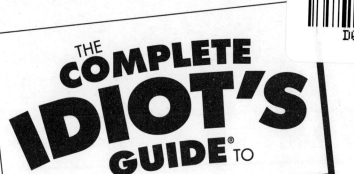

THE COMPLETE IDIOT'S GUIDE® TO

Creating a Web Page and Blog

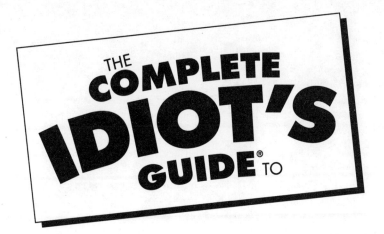
THE
COMPLETE
IDIOT'S
GUIDE® TO

Creating a Web Page and Blog

Sixth Edition

by Paul McFedries

ALPHA

A member of Penguin Group (USA) Inc.

For Karen

Copyright © 2004 by Penguin Group (USA) Inc.

International Standard Book Number: 1-59257-267-7
Library of Congress Catalog Card Number: 2004106748

06 05 04   8 7 6 5 4 3 2 1

Interpretation of the printing code: The rightmost number of the first series of numbers is the year of the book's printing; the rightmost number of the second series of numbers is the number of the book's printing. For example, a printing code of 04-1 shows that the first printing occurred in 2004.

Printed in the United States of America

Note: This publication contains the opinions and ideas of its author. It is intended to provide helpful and informative material on the subject matter covered. It is sold with the understanding that the author and publisher are not engaged in rendering professional services in the book. If the reader requires personal assistance or advice, a competent professional should be consulted.

The author and publisher specifically disclaim any responsibility for any liability, loss, or risk, personal or otherwise, which is incurred as a consequence, directly or indirectly, of the use and application of any of the contents of this book.

Most Alpha books are available at special quantity discounts for bulk purchases for sales promotions, premiums, fund-raising, or educational use. Special books, or book excerpts, can also be created to fit specific needs.

For details, write: Special Markets, Alpha Books, 375 Hudson Street, New York, NY 10014.

Publisher: *Marie Butler-Knight*
Product Manager: *Phil Kitchel*
Senior Managing Editor: *Jennifer Chisholm*
Acquisitions Editor: *Mikal E. Belicove*
Development Editor: *Ginny Bess Munroe*
Production Editor: *Janette Lynn*
Copy Editor: *Anja Mutic-Blessing*
Illustrator: *Chris Eliopoulos*
Cover/Book Designer: *Trina Wurst*
Indexer: *Brad Herriman*
Layout/Proofreading: *Becky Harmon, Donna Martin*

Contents at a Glance

Contents

Foreword

All over the world people create Web pages and have been doing so for years. Some websites are for business, but many are just about people and the things they believe in. Anyone can create a website, if they want to, and the website they create can be about anything they want. Creating a personal website is a great way to express yourself and tell people what you think about any subject you find interesting. It can be about your family, your favorite hobby, or about yourself.

When I first discovered that I could write my own personal web page many years ago, I was thrilled. I scoured the Internet for information on how to do it and taught myself. Over the years I took some online courses to teach me more and have read many books on the subject. I created websites for myself, my friends, and even for some of the organizations I belonged to. I found an art form that I was good at, and loved seeing my code turn into something beautiful and informative right in front of my eyes.

A few years later I started writing a website for About.com and began teaching other people how to create their own personal web pages. It's been very rewarding. I love when people e-mail me to tell me how much my site has helped them. I'm fascinated by the creative, wonderful sites that people can build and maintain with just the right kind of help.

If you bought this book then you are probably ready to create your own website. You are ready to show the world who you are, show off your family, or write about something that has always interested you. In this book you will find everything you need to get started. You will learn HTML, the code used to create web pages, and how to put it all together. This is the kind of book I wish I had years ago when I started writing web pages. It's written in such a way that you feel the author, Paul, is actually talking to you. This book is easy to read and even easier to follow along.

Starting from the beginning and working your way through one step at a time is always the best way to learn anything. That's exactly what *The Complete Idiot's Guide to Creating a Web Page and Blog, Sixth Edition*, helps you do. When I read this book, I felt as though I had written it myself. It starts with teaching you to build a simple web page and what the basic codes are you need to know. As you read through the book, you will be taken one step at a time, and shown examples along the way, of how to add to that basic web page until you have a complete site full of graphics, links, colors, and many other fun things.

When you are finished with the book you will no longer be a beginner. You'll have a fun, informative, productive website that tells the world who you are. Have fun with it. It's only worth it while you like doing it.

—Linda Roeder, About.com's Guide to Personal Web Pages

Linda Roeder is the writer and guide to the Personal Web Pages site on About.com (http://personalweb.about.com). She earned her Bachelor's degree in accounting from Alvernia College (Reading College) in 1996, and she runs another website, on raising boys, which can be found at http://raisingboys.allinfoabout.com.

Introduction

Creating a web page or blog sounds like tough stuff, doesn't it? I mean, have you ever *seen* the code that comprises a web page? It looks as though someone took a bunch of letters, numbers, and symbols, put them through some kind of linguistic blender, and then poured the result onto the web. It's ugly, it's messy, and it's downright intimidating. But it's also one more thing:

It's easy.

Yes, you read that right. Creating web pages and blogs is really quite easy. Actually, let me qualify that: Creating web pages and blogs is easy *if* you approach it in the right way. What's the right way? Starting at the very beginning with the most basic structure of a page, and then slowly working step-by-step through the rest of it, tacking on bits and pieces as you go along. This way you slowly build your HTML knowledge until, before you know it, you have your very own web page for all to see.

The good news is that this step-by-step, piece-by-piece method is exactly the approach I use in this book. To that end, this book doesn't assume you have any previous experience with web page production. All the information is presented in short, easy-to-digest chunks that make building a page fun and easy on the brain.

Sounds great! But why are you calling me an idiot?

Well, when it comes to producing content for the World Wide Web, a "complete idiot" is someone who, despite having the normal complement of gray matter, wouldn't know HTML from H. G. Wells. This is, of course, perfectly normal and, despite what many so-called Internet gurus may tell you, it does not imply any sort of character defect on your part.

So I might as well get one thing straight right off the bat: The fact that you're reading *The Complete Idiot's Guide to Creating a Web Page and Blog* (my, that *is* a mouthful, isn't it?) does *not* make you an idiot. On the contrary, it shows that …

- ◆ You don't take yourself—or any of this web page malarkey—too seriously, so you're willing to have a little irreverent fun as you go along.

- ◆ You're determined to learn this HTML thing, but you don't want to be bothered with a lot of boring, technical details.

- ◆ You realize it doesn't make sense to learn absolutely everything about HTML. You just need to know enough to get your web page or blog up and running.

- ◆ You're smart enough not to spend your days reading five bazillion pages of arcane (and mostly useless) information. You do, after all, have a life to lead.

How This Book Is Set Up

I'm assuming you have a life away from your computer screen, so *The Complete Idiot's Guide to Creating a Web Page and Blog* is set up so you don't have to read it from cover to cover. If you want to know how to add a picture to your web page, for example, just turn to the chapter that covers working with images. (Although, having said that, beginners will want to read at least Chapter 2, "Laying the Foundation: The Basic Structure of a Web Page," before moving on to more esoteric topics.) To make things easier to find, I've organized the book into half a dozen more or less sensible sections.

Part 1: "Creating Your First Web Page and Blog"

After dipping a toe into the web publishing waters with some introductory material in Chapter 1, you then dive right in to the hurly-burly of web page construction. The next five chapters take you step-by-step, piece-by-piece through the process of building a spanking new web page. These chapters build your knowledge of basic HTML slowly and with lots of examples. Then Chapters 7 and 8 show you how to successfully negotiate the big moment: getting your page on the web for your friends and family to admire.

Part 2: "A Grab Bag of Web Page and Blog Wonders"

Part 2 takes you beyond the basics by presenting you with a hodgepodge of web page topics. You get oh-so-simple instructions on web page knickknacks such as image links (Chapter 9), tables (Chapter 10), multimedia (Chapter 11), forms (Chapter 12), and frames (Chapter 13).

Part 3: "Building Your Best Blog"

This part of the book features five chapters designed to help you get your blog off the ground. You learn the basic blog building blocks in Chapter 16. From there, you learn some extra goodies to take your blogging up a notch (Chapter 17); getting and keeping a readership (Chapter 18); learning how to live in harmony with your fellow bloggers (Chapter 19); and making blogging easier by using the available programs and sites (Chapter 20).

Part 4: "High HTML Style: Working with Style Sheets"

Style sheets are the wave of the future in web page design, so Part 4 devotes no less than three chapters to mastering them. I explain the basics in Chapter 21, and then I show you how to wield styles for fonts, colors, and backgrounds (Chapter 15), as well as dimensions, borders, and margins (Chapter 16).

On the companion CD: "Working with JavaScripts"

The two chapters that you'll find on the CD show you how to add tiny little programs to your web pages to give them that interactive boost. Chapter 24 tells you all about this JavaScript thing that everyone always blathers on about. It also gives you quite a few examples of scripts that you can plop right inside your pages. Chapter 25 takes the JavaScript ball and runs with it by showing you a whack of other examples that do all kinds of amazingly useful things.

You Want More? You've Got It!

Happily, there's more to this book than 25 chapters of me yammering away. To put a feather in your HTML cap and to make your page-publishing adventures a bit easier, I've included a few other goodies:

- **Appendix A: Frequently Asked Questions About HTML.** This appendix runs through a few dozen of the most common questions asked by beginning webmasters and, of course, offers simple solutions to each problem.

- **Appendix B: HTML Codes for Cool Characters.** This appendix lists all the HTML codes you can use to incorporate characters such as ¢ in your web page. (This is all explained in more detail in Chapter 3.)

- **Appendix C: The CD: The Webmaster's Toolkit.** The book's major bonus is the CD that's glued onto the back cover. This little plastic Frisbee contains a complete Webmaster's Toolkit with tons of HTML-related doodads, including Chapters 24 and 25, all the HTML examples I use in the book, some sample web pages, HTML programs, lots of graphics you can put in your web page, and tons more. This appendix tells you what's on the CD and where to find it.

- **The Complete Idiot's HTML Tag Reference.** This is also on the CD, and it gives you a complete list of all the HTML tags in the known universe.

- **The Complete Idiot's Style Sheet Reference.** This CD reference runs through all the available style sheet properties, tells you which browsers support them, lists all the possible values, and gives you lots of examples.

Also, as you're trudging through the book, look for the following features that point out important info:

Webmaster Wisdom

These boxes contain notes, tips, and asides that provide you with interesting and useful (at least theoretically!) nuggets of web page lore.

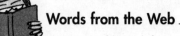

Words from the Web

This type of box defines words and phrases that every budding webmaster needs to know.

Page Pitfalls

These boxes contain web page cautionary tales that warn you of traps to avoid and hurdles to jump over.

Blog On

These asides give you extra tips and tidbits aimed specifically at the blog builders in the crowd.

Acknowledgments (The Giving Credit Where Credit Is Due Department)

Remember the waterfront shack with the sign FRESH FISH SOLD HERE? Of course it's fresh, we're on the ocean. Of course it's for sale, we're not giving it away. Of course it's here, otherwise the sign would be someplace else. The final sign: FISH.

—Peggy Noonan

The wonderful editors at Alpha Books have taken my FRESH FISH SOLD HERE manuscript and turned it into a FISH book. That's good news for you because it means you get a book that has no fluff, chaff, or anything else that isn't bookworthy. This takes skillful editing, and the following folks had the necessary skills to get the job done: acquisitions editor Mikal Belicove, development editor Ginny Bess, production editor Jan Lynn, copy editor Anja Mutic-Blessing, technical editor Luke Seemann, and software specialist Dan Scherf.

The members of the editorial team aren't the only people who had their fingers in this publishing pie. Flip back a few pages and you'll find a list of the designers, illustrators, indexers, and other professionals who worked long and hard to produce this book. I tip my authorial hat to all of them. I'd also like to thank the thousands and thousands of readers who have written to me over the years to offer compliments and suggestions. If this is the best edition yet (and I lack just enough humility to think that it is), it's thanks in no small measure to your willingness to offer a couple of cents' worth.

Trademarks

All terms mentioned in this book that are known to be or are suspected of being trademarks or service marks have been appropriately capitalized. Alpha Books and Penguin Group (USA) Inc. cannot attest to the accuracy of this information. Use of a term in this book should not be regarded as affecting the validity of any trademark or service mark.

Part 1

Creating Your First Web Page and Blog

I know you must be champing at the bit to get started creating a web page or blog to call your own. Well, I'm happy to say, your big moment is just around the corner. The eight chapters here in Part 1 will take you through the entire web page production process, from go to whoa. You'll see that it's really not all that hard to get a page from in here (your computer) to out there (the World Wide Web). When the dust settles, you'll have an actual, honest-to-goodness, "Look, Ma, I'm in cyberspace!" web page. You will be, in short, a full-fledged member of the Royal Order of Webmeisters and the envy of all your pathetic pageless friends.

A Brief HTML Primer

In This Chapter

◆ What in the name of blue blazes is HTML?

◆ A look at what kind of havoc you can wreak with HTML

◆ Answers to pressing HTML questions

◆ A veritable cornucopia of web page and blog examples that show HTML in its best light

Before you go off half-cocked and start publishing pages willy-nilly on the World Wide Web, it helps to have a bit of background on HTML. After all, you wouldn't try to set up shop in a new country without first understanding the local geography and customs and learning a few choice phrases, such as "I am sorry I insulted your sister" and "You don't buy beer, you rent it!"

This chapter gives you a handle on the HTML hoo-ha that seems to be such an integral part of web page and blog construction. What is HTML? Why bother with it? What can you do with it? Why does it sound so darned scary? Will it turn your brain to mush? This chapter answers all these questions and more.

Okay, So Just What Is HTML?

I have some good news, and I have some bad news. The bad news is that HTML stands for—brace yourself—*HyperText Markup Language*. (I'll pause for a sec to let you get the inevitable jargon-induced shudders out of the way.)

The good news, however, is that HTML doesn't stand for Hard To Master Lingo. HTML is, in fact, really a sheep in wolf's clothing: It looks nasty, but it's really quite tame. (And, no, it won't turn even a small part of your brain to mush.) Learning basic HTML—which is what 90 percent of all web pages and blogs use—isn't much tougher than reciting the alphabet, and it's way easier than programming your VCR. (This is, I'm sure, good news for those of you who sport that scarlet letter of modern technology: the flashing 12:00 on your VCR clock.)

That's all well and good, Author Boy, but HyperText Markup Language isn't exactly a phrase that trips lightly off the tongue; it really sounds intimidating.

Well, you're right, it does. So, in the spirit of self-help books everywhere, you need to face your fears and look HTML squarely in the eye. Specifically, you need to examine what each element of the phrase "HyperText Markup Language" means in plain English:

◆ **HyperText.** As I'm sure you know, a *link* is a special word or phrase in a web page that "points" to another web page. When you click one of these links, your browser transports you immediately to the other page, no questions asked. The eggheads who invented the web actually used the highfalutin term *hypertext link* for this special text (the prefix *hyper-* means "beyond"). Because these hypertext links are really the distinguishing feature of the World Wide Web, web pages are often known as *hypertext documents*. So HTML has the word "HyperText" in it because you use it to create these hypertext documents. (It would be just as accurate to call it WPML—Web Page Markup Language.)

◆ **Markup.** My dictionary defines "markup" as (among other things) "detailed stylistic instructions written on a manuscript that is to be typeset." For our purposes, I can rephrase this definition as follows: "detailed stylistic instructions typed into a text document that is to be published on the World Wide Web." That's HTML in a nutshell. It has a few simple codes for detailing things such as making text bold or italic, creating bulleted lists, inserting images, and, of course, defining links. You just type these codes into the appropriate places in an ordinary text document and the web browser software does the dirty work of translating the codes. The result? Your page is displayed the way you want, automatically.

♦ **Language.** This word might be the most misleading of them all. Many people interpret this to mean that HTML is a programming language, and they wash their hands of the whole thing right off the bat. "You mean I gotta learn *programming* to get my two cents worth on the web?" Not a chance, Vance. HTML has nothing, I repeat, *nothing* whatsoever to do with computer programming. Rather, HTML is a "language" in the sense that it has a small collection of two- and three-letter combinations and words that you use to specify styles such as bold and italic.

What Can You Do with HTML?

All right, so HTML isn't the Hideous, Terrible, Mega-Leviathan that its name might suggest, but rather a Harmless, Tame, Mini-Lapdog. What can you do with such a creature? Well, lots of things, actually. After all, people aren't flocking to the web because it's good for their health. Just the opposite, in fact. They're surfing 'til they drop because the web presents them with an attractive and easily navigated source of information and entertainment (or *infotainment*, as the wags like to call it). It's HTML that adds the attractiveness and ease of navigation. To see what I mean, the next few sections take you through examples of the basic HTML elements.

Words from the Web
Creating something (such as a web page or blog) for no other reason than the sheer fact that you *can* create it is called **inverse vandalism**.

You Can Format Text

A high Jolts Per Minute (JPM) count is what turns the crank of your average web-surfing dude and dudette. However, nothing generates fewer jolts (and is harder on the eyes to boot) than plain, unadorned text. To liven things up, you need to use different sizes and styles of type for your web page text. Happily, HTML is no slouch when it comes to dressing up text for the prom:

♦ You can display your web prose as bold.

♦ You can emphasize text with italics.

♦ You can make text look as though it was produced by a typewriter.

♦ You can display text using different colors, such as red, white, and blue.

♦ You can use different font sizes for words and even individual characters.

Figure 1.1 shows examples of each kind of style. (I show you how to use HTML to format web page text in Chapter 3.)

Figure 1.1

Some examples of HTML text styles.

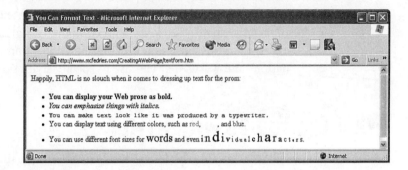

You Can Create Lists of Things

If you're presenting information on your web page or log, it helps if you can display your data in a way that makes sense and is easy to read. In some cases, this means arranging the data in lists, such as a numbered list or a bulleted list (see Figure 1.1 for an example of the latter). I fill you in on how to use HTML to create these and other kinds of lists in Chapter 4.

You Can Set Up Links to Other Pages

Web sessions aren't true surfin' safaris unless you take a flying leap or two. I'm speaking, of course, of selecting links that take you to the far-flung corners of the web world.

You can give the readers of your web pages or blogs the same kicks by using HTML to create links anywhere on a page. You can set up three kinds of links:

- Links to another page of yours.
- Links to a different location in the same page. (This is useful for pages that contain several sections; you could, for example, put a "table of contents" at the top of the page that consists of links to the various sections in the document.)
- Links to any page anywhere on the web.

There are even plenty of sites that exist only to provide a web "mouse potato" (like a couch potato, only with a computer) with huge lists of links to pages that are informative, entertaining, or simply "cool."

You find out how to use HTML to sprinkle links all over your web pages in Chapter 5.

You Can Insert Images

Fancy text effects, lists, and lots of links go a long way toward making a web page a hit. But for a real crowd-pleasing page, you want to throw in an image or two. It could be a picture of yourself, a drawing the kids made, some clip art, or any of the images that are on this book's CD. As long as you have the image in a graphics file, you can use HTML to position the image appropriately on your page. I give you the details (as well as info on the types of graphics files you can use) in Chapter 6.

Figure 1.2 shows an example page with an image. This is a page from my Word Spy blog site (wordspy.com), and the image is used to illustrate a point from the text.

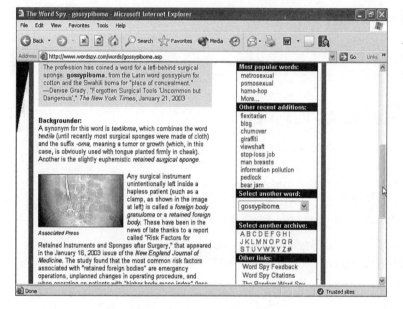

Figure 1.2

A well-chosen image or two can do wonders for otherwise drab web pages or blogs.

You Can Format Information in Tables

If your web page needs to show data formatted in rows and columns, you could try using tabs and spaces to line things up all nice and neat. However, you'll groan in disappointment when you view the page in a browser. Why? Because HTML reduces multiple spaces to a single space, and it ignores tabs completely! This sounds like perverse behavior, but it's just the way HTML was set up.

You're not out of luck, though. You can use HTML to create tables to slot your data into slick-looking rows and columns. Figure 1.3 shows an example of a table. I tell you how to use HTML to construct tables in Chapter 10.

Figure 1.3

Tables: a blessing for neat freaks everywhere.

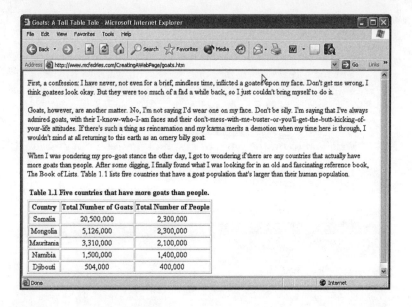

The following text appears within the browser window image:

First, a confession: I have never, not even for a brief, mindless time, inflicted a goatee upon my face. Don't get me wrong, I think goatees look okay. But they were too much of a fad a while back, so I just couldn't bring myself to do it.

Goats, however, are another matter. No, I'm not saying I'd wear one on my face. Don't be silly. I'm saying that I've always admired goats, with their I-know-who-I-am faces and their don't-mess-with-me-buster-or-you'll-get-the-butt-kicking-of-your-life attitudes. If there's such a thing as reincarnation and my karma merits a demotion when my time here is through, I wouldn't mind at all returning to this earth as an ornery billy goat.

When I was pondering my pro-goat stance the other day, I got to wondering if there are any countries that actually have more goats than people. After some digging, I finally found what I was looking for in an old and fascinating reference book, The Book of Lists. Table 1.1 lists five countries that have a goat population that's larger than their human population.

Table 1.1 Five countries that have more goats than people.

Country	Total Number of Goats	Total Number of People
Somalia	20,500,000	2,300,000
Mongolia	5,126,000	2,300,000
Mauritania	3,310,000	2,100,000
Namibia	1,500,000	1,400,000
Djibouti	504,000	400,000

Pages from All Walks of Web Life

Now that you've got some idea of what HTML can do, wouldn't you like to see the rabbits various web magicians have pulled from their HTML hats? To that end, the next few sections present some real-world examples of web pages and blogs that show you what you can do with a little HTML know-how. In fact, a reader of previous editions of this book created all of the pages featured in these sections!

Of course, these examples represent only the smallest subset of the web world. There are billions of web pages and blogs out there, and each one is like a digital fingerprint—a unique expression of its creator's individuality.

The Personal Touch: Personal Home Pages

The simplest, and probably the most common, type of web page is the personal home page. This is a page that an individual sets up to tell the web world a little bit about himself. They're the web equivalent of those "Hi! My Name is…" stickers that people wear at parties and receptions. They range from warm and fuzzy ("Welcome, friend, to my home page"), to downright vainglorious ("Let me tell you everything there is to know about me"), to frighteningly personal ("Dear diary…"). Figure 1.4 shows an excellent personal home page created by a reader named, more than a little appropriately, Gordon Reeder.

Words from the Web

A website that's run by an expert in a particular field and that contains lots of useful, accurate information is called a guru site.

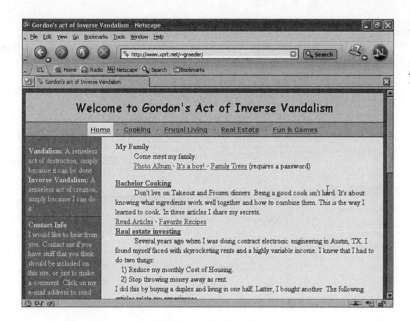

The Blog Revolution

I hinted in the previous section that some personal pages are diarylike. In fact, there are *several* sites that maintain digital diaries—so many that this type of site now has its own category, called a *web log* or, most often, just a *blog*.

A blog can be whatever you want it to be, but most blogs satisfy some of the following criteria:

- ♦ It must contain multiple entries—or *posts* as they're often called in blogland— listed in reverse-chronological order, with the most recent on top.

- ♦ The posts should cover a particular topic.

- ♦ The page should be updated frequently; several times a day is best, but at least a few times per week.

- ♦ The page should link to and comment on other sites and other blogs. The earliest web logs, after all, were "logs" of where a person had been on the web.

For most blogs, the "topic" is the blogger (that is, the person who maintains the site). These personal blogs are by far the most common, and the posts cover everything from what's going on in the blogger's life to interesting news tidbits found by the blogger, to the blogger's personal opinions on politics or ice cream. An excellent example of this kind of blog is the Beli-Blog run by Mikal Belicove, who is the acquisitions editor for this book. Figure 1.5 shows a typical entry from the always-interesting Beli-Blog.

Figure 1.5

The subject of most blogs is the blogger himself.

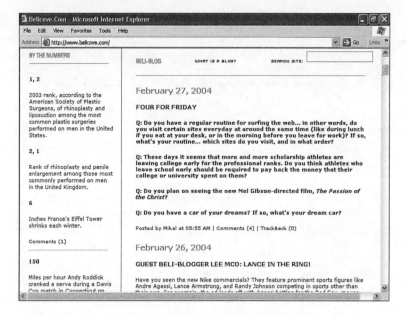

Other blogs are dedicated to particular topics, such as politics, the media, or technology. In these kinds of blogs, the blogger's goal is to illuminate the underlying topic by posting related blurbs that are interesting, informative, or controversial (some rare and talented bloggers manage to be all three).

My Word Spy site, which is dedicated to new words and to old words that are being used in new ways, contains an example of such a blog. Figure 1.6 shows the site in action.

Figure 1.6

Other blogs focus on a particular topic.

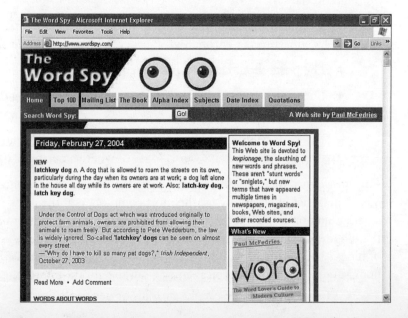

Hobbyists Do It Themselves with HTML

Sometimes the hardest thing about putting together a web page or blog is coming up with something to say. (Although there are plenty of garrulous guys and gals out there for whom this is definitely not a problem!) So, what's a body to do about a bad case of web writer's block? Well, lots of people go with what they know: They talk about their hobbies and interests. Hey, it makes sense. You're more likely to sound enthusiastic and excited about a topic you're keen on, so you're also more likely to hold your reader's interest. You can do lots of things to fill up your page—introduce the hobby to novices, talk about how you got started, show some samples of your work (depending on the hobby, of course), include links to related web pages, and much more.

As you might imagine, there's no shortage of hobby-related pages on the World Wide Web. You can find info on everything from amateur radio to beekeeping to wood-working. Figure 1.7 shows a gardening page put together by reader Paula Graham.

Figure 1.7

Hobby pages abound on the web.

Corporate Culture Hits the Web

In the late 1990s, one of the biggest engines that drove the growth of the web was the influx of businesses scrambling to get a "presence" in cyberspace. Companies from mom 'n' pop shops to Fortune 500 behemoths set up on the web in anticipation of, well, *something*. Nobody was quite sure why they needed a website, but they were happy to put one up, just in case something *big* happened one of these days. Hey, who can blame them? With all the Internet hype that was floating around, no self-respecting CEO was going to be caught with his or her pants down.

Many readers of previous editions of this book have leveraged their new HTML skills to build pages for their companies. And a few even managed to get paid to create sites for other companies! For example, Figure 1.8 shows a nice website crafted by reader David Colliver for his BMC Weddings client.

Figure 1.8

With your newfound HTML skills, you can build pages for businesses that want a place in cyberspace.

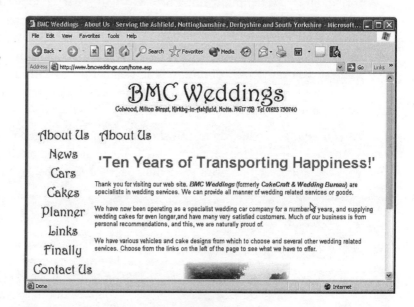

Helping Hands: Government and Public Service Pages

While Big Business was rushing to get on the web, you better believe Big Brother wasn't going to be left behind. Yes, governments—local, state, and federal—have put up web pages to beat the band. Granted, many of these sites are quite useful. You can use them to contact representatives, read government reports and studies, do research, renew your license, and even file taxes. Some of the pages are even—gasp!—creative.

There are also many pages devoted to public service organizations, nonprofits, and other institutions that are in the business of helping people. A good example is Parent Help U.S.A., a site designed by reader Nancy Palmer and shown in Figure 1.9.

Figure 1.9

Parent Help U.S.A.'s home page.

The Least You Need to Know

♦ HTML sounds evil, but it's really just a relatively small collection of codes that tell the browser how to display text, where to put images, how to set up links, and so on.

♦ With HTML, you can format text using bold, italics, colors, and sizes, create lists and links, insert images, and build tables.

♦ Tens of thousands of my readers have cobbled together handsome and creative pages and blogs of their own, so there's no reason in the world why *you* can't do it, too.

Chapter 2

Laying the Foundation: The Basic Structure of a Web Page or Blog

In This Chapter

- A laundry list of things you need to get started
- A quick course on tags, the building blocks of HTML
- The basic blueprint for all web pages and blogs
- How to add a title, toss in some text, and split your prose into paragraphs
- Your field guide to the most fundamental of HTML flora and fauna

This book's goal is to help you create your own web pages or blogs and thus lay claim to a little chunk of personal cyberspace real estate: a home page away from home, if you will. Before you can live in this humble abode, however, you have to "pour the concrete" that serves as the foundation for the rest of your digital domicile. In this chapter, I show you a few HTML basics that constitute the underlying structure of all web pages and blogs.

Getting Started

As you saw in Chapter 1, some web pages and blogs look truly spectacular. To achieve these impressive effects, you might think you need to stretch a fancy word processing or page layout program to its limits. Or you might think you have to rush out and spend big bucks for some kind of highfalutin "HTML generator" that's designed specifically for cranking out web pages. Nah, you're way off. All you really need for creating a basic page or blog is a lowly text editor. Yes, even a brain-dead program such as Windows Notepad is more than adequate for doing the HTML thing.

Surely a plain old run-of-the-mill text editor won't let me create anything resembling those beautiful pages I see on the web.

Yes, it will—and stop calling me "Shirley." The vast majority of all the web pages in the world are really just simple text files.

So why in the name of Sam Hill do those pages look so good? Text files I've seen have been ugly with a capital Ugh!

The web's beauty secret is that it's actually the web browsers that determine how a page looks. When you surf to a web page, the browser reads the text, scours the file for HTML markings, and then displays the page accordingly. So, for example, you can mark inside your text file that you want a certain word to appear as bold. When the browser comes to that part of the document, it goes right ahead and formats the word in a bold font. The browser handles all this dirty work behind the scenes, and you never have to give it a second thought (or even a first thought, for that matter).

First, Crank Out a New Text File

So, to get to the point at long last, your first step whenever you want to create a web page is to create a text file. To do that, not surprisingly, you need to fire up your favorite text editor:

- For most versions of Windows, you start the Notepad text editor by selecting **Start, Programs, Accessories, Notepad.**

- If you have Windows XP, you launch Notepad by selecting **Start, All Programs, Accessories, Notepad.**

- Mac fans can use the SimpleText program, the icon for which is in the **Applications** folder on their hard drive.

- If you have another text editor, launch it the way you normally do.

Both Notepad and SimpleText display a brand-new text document automatically when you start each program. If you ever need to start a new document by hand, select the **File, New** command.

If you prefer, it's okay to use a word processor such as WordPad, the program that comes with most versions of Windows, or Microsoft Word. Again, launch the program and a new document will be staring at you in a few seconds (or choose **File, New** to do it yourself). If you take the word processor route, please keep the following caveats in mind:

- ◆ **Don't use the program's commands to format the document in any way (such as adding italics or centering paragraphs).** Not only do you run the risk of having a browser choke on these extra formatting codes, but every web browser on the face of the earth will completely ignore your efforts. Remember, the only way to make a browser do your bidding and display your web page properly is to use the appropriate HTML codes.

- ◆ **Don't save the file in the word processor's native format.** Be sure to save the file as pure text, sometimes referred to as ASCII text. More on this in a sec.

Notes About Saving HTML Files

While slaving away on the text file that will become your web page, make sure you practice safe computing. That is, make sure you save your work regularly. However, from the thousands of notes that I've received from readers, I can tell you that the number-one thing that trips up wet-behind-the-ears webmeisters is improperly saving their HTML files. To help you easily leap these saving hurdles, here are a few notes to pore over:

- ◆ **The Save command.** You save a file by selecting the program's **File, Save** command. The first time you do this with a new file, the **Save As** dialog box shows up for work. You use this dialog box to specify three things: the file name, the file type, and the file's location on your hard disk. The next few notes discuss some tidbits about the name and type.

- ◆ **Use the right file extension.** For garden-variety web pages, your file names must end with either the .htm or the .html file extension (for example, mypage.html). Therefore, when you name your file, be sure to specify either .htm or .html.

Webmaster Wisdom

Many new HTMLers get confused about whether to use .htm or .html when naming their files. Actually, you're free to use either one because it doesn't make any difference.

♦ **Use lowercase file names only.** The majority of web servers (computers that store web pages) are downright finicky when it comes to uppercase letters versus lowercase letters. For example, the typical server thinks that index.html and INDEX.HTML are two different files. It's dumb, I know. So, to be safe, always enter your file names using only lowercase letters.

♦ **Don't use spaces.** Most versions of Windows and the Mac are happy to deal with file names that include spaces. Internet Explorer, too, is space-savvy. However, Netscape gets *really* confused if it comes upon any file name that has one or more spaces. So, to be safe, avoid using spaces in your file names. If you want to separate words in file and directory names, use an underscore (_) or a hyphen (-).

♦ **Use the right file type.** While in the Save As dialog box, you need to select the correct "file type" for your HTML file. How you do this depends on what program you're using:

If you're using Notepad: Use the **Save as type** list to select **All Files (*.*).** This ensures that Notepad uses your .htm or .html extension (and not its normal .txt extension).

If you're using Windows WordPad: Use the **Save as type** list to select **Text Document.** You also need to surround your file name with quotation marks (for example, "index.html") to ensure that WordPad uses your .htm or .html extension.

If you're using Microsoft Word: Use the **Save as type** list to select **Text Only (*.txt).** Again, you need to surround your file name with quotation marks.

♦ When you've done all that, click **Save** in the Save As dialog box to save the file. (If you're using WordPad, the program might ask if you're sure you want to save the file in "Text-Only format." Say "Duh!" and click **Yes.**)

The Edit-Save-Browse Cycle

By now you've probably figured out the biggest problem associated with fashioning a web page out of a text file: There's no way to know what the page will look like after it's been foisted on to the web! Fortunately, all is not lost. Most browsers are more than happy to let you load a text file right from the confines of your computer's hard disk. This means you can test drive your page without first having to put it on the web. So here's the basic cycle you'll use to build your pages:

1. In your text editor or word processor, either start a new file (if one isn't started for you already) or use the **File, Open** command to open an existing file. (If you're opening an existing HTML file in Microsoft Word, you need to select the **View, HTML Source** command to see the tags.)

2. Add some text and HTML stuff (I'll define what this "stuff" is in the next section) to your file.

3. Select the program's **File, Save** command to save the file using the points I mentioned above.

4. Load the file into your browser of choice to see how things look. As a public service, here are the appropriate instructions for loading a file from your hard disk using the Big Two browsers:

   ♦ In Internet Explorer for Windows, select the **File** menu's **Open** command (or press **Ctrl+O**), click the **Browse** button in the Open dialog box that appears, and then pick out the file you need. You can reload the file by selecting the **View** menu's **Refresh** command, or by pressing **F5**.

   ♦ In Internet Explorer for the Mac, select the **File, Open File** command (or press ⌘**+O**) and then use the Open dialog box to choose your file. You can reload the page by selecting **View, Refresh,** or pressing ⌘**+R**.

   ♦ In Netscape Navigator 4, pull down the **File** menu, select the **Open Page** command (or you can press **Ctrl+O**), click the **Choose File** button, and then find the file by using the Open dialog box that appears. To reload the file, pull down the **View** menu and select **Reload** (or press **Ctrl+R**).

   ♦ In Netscape 7, select **File, Open File** (or press **Ctrl+O**) and then use the Open File dialog box. To reload, select **View, Reload,** or **Ctrl+R**.

> **Webmaster Wisdom**
>
> When you run the **File, Open** command, the Open dialog box probably won't show your HTML files. To see them, use the **Files of type** list to select **All Documents (*.*)** (Some programs use **All Files (*.*)** instead).

> **Page Pitfalls**
>
> If you find that Netscape stubbornly refuses to update your edited page, give Netscape a kick in the pants by exiting the program and then restarting it. Alternatively, hold down the Shift key and click the Reload button.

5. Lather. Rinse. Repeat steps 2 and 3. Note that after the file is loaded in the browser, you need only choose the program's **Reload** command to see the effects of your changes.

Tag Daze—Understanding HTML's Tags

As I mentioned earlier, the magic of the web is wrought by browser programs that read text files and then decipher the HTML nuggets that you've sprinkled hither and thither. These HTML tidbits are markers—called *tags*—that spell out how you want things to look. For example, if you want a word on your page to appear in bold text, you surround that word with the appropriate tags for boldfacing text.

In general, tags use the following format:

```
<TAG>The text to be affected by the tag</TAG>
```

The *TAG* part is a code (usually a one- or two-letter abbreviation, but sometimes an entire word) that specifies the type of effect you want. You always surround these codes with angle brackets <>; the brackets tell the web browser that it's dealing with a chunk of HTML and not just some random text.

For example, the tag for bold is <B>. So if you want the phrase "BeDazzler Home Page" to appear in bold, you type the following into your document:

```
<B>BeDazzler Home Page</B>
```

The first <B> says to the browser, in effect, "Listen up, Browser Boy! You know the text that comes after this? Be a good fellow and display it in bold." This continues until the browser reaches the </B>. The slash (/) defines this as an *end tag*, which lets the browser know it's supposed to stop what it's doing. So the </B> tells the browser, "Okay, okay. Ixnay on the oldbay!" As you'll see, there are tags for lots of other effects, including italics, paragraphs, headings, page titles, links, and lists. HTML is just the sum total of all these tags.

Page Pitfalls

One of the most common mistakes that rookie web weavers make is to forget the slash (/) that identifies a tag as an end tag. If your page looks wrong when you view it in a browser, a missing slash is the first thing you should look for. The second thing you should look for is another common error: using the backslash (\). Zees ees verboten in zee HTML!

And Now, Some Actual HTML

Okay, you're ready to get down to some brass HTML tacks. (Halle-freakin'-lujah, I hear you saying.) You'll begin by cobbling together a few HTML tags that constitute the underlying skeleton of all web pages and blogs.

Your HTML files will always lead off with the <HTML> tag. This tag doesn't do a whole heckuva lot except tell any web browser that tries to read the file that it's dealing with a file that contains HTML knickknacks. Similarly, the last line in your document will always be the corresponding end tag: </HTML>. You can think of this end tag as the HTML equivalent for "The End." So each of your web pages will start off with this:

```
<HTML>
```

and end with this:

```
</HTML>
```

The next items serve to divide the page into two sections: the header and the body. The header section is like an introduction to the page. Web browsers use the header to glean various types of information about the page. Although a number of items can appear in the header section, the only one that makes any real sense at this early stage is the title of the page, which I talk about in the next section.

To define the header, add a <HEAD> tag and a </HEAD> tag immediately below the <HTML> tag you typed in earlier. So, your web page should now look like this:

```
<HTML>
<HEAD>
</HEAD>
</HTML>
```

Webmaster Wisdom _____

It makes absolutely no difference if you enter your tag names in uppercase letters or lowercase letters. Uppercase letters are easier to read and to distinguish from regular text, so that's the style I use in this book. Note, however, that the latest HTML standard suggests that all HTML tags be entered using lowercase letters. For this reason, you might want to get into the habit of using lowercase letters in your tags.

Page Pitfalls

Another common page error is to include two or more copies of these basic tags (particularly the <BODY> tag). For best results, make sure you use each of these six basic structural tags only one time on each page.

The body section is where you enter the text and other fun stuff that the browser will actually display. To define the body, you place a <BODY> tag and a </BODY> tag after the header section (that is, below the </HEAD> tag), as follows:

```
<HTML>
<HEAD>
</HEAD>
<BODY>
</BODY>
</HTML>
```

Hmm. It's not exactly a work of art, is it? On the excitement scale, these opening moves rank right up there with watching the grass grow and tuning in to C-SPAN on a slow news day. Let's just file this stuff in the "Necessary Evils" section and move on to more interesting things.

A Page by Any Other Name: Adding a Title

If you try loading your web page or blog into a browser, you'll just get a whole lot of nothingness because you haven't given the browser anything meaty that it can sink its teeth into. The first snack you can offer a hungry browser program is the title of the web page. The page's title is just what you might think it is: the overall name of the page (not to be confused with the name of the file you're creating). When a person views the page, the title appears in the title bar of the browser's window.

Webmaster Wisdom

To relieve some of the inevitable boredom of these early stages of web page creation, you'll find some help on the CD that comes with this book. I've included a file named **skeleton.htm** that contains all the tags that make up the bare bones of a web page. You can use this file as a template each time you start a new web page.

The <TITLE> Tag

To define a title, you surround the title text with the <TITLE> and </TITLE> tags. For example, if you want the title of your page to be "My Home Sweet Home Page," you enter it as follows:

```
<TITLE>My Home Sweet Home Page</TITLE>
```

Note that you always place the title inside the head section, so your basic HTML document now looks like this:

```
<HTML>
<HEAD>
<TITLE>My Home Sweet Home Page</TITLE>
</HEAD>
<BODY>
</BODY>
</HTML>
```

Figure 2.1 shows this document loaded into the Windows version of Internet Explorer. Notice how the title appears in the browser's title bar.

The page title

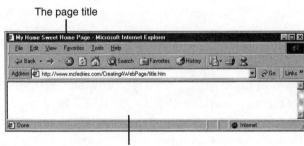

The body text will appear here.

Figure 2.1

Most Windows web browsers display the title in the title bar (duh).

Title Do's and Don'ts

Here are a few things to keep in mind when thinking of a title for your page:

♦ Do make sure your title describes what the page or blog is all about.

♦ Don't make your title too long. If you do, the browser might chop it off because there's not enough room to display it in the title bar. Fifty or sixty characters are usually the max.

♦ Do use titles that make sense when someone views them out of context. For example, if someone really likes your page or blog, that person might add it to his or her list of favorites or bookmarks (hey, it could happen). The browser displays the page title in the favorites list, so it's important that the title makes sense when that person looks at the bookmarks later on.

♦ Don't use titles that are cryptic or vague. Titling a page "Link #42" or "A Blog" might make sense to you, but your readers might not appreciate it.

Fleshing Out Your Page with Text

With your page title firmly in place, you can now think about putting some flesh on your web page's bones by entering the text you want to appear in the body of the page. For the most part, you can simply type the text between the <BODY> and </BODY> tags, like this:

```
<HTML>
<HEAD>
<TITLE>My Home Sweet Home Page</TITLE>
</HEAD>
<BODY>
This text appears in the body of the web page.
</BODY>
</HTML>
```

Before you start typing willy-nilly, however, there are a few things you should know:

- ◆ You might think you can line things up and create some interesting effects by stringing together two or more spaces. Ha! Web browsers chew up all those extra spaces and spit them out into the nether regions of cyberspace. Why? Well, the philosophy of the web is that you can use only HTML tags to lay out a document. So, a run of multiple spaces (or white space, as it's called) is ignored. (There are a couple of tricks you can use to get around this, however. I tell you about them in the next chapter.)

- ◆ Tabs also fall under the rubric of white space. You can enter tabs all day long, but the browser ignores them completely.

- ◆ Another thing that browsers like to ignore is the carriage return. It might sound reasonable to the likes of you and me that pressing **Enter** starts a new paragraph, but that's not so in the HTML world. I talk more about this in the next section.

- ◆ If HTML documents are just plain text, does that mean you're out of luck if you need to use characters such as ©, ™, and ¶? Luckily, no, you're not. HTML has special codes for these kinds of characters, and I talk about them in the next chapter.

CAUTION

Page Pitfalls

Note, too, that the angle bracket characters (< and >) can't be displayed directly in HTML pages because the browser uses them to identify tags. Again, if you need to use them, I show you some special codes in the next chapter that get the job done.

♦ Word processor users, it bears repeating here that it's not worth your bother to format your text using the program's built-in commands. The browser cheerfully ignores even the most elaborate formatting jobs because, as usual, browsers understand only HTML-based formatting. (And besides, a document with formatting is, by definition, not a pure text file, so a browser might bite the dust trying to load it.)

How to Do Paragraphs

As I mentioned earlier, carriage returns aren't worth a hill of beans in the World Wide Web. If you type one line, press **Enter,** and then type a second line, the browser simply runs the two lines together, side-by-side.

If a new paragraph is what you need, you have to stick the browser's nose in it, so to speak, by using the <P> tag. For example, consider the following text:

```
<HTML>
<HEAD>
<TITLE>My Home Sweet Home Page</TITLE>
</HEAD>
<BODY>
This text appears in the body of the web page.
This is the second line (not!).
<P>
This is the third line.
</P>
</BODY>
</HTML>
```

Figure 2.2 shows how this text looks in the browser. As you can see, the first two lines appear beside each other, despite the fact that they're on separate lines in the original text. However, the third line sits nicely in its own paragraph thanks to the <P> tag that precedes it. Note, too, that I used the </P> end tag to finish the paragraph.

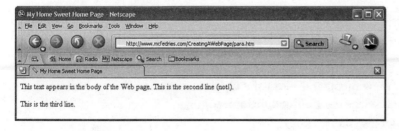

Figure 2.2

You need to use the <P> tag to create paragraphs in HTML.

Help! The Browser Shows My Tags!

When you view your HTML file in the browser, you might be dismayed to see that it shows not only your page text, but all the HTML tags as well (see Figure 2.3).

Figure 2.3

The browser might show your tags along with your text.

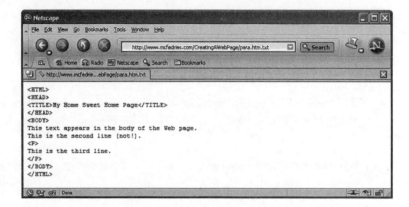

This kind of problem is almost always caused by one of the following:

◆ The file isn't a pure text file but is, rather, in a word processor format. As I mentioned earlier, if you're using a word processor to create your HTML files, make sure that when you save the file, you save it as a text file.

◆ The file doesn't have an .htm or .html extension. If you're using Windows and saving a file as text, Windows has a perverse tendency to always want to add the .txt extension to the end of the file name. Even if you specify the .htm or .html extension when you save the file, Windows just adds the .txt extension anyway (so you end up with something like index.htm.txt).

Assuming the latter is the problem, you saw earlier how you can overcome it by surrounding your file name with quotes in the Save As dialog box. To avoid that hassle, tell Windows to display file extensions. That way, the system always honors the extensions you enter by hand and won't force documents saved as text to always use the .txt extension. Here's how you do it:

1. Select **Start, Programs, Windows Explorer.** (In Windows XP, select **Start, My Computer.**)

2. Pull down the **View** menu and select the **Options** command (or pull down the **Tools** menu and select the **Folder Options** command, depending on which version of Windows you're using).

3. In the Options dialog box (you might need to select the **View** tab, again depending on which flavor of Windows you have), deactivate the **Hide MS-DOS extensions for the file types that are registered** check box. (In Windows XP, this check box is called **Hide extensions for known file types.**)

4. Click **OK.**

After that's done, you're able to add the .htm or .html extension to the end of your file names without having to use quotation marks.

Note, too, that you should check your existing HTML files to see if they have .txt extensions. For example, you might have files named index.htm.txt, or whatever. If so, edit the file name to remove the .txt at the end.

The Least You Need to Know

♦ You can create perfectly good web pages and blogs using a lowly text editor such as Notepad (Windows) or SimpleText (Mac).

♦ If you prefer to use WordPad, Word, Microsoft Works, or some other word processor, don't use the program's formatting commands and be sure to save the file as a text file.

♦ When naming your files, use the .htm or .html extension, use only lowercase letters, and avoid spaces like the plague.

♦ Always start your page or blog with the following eight tags:

```
<HTML>
<HEAD>
<TITLE>
</TITLE>
</HEAD>
<BODY>
</BODY>
</HTML>
```

♦ Other than the page title, the text and tags that you want other folks to see go inside the body section (that is, between the <BODY> and </BODY> tags).

♦ To start a new paragraph in your page, plop the <P> tag at the point where you want the paragraph to begin. At the end of the paragraph, don't forget the </P> end tag.

From Buck-Naked to Beautiful: Dressing Up Your Page or Blog

In This Chapter

◆ HTML tags for formatting characters

◆ How to create impressive-looking headings

◆ Miscellaneous text tags

◆ How to insert special characters in your page

◆ A complete makeover for your web page text

In the early, pre-text stages of the web page production process, your page is essentially naked. It passes its days exposed to the elements, shivering and teeth-chatteringly cold. Brrr! To put some color in your page's cheeks and prevent it from catching its death, you need to clothe it with the text you want everyone to read, as described in Chapter 2. These new text garments might be warm, but they aren't much to look at. I mean, face it, a plain-text web page just doesn't present your prose in the best light. I'm definitely talking Worst Dressed List here.

However, this really doesn't matter for those times when you're just kicking around the web house. At this stage, you're the only one who sees your web page, so you usually don't care how it looks. But what about when it's time to go out on the town? What do you do when you want the rest of the web world to see your creation? Heck, you can't send your web page out into cyberspace looking like *that!*

Before your page has its coming-out party, you need to dress it up in apparel appropriate for the occasion. In short, you need to format your text so it looks its best. This chapter is your web page fashion consultant as it examines the various ways you can use HTML to beautify your words.

Sprucing Up Your Text

The first of our web page makeover chores is to examine some tags that alter the look of individual words and phrases. The next few sections fill you in on the details.

Some Basic Text Formatting Styles

The good news about text formatting is that you'll mostly deal with four basic kinds: **bold,** *italic,* <u>underline</u>, and `monospace`. The bad news is that HTML seemingly has about a billion different tags that produce these styles. However, I'll take mercy on you and only let you in on the easiest tags to use. Table 3.1 shows the tags that produce each of these formats.

Table 3.1 The Basic Text Formatting Tags

Text style	Begin tag	End tag
Bold	<B>	</B>
Italic	<I>	</I>
<u>Underline</u>	<U>	</U>
`Monospace`	<TT>	</TT>

Here's a sample HTML document (bookstor.htm on this book's CD) that shows each of these styles in action. Figure 3.1 shows how the styles look when viewed with Internet Explorer.

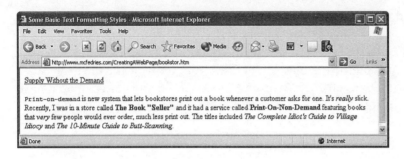

Figure 3.1

A web page showing the four basic text-formatting styles.

```
<HTML>
<HEAD>
<TITLE>Some Basic Text Formatting Styles</TITLE>
</HEAD>
<BODY>
<P>
<U>Supply Without the Demand</U>
</P>
<P>
<TT>Print-on-demand</TT> is a new system that lets bookstores print out a book
whenever a customer asks for one. It's <I>really</I> slick. Recently, I was in
a store called <B>The Book "Seller"</B> and it had a service called <B>Print-
On-Non-Demand</B> featuring books that <I>very</I> few people would ever
order, much less print out. The titles included <I>The Complete Idiot's Guide
to Village Idiocy</I> and <I>The 10-Minute Guide to Butt-Scanning</I>.
</P>
</BODY>
</HTML>
```

Webmaster Wisdom

Just in case you're a glutton for punishment, here's a rundown of some alternative tags you can use for these text styles:

Text style	Alternative tags
Bold	<STRONG>
Italic	*<EM> or <CITE> or <ADDRESS>*
`Monospace`	<CODE> or <KBD>

(Note that, to keep things simple, I've left out the corresponding end tags, such as </STRONG> and </EM>.) I should also mention here that you might want to think twice (or even three times) before using the <U> tag for underlining. As you can see in Figure 3.1, underlined text looks suspiciously like a link, which will only serve to confuse your readers.

Keep in mind that this book's CD includes all the HTML examples you read about in the book. (For more about the CD, see Appendix B.) This helps make your web-building chores easier because you can use the examples to get started with your own pages. To get your mitts on the example I used previously, look for the file named bookstor.htm on the CD. If you don't have a CD-ROM drive on your computer, or if the CD is damaged, you can get the examples from my website at the following URL:

```
www.mcfedries.com/CreatingAWebPage/examples.html
```

Combining Text Formats

You should note, as well, that it's perfectly okay to combine these text styles. So, for example, if you need bold italic text, you can get it by throwing the <B> and <I> tags together, like this:

```
<B><I>This'll give you, like, bold italic text</I></B>
```

Accessorizing: Displaying Special Characters

You might think that because HTML is composed in text-only documents (documents that include only the characters and symbols you can peck out from your keyboard), nonstandard characters such as ¢ and ¥ would be taboo. It's true that there's no way to add these characters to your page directly, but the web wizards who created HTML thought up a way around this limitation. Specifically, they came up with special codes called *character entities* (which is surely a name only a true geek would love) that represent these and other oddball symbols.

These codes come in two flavors: a *character reference* and an *entity name*. Character references are basically just numbers, and the entity names are friendlier symbols that describe the character you're trying to display. For example, you can display the registered trademark symbol ® by using either the ® character reference or the ® entity name, as shown here:

```
Print-On-Non-Demand&#174;
```

or

```
Print-On-Non-Demand&reg;
```

Page Pitfalls

To ensure that all browsers render your characters properly, use only lowercase letters when typing the entity names.

Note that both character references and entity names begin with an ampersand (&) and end with a semicolon (;). Don't forget either character when using special characters in your own pages.

Table 3.2 lists a few other popular characters and their corresponding codes. You'll find a more complete list in Appendix B.

Table 3.2   A Few Common Characters

Symbol	Character Reference	Entity name
<	&#060;	&lt;
>	&#062;	&gt;
Nonbreaking space		
¢	&#162;	&cent;
£	&#163;	&pound;
¥	&#165;	&yen;
©	&#169;	&copy;
®	&#174;	&reg;
°	&#176;	&deg;
¼	&#188;	&frac14;
½	&#189;	&frac12;
¾	&#190;	&frac34;
×	&#215;	&times;

Webmaster Wisdom _____

The table contains a bizarre entry called a "nonbreaking space." What's up with that? Remember in Chapter 2 when I told you that HTML simply scoffs at white space (multiple spaces and tabs)? Well, you use the nonbreaking space thingamajig when you want to force the browser to display white space. For example, if you want to indent the first line of a paragraph by three spaces, you'd start it like so:

```
   This line appears indented by three spaces.
```

You can also use the nonbreaking space to position images, line up text, and much more.

A Few Formatting Features You'll Use All the Time

This section takes you through five more formatting tags that should stand you in good stead throughout your career as a web engineer. You use these tags for adding headings, aligning paragraphs, displaying "preformatted" text, inserting line breaks, and displaying horizontal lines. The next few sections give you the details.

Sectioning Your Page with Headings

Many web designers divide their page contents into several sections, like chapters in a book. To help separate these sections and thus make life easier for the reader, you can use headings. Ideally, headings act as minititles that convey some idea of what each section is all about. To make these titles stand out, HTML has a series of heading tags that display text in larger, bold fonts. There are six heading tags in all, ranging from <H1>, which uses the largest font, down to <H6>, which uses the smallest font.

What's with all the different headings? Well, the idea is that you use them to outline your document. As an example, consider the headings I've used in this chapter and see how I'd format them in HTML.

> **Blog On**
>
> Headings are useful for blogs, too. For example, when you're starting a new day of blog entries, you could put the date in a heading (such as <H2>). Then, for each of that day's posts, you could use a smaller heading (such as <H3>) as the blurb headline.

Webmaster Wisdom

Notice that I force the browser to display a less-than sign (<) by using the character code < and to display a greater-than sign (>) by using the code >.

The overall heading, of course, is the chapter title, so I'd display it using, say, the <H1> tag. The first main section is the one titled "Sprucing Up Your Text," so I'd give its title an <H2> heading. That section contains three subsections, "Some Basic Text Formatting Styles," "Combining Text Formats," and "Accessorizing: Displaying Special Characters." I'd give each of these titles the <H3> heading. Then I come to the section called "A Few Formatting Features You'll Use All the Time." This is another main section of the chapter, so I'd go back to the <H2> tag for its title, and so on.

The following HTML document (look for headings.htm on the CD in this book) shows how I'd format all the section titles for this chapter, and Figure 3.2 shows how they appear in Netscape. (Notice that I don't need to use a <P> tag to display headings on separate lines; that's handled automatically by the heading tags.)

```
<HTML>
<HEAD>
<TITLE>Some Example Headings</TITLE>
</HEAD>
<BODY>
<H1>From Buck-Naked to Beautiful: Dressing Up Your Page</H1>
<H2>Sprucing Up Your Text</H2>
<H3>Some Basic Text Formatting Styles</H3>
<H3>Combining Text Formats</H3>
<H3>Accessorizing: Displaying Special Characters</H3>
<H2>A Few Formatting Features You'll Use All the Time</H2>
```

```
<H3>Sectioning Your Page With Headings</H3>
<H3>Aligning Paragraphs</H3>
<H3>Handling Preformatted Text</H3>
<H3>Them's the Breaks: Using &lt;BR&gt; for Line Breaks</H3>
<H3>Inserting Horizontal Lines</H3>
<H2>Textras: Fancier Text Formatting</H2>
<H3>The &lt;FONT&gt; Tag I: Changing the Size of Text</H3>
<H3>The &lt;BASEFONT&gt; Tag</H3>
<H3>The &lt;FONT&gt; Tag II: Changing the Typeface</H3>
<H3>Changing the Color of Your Page Text</H3>
<H3>The &lt;FONT&gt; Tag III: Changing the Color</H3>
<H3>The Dreaded &lt;BLINK&gt; Tag</H3>
</BODY>
</HTML>
```

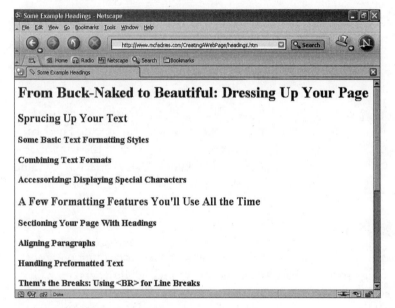

Figure 3.2

Examples of HTML's heading tags.

Aligning Paragraphs

Centering text and graphics is a time-honored way to give reports and brochures a professional look and feel. To provide the same advantage to your web pages, the <CENTER> tag gives you centering capabilities for your page headings, paragraphs, lists, and even graphics. Here's how <CENTER> works:

```
<CENTER>
[Headings, text, and graphics that you want centered go here.]
</CENTER>
```

The <CENTER> tag is a nice, simple way to shift things to the middle of a page. However, you can also use the <P> tag and the heading tags by shoehorning some extra text inside the tag. This extra text is called an *attribute* and it tells the browser to modify how it normally displays the tag.

For example, to center a paragraph, you use the following variation on the <P> tag theme:

```
<P ALIGN="CENTER">
```

When the browser stumbles upon the "ALIGN" attribute, it knows that it's going to have to modify the behavior of the <P> tag in some way. The exact modification is supplied by the value of the attribute, which is "CENTER" in this case. This orders the browser to display the entire contents of the following paragraph centered in the browser window.

Similarly, you can center, say, an <H1> heading like this:

```
<H1 ALIGN="CENTER">
```

The advantage to this approach is that you can also use either LEFT or RIGHT with the ALIGN attribute to further adjust your paragraph alignment. The LEFT value aligns the text on the left side of the window (that is, the normal alignment), and the RIGHT value aligns the text on the right side of the window.

> **⚠ CAUTION**
>
> **Page Pitfalls**
>
> Always surround attribute values with quotation marks, like this:
>
> ```
> <P ALIGN="RIGHT">
> ```
>
> And if your page doesn't display properly when you view it in the browser, immediately check to see if you left off either the opening or closing quotation mark in an attribute value.

Handling Preformatted Text

In the previous chapter, I told you that web browsers ignore white space (multiple spaces and tabs) as well as carriage returns. Well, I lied. Sort of. You see, all browsers normally *do* spit out these elements, but you can talk a browser into swallowing them whole by using the <PRE> tag. The "PRE" part is short for "preformatted," and you normally use this tag to display preformatted text exactly as it's laid out. Here, "preformatted" means text in which you use spaces, tabs, and carriage returns to line things up.

Let's look at an example. The following bit of code is an HTML document (look for pre.htm on this book's CD) in which I set up two chunks of text in a pattern that uses spaces and carriage returns. The first bit of doggerel doesn't make use of the <PRE> tag, but I've surrounded the second poem with <PRE> and </PRE>. Figure 3.3 shows the results. Notice that the lines from the first poem are strung together, but that when the browser encounters <PRE>, it displays the white space and carriage returns faithfully.

```
<HTML>
<HEAD>
```

```
<TITLE>The &lt;PRE&gt; Tag</TITLE>
</HEAD>
<BODY>
<H3>Without the &lt;PRE&gt; Tag:</H3>
        Here's
       some ditty,
     specially done,
   to lay it out all
  formatted and pretty.
Unfortunately, that is all
  this junk really means,
      because I admit I
        couldn't scrawl
          poetry for
            beans.
<H3>With the &lt;PRE&gt; Tag:</H3>
<PRE>
        Here's
       some ditty,
     specially done,
   to lay it out all
  formatted and pretty.
Unfortunately, that is all
  this junk really means,
      because I admit I
        couldn't scrawl
          poetry for
            beans.
</PRE>
</BODY>
</HTML>
```

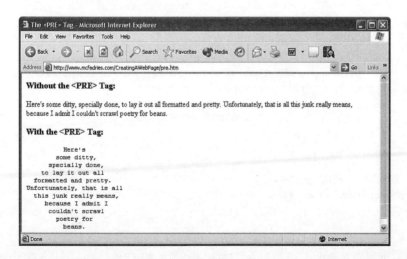

Figure 3.3

How preformatted text appears in Internet Explorer.

Webmaster Wisdom _____

You'll notice one other thing about how the browser displays text that's ensconced within the <PRE> and </PRE> tags: It formats the text in an ugly monospaced font. The only way to get around this is to use something called a "style sheet" to specify the font you want the browser to use with the <PRE> tag. I show you how this works in Part 4.

Them's the Breaks: Using ‹BR› for Line Breaks

As you saw in the previous chapter, you use the <P> tag when you need to separate your text into paragraphs. When a browser spies a <P> tag, it starts a new paragraph on a separate line and inserts an extra, blank line after the previous paragraph. However, what if you don't want that extra line? For example, you might want to display a list of items with each item on a separate line and without any space between the items. (Actually, there are better ways to display lists than the method I show you here; see Chapter 4.)

Well, you could use the <PRE> tag, but your text would appear in that ugly, monospaced font. A better solution is to separate your lines with <BR>, the line break tag. A browser starts a new line when it encounters <BR>, but it doesn't toss in an extra blank line. Here's an example (it's the file named breaks.htm on the CD):

```
<HTML>
<HEAD>
<TITLE>Line Breaks</TITLE>
</HEAD>
<BODY>
<H2>Supply Without the Demand</H2>
<HR>
<TT>Print-on-demand</TT> is a new system that lets bookstores print out a book
whenever a customer asks for one. It's <I>really</I> slick. Recently, I was in
a store called <B>The Book "Seller"</B> and it had a service called <B>Print-
On-Non-Demand</B>&#174; featuring books that <I>very</I> few people would ever
order, much less print out. The titles included the following:
<P>
The Complete Idiot's Guide to Village Idiocy<BR>
The 10-Minute Guide to Butt-Scanning<BR>
Baby's First Book of Java<BR>
Leashes Unleashed<BR>
Programmer's Guide to Basic Hygiene<BR>
Teach Yourself the Presidency in 4 Years
</P>
</BODY>
</HTML>
```

In the list of books, I added the <BR> tag to the end of each line (except the last one; I don't need it there). As you can see in Figure 3.4, Internet Explorer dutifully displays each line separately, with no space in between.

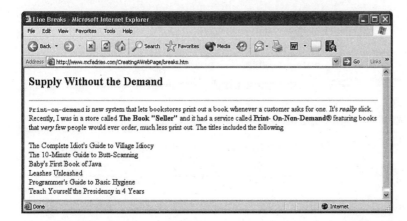

Figure 3.4

Use the <BR> tag to force a line break in your text.

Inserting Horizontal Lines

If you're particularly eagle-eyed, you might have noticed a horizontal line extending across the browser screen shown in Figure 3.4. What gives? Well, while you weren't looking, I surreptitiously inserted an <HR> tag into the HTML text. <HR>, which stands for "horizontal rule," produces a line across the page, which is a handy way to separate sections of your document.

If you use <HR> by itself, you get a standard line that goes right across the page. However, there are various attributes associated with the <HR> tag that enable you to change the line's size, width, alignment, and more. Table 3.3 shows a rundown.

> **Blog On**
>
> Many bloggers use <HR> tags to separate one day from another, or sometimes to separate each post.

> **Webmaster Wisdom**
>
> The <HR> tag draws a plain horizontal line. You might notice some web pages have fancier lines that use color and other neat texture effects. Those lines are actually images; I show you how to add images to your page in Chapter 6.

Table 3.3 Extra Attributes for the ‹HR› Tag

<HR> Extension	What It Does
<HR WIDTH="x">	Sets the width of the line to x pixels
<HR WIDTH="y%">	Sets the width of the line to y percent of the window
<HR SIZE="n">	Sets the thickness of the line to n pixels (where the default thickness is 1 pixel)
<HR ALIGN="LEFT">	Aligns the line with the left margin
<HR ALIGN="CENTER">	Centers the line
<HR ALIGN="RIGHT">	Aligns the line with the right margin
<HR NOSHADE>	Displays the line as a solid line (instead of appearing etched into the screen)

Note that you can combine two or more of these attributes in a single <HR> tag. For example, if you want a line that's half the width of the window and is centered, then you'd use the following tag:

```
<HR WIDTH="50%" ALIGN="CENTER">
```

Textras: Fancier Text Formatting

As you saw a bit earlier in this chapter, you can display your text in a different font size by using one of the heading tags (such as <H1>). Unfortunately, you can't use heading tags to adjust the size of individual characters because headings always appear on a line by themselves. To fix this, you use two tags: <FONT> and <BASEFONT>, which I discuss in the next couple of sections. I'll also show you how to change the typeface and color of your text.

The ‹FONT› Tag, Part I: Changing the Size of Text

The <FONT> tag adjusts (among other things) the size of any text placed between <FONT> and its corresponding end tag, </FONT>. Here's how it works:

```
<FONT SIZE="size">Affected text goes here</FONT>
```

The size part is a number that pinpoints how big you want the text to appear. You can use any number between 1 (tiny) and 7 (gargantuan); 3 is the size of standard-issue text. Here's an example (see fontsize.htm on the CD in this book):

```
<HTML>
<HEAD>
<TITLE>Changing the Size of Text</TITLE>
</HEAD>
```

```
<BODY>
<H1>Changing Font Size with the &lt;FONT&gt; Tag</H1>
<HR>
<P>
<FONT SIZE="7">This text uses a font size of 7.</FONT><BR>
<FONT SIZE="6">This text uses a font size of 6.</FONT><BR>
<FONT SIZE="5">This text uses a font size of 5.</FONT><BR>
<FONT SIZE="4">This text uses a font size of 4.</FONT><BR>
<FONT SIZE="3">This text uses a font size of 3 (normal).</FONT><BR>
<FONT SIZE="2">This text uses a font size of 2.</FONT><BR>
<FONT SIZE="1">This text uses a font size of 1.</FONT><BR>
</P>
<HR>
<P>
<FONT SIZE="7">Y</FONT>ou can mix and match sizes:
</P>
<BR>
<P>
Here at Shyster & Son Brokerage, you'll see your investments
<FONT SIZE="7">s</FONT><FONT SIZE="6">h</FONT><FONT SIZE="5">r</FONT>
<FONT SIZE="4">i</FONT><FONT SIZE="3">n</FONT><FONT SIZE="2">k</FONT>
while our commissions
<FONT SIZE="4">g</FONT><FONT SIZE="5">r</FONT><FONT SIZE="6">o</FONT>
<FONT SIZE="7">w!</FONT>
</P>
</BODY>
</HTML>
```

Figure 3.5 shows the results as they appear with Internet Explorer.

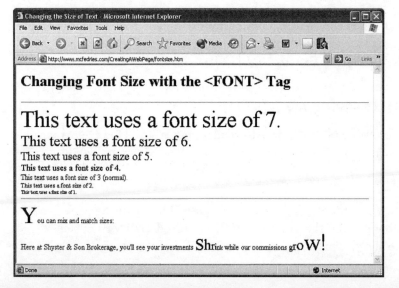

Figure 3.5

Use the <FONT> tag to adjust the size of your web page text.

The ‹BASEFONT› Tag

I mentioned earlier that the standard font size in a web page is 3. This is called the *base font*, and you'll be interested to know that it's not set in stone. To change it, use the <BASEFONT> tag:

```
<BASEFONT SIZE="size">
```

Once again, *size* is a number between 1 and 7 that specifies the base font size you want. For example, if you enter **<BASEFONT SIZE="7">** at the top of your document (that is, immediately after the <BODY> tag), then all the text will appear with font size 7.

You might be wondering what the heck's the big deal with <BASEFONT>. After all, couldn't you just insert a <FONT SIZE="7"> tag at the top of the document? Good point. (Gee, you *are* paying attention, aren't you?) The beauty (if beauty is the right term) of base fonts is that they enable you to set up relative font sizes. A relative font size is one that's so many sizes larger or smaller than the base font. Here's an example:

```
<BASEFONT SIZE="6">
This text is displayed in the base font size. However
<FONT SIZE="-2">these three words</FONT> were displayed in
a font size that's two sizes smaller than the base font.
```

The <FONT SIZE="-2"> tag tells the browser to display the text in a font size that's two sizes smaller than the base font (to get larger fonts, you'd use a plus sign (+), instead). Therefore, because I specified a base font of 6, the text between the <FONT> and </FONT> tags appears with a font size of 4.

Why not simply use <FONT SIZE="4">, instead? Well, suppose you plaster your document with dozens of font changes and then, when you display it in the browser, the fonts appear too small. If you're using explicit font sizes, you have to painstakingly adjust each <FONT> tag. However, if you're using relative font sizes, you only have to change the single <BASEFONT> tag.

The ‹FONT› Tag, Part II: Changing the Typeface

By default, the browser uses a plain typeface to render your pages. However, you can change that by shoehorning the FACE attribute into the <FONT> tag, like this:

```
<FONT FACE="typeface">
```

Here, *typeface* is the name of the typeface you want to use. The following page (it's typeface.htm on this book's CD) shows a few FACE-enhanced <FONT> tags in action, and Figure 3.6 shows what Internet Explorer thinks of the whole thing.

```
<HTML>
<HEAD>
<TITLE>Changing the Typeface</TITLE>
</HEAD>
<BODY>
<H1>The &lt;FONT&gt; Tag Can Also Do Different Typefaces</H1>
<HR>
<P>
<FONT SIZE="6">
This is the default browser typeface (Times New Roman).<BR>
<FONT FACE="Arial">This is the Arial typeface.</FONT><BR>
<FONT FACE="Courier New">This is the Courier New typeface.</FONT><BR>
<FONT FACE="Comic Sans MS">This is the Comic Sans MS typeface.</FONT><BR>
<FONT FACE="Whatever">Doh! This is NOT the Whatever typeface!</FONT>
</FONT>
</P>
<BODY>
<HTML>
```

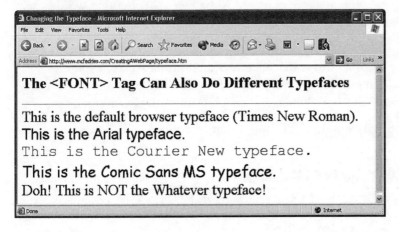

Figure 3.6

Use the <FONT> tag's FACE attribute to try on different typefaces for size.

Sounds easy, right? Not so fast, bucko. The problem with the FACE attribute is that it works only if the typeface you specify is installed on the user's computer. If it's not, you're out of luck because the browser will just use its default typeface. In the previous example, notice that the browser doesn't render anything for the Whatever typeface because it's not installed. (It doesn't even exist because I just made up the name!)

To increase your chances, however, you're allowed to add multiple typeface names to the FACE attribute:

```
<FONT FACE="Arial, Verdana, Helvetica, sans-serif">
```

If Arial's not installed, the browser will try Verdana, instead; if Verdana's not installed, the browser tries Helvetica; if that's a no-go, the computer's default sans serif typeface is used. (The FACE attribute values "serif" and "sans serif" tell the browser to use the computer's default serif and sans serif typefaces.)

Some Notes About Working with Colors

The next couple of sections show you how to change text colors. You'll find that you often have to work with colors when constructing web pages, so it's probably a good idea to take a minute or two now and get the HTML color techniques down pat.

Most of the time, you specify a color by entering a six-digit code that takes the following form:

```
#rrggbb
```

This sure looks weird, but there's method in its mathematical madness. Here, *rr* is the red part of the color, *gg* is the green part, and *bb* is the blue part. In other words, each code represents a combination of the three primary colors, and it's this combination that produces the final color. These are called *RGB values*.

The truly nerdish aspect of all this is that each two-digit primary color code uses *hexadecimal* numbers. These are base 16 (instead of the usual base 10 in decimal numbers), so they run from 0 through 9, then A through F. Yeah, my head hurts, too.

Table 3.4 lists the appropriate values for some common colors.

Table 3.4   RGB Codes for Common Colors

If You Use This Value	You Get This Color
#000000	Black
#FFFFFF	White
#FF0000	Red
#00FF00	Green
#0000FF	Blue
#FF00FF	Magenta
#00FFFF	Cyan
#FFFF00	Yellow

Rather than working with these bizarre RGB values, you might prefer to use the standard HTML color names. These color names use nice English words such as "Blue" and "Tan" (as well as plenty of bizarre words such as "Bisque" and "Orchid"). A complete list of the color names, their corresponding RGB values, and a swatch that shows the color are available in the file x11color.htm on the CD in this book (see Figure 3.7 for a black-and-white version of that document).

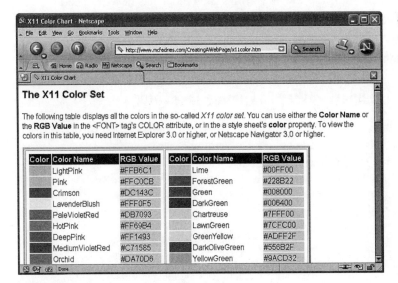

Figure 3.7

The colors, color names, and their RGB equivalents.

Changing the Color of Your Page Text

Browsers display your text in basic black, which is readable but not all that exciting. To put some color in your text's cheeks, let's look at a few extra goodies.

For starters, the <BODY> tag has a TEXT attribute:

```
<BODY TEXT="color">
```

Here, *color* is either a color name or an RGB value that specifies the color you want to use.

Webmaster Wisdom

Because you can change the color of your page's background, links, and text, it's very important that you choose a color combination that makes for easy reading. For example, light yellow text on white or bright green text on red can be a little hard on the eyes.

Changing the Color of Your Links

There are also ways to specify colors for the links you include in your page. Here's how they work:

```
<BODY LINK="color1" VLINK="color2" ALINK="color3">
```

Use LINK to specify the color of new links (links the reader has never clicked before); use VLINK to set up a color for visited links (links the reader *has* clicked before); use ALINK to set up a color for active links. (An *active link* is a link you've clicked but haven't yet unclicked.)

The ‹FONT› Tag, Part III: Another Way to Change Text Color

The problem with these <BODY> tag attributes is that they affect the entire page. What if you only want to change the color of a heading, a word, a link, or even a single letter? For that you need to return to our old friend the <FONT> tag, which also supports a COLOR attribute:

```
<FONT COLOR="color">
```

Here's an example:

```
<FONT COLOR="#FF0000">This text is red.</FONT>
```

> **Page Pitfalls** _____
>
> The HTML elements you learned about in this chapter (and many that you'll learn about in subsequent chapters) can actually make a web page or blog look worse if you misuse or overuse them. If you're interested in making your pages look their best, be sure to read Chapter 15, which discusses the do's and don'ts of web page and blog design.

The Least You Need to Know

- Use the <B> tag for bold text, <I> for italics, <U> for underlining, and <TT> for monospace.

- The heading tags run from <H1> (the largest) through <H6> (the smallest). Remember, too, that text between heading tags always appears in a separate paragraph.

◆ Many tags can take one or more attributes that change the way the browser handles the tag. When specifying attributes, always surround the values with quotation marks.

◆ To align your text, the <P> tag and the heading tags accept the ALIGN attribute, which can take any of three values: LEFT, CENTER, and RIGHT.

◆ To format text, use the <FONT> tag's various attributes, including SIZE (to change the size of the text), FACE (to change the typeface), and COLOR (to change the color).

◆ You'll most often specify a color using the code *#rrggbb*, where *rr* is the red value, *gg* is the green value, and *bb* is the blue value. Each value is a hexadecimal number that runs from 00 to FF.

Chapter 4

The Gist of a List: Adding Lists to Your Page

In This Chapter

- ◆ Creating numbered lists
- ◆ How to set up bulleted lists
- ◆ Cobbling together a definition list
- ◆ More list examples than you can shake a stick at

Are you making a list and checking it twice? Gonna find out who's naughty and … oops, drifted off to the North Pole for a second! But if you do want to include a list in your web page or blog, what's the best way to go about it? You saw in the previous chapter how you can use the
 (line break) tag to display items on separate lines. That works well enough, I guess, but hold your list horses—there's a better way. HTML has a few tags that are specially designed to give you much more control over your list-building chores. In fact, HTML offers no fewer than three different list styles: numbered lists, bulleted lists, and definition lists. This chapter takes you through the basics of each list type and provides you with plenty of examples.

Putting Your Affairs in Order with Numbered Lists

If you want to include a numbered list of items—it could be a top-ten list, bowling league standings, or any kind of ranking—don't bother adding in the numbers yourself. Instead, you can use HTML ordered lists to make the web browser generate the numbers for you.

Ordered lists use two types of tags:

- ◆ The entire list is surrounded by the <OL> (ordered list) and </OL> tags.

- ◆ Each item in the list is preceded by the <LI> (list item) tag and is closed with the </LI> end tag.

The general setup looks like this:

```
<OL>
<LI>First item.</LI>
<LI>Second item.</LI>
<LI>Third item.</LI>
<LI>You get the idea.</LI>
</OL>
```

Here's an example (see numlist1.htm on the CD in this book):

```
<HTML>
<HEAD>
<TITLE>Numbered Lists - Example #1</TITLE>
</HEAD>
<BODY>
<H3>My Ten Favorite U.S. College Nicknames</H3>
<OL>
<LI>Missouri-Kansas City Kangaroos</LI>
<LI>Delaware Fightin' Blue Hens</LI>
<LI>Texas Christian Horned Frogs</LI>
<LI>Coastal Carolina Chanticleers</LI>
<LI>Kent State Golden Flashes</LI>
<LI>Marshall Thundering Herd</LI>
<LI>Idaho Vandals</LI>
<LI>Purdue Boilermakers</LI>
<LI>South Carolina Fighting Gamecocks</LI>
<LI>Wake Forest Demon Deacons</LI>
</OL>
</BODY>
</HTML>
```

Notice that I didn't include any numbers before each list item. However, when I display this document in a browser (see Figure 4.1), the numbers get inserted automatically. Pretty slick, huh?

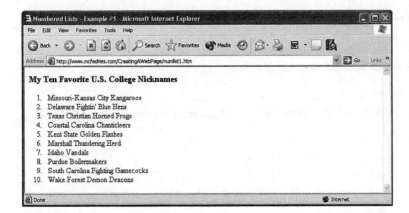

Webmaster Wisdom _____

Your list items don't have to be just plain text, so you're free to go crazy and insert other HTML tags. For example, you could use <B> and </B> to boldface a word or two in the item, you could use the <FONT> tag to change the font size or typeface of the item, or you could make an item a link to another web page. (Chapter 5 discusses linking.) Just make sure to start each line with the <LI> tag.

The items you toss into your numbered lists don't have to be short words and phrases, however. For example, if you're explaining how to perform a certain task, a numbered list is the perfect way to take your readers through each step. Here's a more involved example (it's numlist2.htm on this book's CD) that uses a numbered list to explain how to juggle:

```
<HTML>
<HEAD>
<TITLE>Numbered Lists-Example #2</TITLE>
</HEAD>
<BODY>
<H3>The Complete Idiot's Guide to Juggling</H3>
<HR>
<P>
Here are the basic steps for the most fundamental of juggling
moves&#151;the three-ball cascade:
</P>
```

```
<OL>
<LI>Place two balls in your dominant hand, one in front of the other,
and hold the third ball in your other hand. Let your arms dangle
naturally and bring your forearms parallel to the ground (as though
you were holding a tray).</LI>
<LI>Of the two balls in your dominant hand, toss the front one toward
your left hand in a smooth arc. Make sure the ball doesn't spin too
much and that it goes no higher than about eye level.</LI>
<LI>Once the first ball has reached the top of its arc, you need to
release the ball in your other hand. Throw it toward your dominant
hand, making sure it flies <I>under</I> the first ball. Again, watch
that the ball doesn't spin or go higher than eye level.</LI>
<LI>Now things get a little tricky (!). Soon after you release the
second ball, the first ball will approach your other hand (gravity
never fails). Go ahead and catch the first ball.</LI>
<LI>When the second ball reaches its apex, throw the third ball (the
remaining ball in your dominant hand) under it.</LI>
<LI>At this point, it just becomes a game of catch-and-throw-under,
catch-and-throw-under. Keep repeating steps 1-5 and, before you know
it, you'll be a juggling fool. (However, I'd recommend holding off on
the flaming clubs until you've practiced a little.)</LI>
</OL>
</BODY>
</HTML>
```

As you can see, most of the items are quite long, and it's kind of hard to tell where each <LI> item begins and ends. However, as shown in Figure 4.2, the list looks pretty good when viewed in a web browser.

Figure 4.2

Numbered lists are perfect for outlining the steps in a procedure.

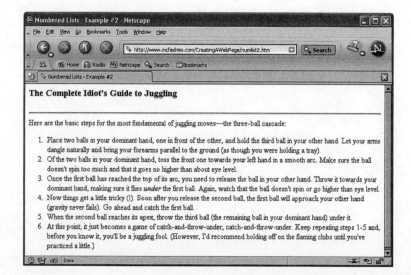

Using a Different Numbering Scheme

The <OL> tag's TYPE attribute enables you to define a different numbering scheme. Here's how it works:

```
<OL TYPE="type">
```

Here, *type* is one of the characters shown in Table 4.1.

Table 4.1   The ‹OL› Tag's TYPE Attribute Values

Type	Numbering scheme	Example
1	Standard numbers	1, 2, 3
a	Lowercase letters	a, b, c
A	Uppercase letters	A, B, C
i	Small Roman numerals	i, ii, iii
I	Large Roman numerals	I, II, III

Here's an example (see oltype.htm on this book's CD):

```
<HTML>
<HEAD>
<TITLE>The TYPE attribute</TITLE>
</HEAD>
<BODY>
<P>
<B>TYPE="a":</B>
</P>
<OL TYPE="a">
<LI>First</LI>
<LI>Second</LI>
<LI>Third</LI>
</OL>
<P>
<B>TYPE="A":</B>
</P>
<OL TYPE="A">
<LI>Win</LI>
<LI>Place</LI>
<LI>Show</LI>
</OL>
<P>
<B>TYPE="i":</B>
```

Webmaster Wisdom

Another useful <OL> tag attribute is START, which enables you to define the starting point of the list number. For example, if you use <OL START="100">, the first item in your numbered list will be 100, the second will be 101, and so on.

```
</P>
<OL TYPE="i">
<LI>Gold</LI>
<LI>Silver</LI>
<LI>Bronze</LI>
</OL>
<P>
<B>TYPE="I":</B>
</P>
<OL TYPE="I">
<LI>Miss America</LI>
<LI>First runner-up</LI>
<LI>Second runner-up</LI>
</OL>
</BODY>
</HTML>
```

Figure 4.3 shows how Internet Explorer handles the various types of lists.

Figure 4.3

The <OL> tag's TYPE attribute in action.

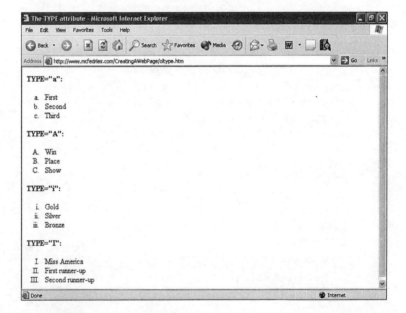

Scoring Points with Bulleted Lists

Numbered lists, of course, aren't the only kinds of lists. If you just want to enumerate a few points, a bulleted list might be more your style. They're called "bulleted" lists because a web browser displays a cute little dot or square (depending on the browser) called a *bullet* to the left of each item.

The HTML tags for a bulleted list are pretty close to the ones you saw for a numbered list. As before, you precede each list item with the same <LI> tag, but you enclose the entire list with the <UL> and </UL> tags. Why "UL"? Well, what the rest of the world calls a bulleted list, the HTML powers-that-be call an *unordered list*. Yeah, that's real intuitive. Ah well, here's how they work:

```
<UL>
<LI>First bullet point.</LI>
<LI>Fifty-seventh bullet point.</LI>
<LI>Sixteenth bullet point.</LI>
<LI>Hey, whaddya want--it's an unordered list!</LI>
</UL>
```

Here's an HTML document (look for bulleted.htm on the CD in this book) that demonstrates how to use the bulleted list tags:

```
<HTML>
<HEAD>
<TITLE>Bulleted List Example</TITLE>
</HEAD>
<BODY>
<H3>Famous Phobias</H3>
<UL>
<LI>Augustus Caesar &#151; Achluophobia (fear of sitting in the dark)</LI>
<LI>Sigmund Freud &#151; Siderodromophobia (fear of trains)</LI>
<LI>Arnold Sch&#246;nberg &#151; Tridecaphobia (fear of the number 13)</LI>
<LI>John Cheever &#151; Gephyrophobia (fear of crossing bridges)</LI>
<LI>Sid Caesar &#151; Tonsurphobia (fear of haircuts)</LI>
</UL>
</BODY>
</HTML>
```

Figure 4.4 shows how the Internet Explorer browser renders this file—little bullets and all.

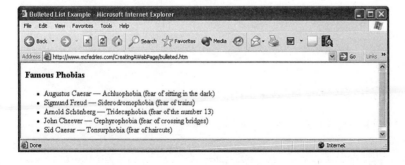

Figure 4.4

A typical bulleted list.

Changing the Bullet Type

The basic bulleted-list bullet is a small circle. However, most browsers also support an extra TYPE attribute that modifies the bullet:

```
<UL TYPE="type">
```

In this case, *type* can be either disc (the standard bullet), circle, or square. (Note that you must use lowercase values here.) Here's a for-instance (look for ultype.htm on this book's CD):

```
<HTML>
<HEAD>
<TITLE>Bulleted List Extensions</TITLE>
</HEAD>
<BODY>
<H3>Using the &lt;UL TYPE="<I>type</I>"&gt; Tag</H3>
<HR>
<UL TYPE="disc">
<LI>Compact disc</LI>
<LI>Disc jockey</LI>
<LI>Disc brake</LI>
</UL>
<UL TYPE="circle">
<LI>Circle the wagons!
<LI>Circle all that apply</LI>
<LI>Chalk circle</LI>
</UL>
<UL TYPE="square">
<LI>Square root</LI>
<LI>Three square meals</LI>
<LI>Times Square</LI>
</UL>
</BODY>
</HTML>
```

And Figure 4.5 shows how it looks from Internet Explorer's point of view.

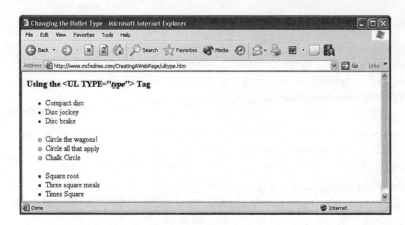

Defining Definition Lists

The final type of list is called a *definition list*. Originally, people used it for dictionary-like lists where each entry had two parts: a term and the definition of the term. As you'll see, though, definition lists are useful for more than just definitions.

To mark the two different parts of each entry in these lists, you need two different tags. The term is preceded by the <DT> tag, and the definition is preceded by the <DD> tag, like this:

> **Webmaster Wisdom**
>
> The best way to get a custom bullet, in my not-so-humble opinion, is to insert a graphic that has a cool bulletlike image. Chapter 6 shows you how this is done.

```
<DT>Term</DT><DD>Definition</DD>
```

You can, if you like, put the <DT> part and the <DD> part on separate lines, but I prefer this style (and either way, they end up looking the same in the browser). You then surround the whole list with the <DL> and </DL> tags to complete your definition list. Here's how the whole thing looks:

```
<DL>
<DT>A Term</DT><DD>Its Definition</DD>
<DT>Another Term</DT><DD>Another Definition</DD>
<DT>Yet Another Term</DT><DD>Yet Another Definition</DD>
<DT>Etc.</DT><DD>Abbreviation of a Latin phrase that means "and so forth."</DD>
</DL>
```

Webmaster Wisdom _____

People often use definition lists for things other than definitions. Some web welders like to use the term (the <DT> part) as a section heading and the definition (the <DD> part) as the section text. You can also leave out the term and just use the <DD> tag by itself. This is handy for those times when you need indented text (say, if you're quoting someone at length).

Let's look at an example. The HTML document shown next (it's on this book's CD in the file named defnlist.htm) uses a definition list to outline a few words and phrases and their definitions. (Notice that I've applied bold face to all the terms; this helps them stand out more when the browser displays them.)

```
<HTML>
<HEAD>
<TITLE>Definition List Example</TITLE>
</HEAD>
<BODY>
<H3>Some Techno-Terms You Should Know</H3>
<DL>
<DT><B>Barney Page</B></DT><DD>A web page that tries to capitalize on a
current craze.</DD>
<DT><B>Bit-Spit</B></DT><DD>Any form of digital correspondence.</DD>
<DT><B>Byte-Bonding</B></DT><DD>When computer users discuss things that
nearby noncomputer users don't understand. See also <I>geeking out</I>.</DD>
<DT><B>Clickstreams</B></DT><DD>The paths a person takes as she negotiates
various web pages.</DD>
<DT><B>Cobweb Page</B></DT><DD>A web page that hasn't been updated in a
while.</DD>
<DT><B>Geek</B></DT><DD>Someone who knows a lot about computers and very
little about anything else.</DD>
<DT><B>Geeking Out</B></DT><DD>When <I>geeks</I> who are <I>byte-bonding</I>
start playing with a computer during a non-computer-related social event.</DD>
</DL>
</BODY>
</HTML>
```

Figure 4.6 shows how the definition list appears in the Netscape 7 scheme of things.

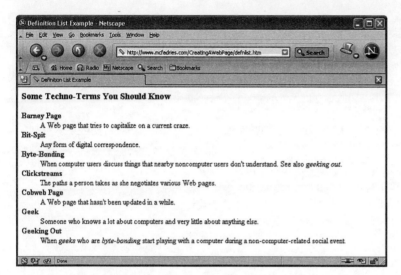

Figure 4.6

A few definitions arrayed, appropriately enough, in a definition list.

Combining Lists Inside Lists

These three types of HTML lists should serve you well for most of your web page and blog productions. However, you're free to mix and match various list types to suit the occasion. Specifically, it's perfectly legal to plop one type of list inside another (this is called *nesting lists*). For example, suppose you have a numbered list that outlines the steps involved in some procedure. If you need to augment one of the steps with a few bullet points, you can simply insert a bulleted list after the appropriate numbered list item.

As an example, I'll take the definition list from the last section and toss in both a numbered list and a bulleted list. Here's the result (I've lopped off some of the lines to make it easier to read; you can find the full document on this book's CD in the file named combo.htm):

```
<DL>
<DT><B>Barney Page</B><DD>A web page that tries to capitalize on a
current craze. Here are some recent Barney page subjects:

<UL>
<LI>The Lord of the Rings</LI>
<LI>Survivor</LI>
<LI>Scooters</LI>
</UL>
```

```
</DD>
<DT><B>Bit-Spit</B><DD>Any form of digital correspondence.
<DT><B>Byte-Bonding</B><DD>When computer users discuss things that
nearby noncomputer users don't understand. Here are the three stages
of byte-bonding that inevitably lead to <I>geeking out</I>:

<OL>
<LI>&quot;Say, did you see that IBM ad where the nuns are talking about surfing
the Net?&quot;</LI>
<LI>&quot;Do you surf the Net?&quot;</LI>
<LI>&quot;Let's go surf the Net!&quot;</LI>
</OL>

</DD>
...
</DL>
```

After the first definition list entry—the one for Barney Page—I've inserted a bulleted list that gives a few examples. (I've added blank lines above and below the bulleted list to make it stand out better. Note that I added these lines for cosmetic purposes only; they don't affect how the page appears in the browser.) Then, after the third definition list entry—Byte-Bonding—I've put in a numbered list. Figure 4.7 shows how all this looks when a browser gets hold of it.

Figure 4.7

HTML is more than happy to let you insert lists inside each other.

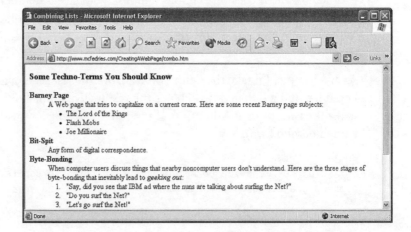

The Least You Need to Know

- For a numbered list, use the <OL> and </OL> tags and surround each list item with <LI> and </LI>.

- To change the number type, add the TYPE attribute to the <OL> tag and set it to one of the following values: a, A, i, or I.

- For a bulleted list, use the <UL> and </UL> tags and surround each list item with <LI> and </LI>.

- To change the bullet type, add the TYPE attribute to the <UL> tag and set it to one of the following values: disc, circle, or square.

- For a definition list, use the <DL> and </DL> tags. For each list item, surround the term with <DT> and </DT> and the definition with <DD> and </DD>.

- The browser won't mind in the least if you insert one type of list inside another.

Making the Jump to Hyperspace: Adding Links

In This Chapter

◆ Some URL fundamentals

◆ Creating links to other web pages

◆ Creating links to other locations in your web page

◆ Creating links that send e-mail messages

◆ Easy hypertext help that'll have your web pages and blogs fully linked in no time flat

As a would-be web page publisher, you've gotta give the people what they want, right? And what today's modern surfer wants more than anything else is to *interact* with a web page. Unfortunately, truly interactive pages require a bit more effort to create. (I'll talk about interaction a bit more in Part 2 and on the companion CD.)

However, there is a way to throw at least a small interactive bone to the readers of your web creations: Give 'em a few links that they can follow to the four corners of the web world (or even just to another part of your own cyberspace plot). It's an easy way to give your pages a dynamic feel that'll have people coming back for more. This chapter explains links and shows you how to put the "hypertext" into HTML.

The URL of Net: A Cyberspace Address Primer

Before the hypertext festivities commence, there's a bit of background info you need to slog through. As I mentioned in Chapter 1, a *hypertext link* is a special word or phrase in a web page that, when the user clicks it, takes him or her to a different web document. Each web page (and, indeed, any Internet resource) has its own address, which is called a *Uniform Resource Locator* (or URL, for short).

When you combine these two factoids, you realize that for a link to work properly, you need to know the correct address of the resource to which you're linking. To do that, you need to understand the anatomy of these URL things. Unfortunately, the whole URL concept seems to have been invented by some insane Geek of Geeks who never believed normal human beings would actually use the darn things. They're long, they're confusing, they're messy, and they're almost impossible to type correctly the first time. Not to worry, though. I've gone *mano-a-mano* with this URL foofaraw, and I've come up with a plan that's designed to knock some sense into the whole mess.

> **Words from the Web**
>
> A Uniform Resource Locator is geekspeak for an address of something on the Internet. This mouthful is usually shorted to URL and pronounced YOO-ar-ell (or, occasionally, ERL).

The idea is that, like journalists and their five Ws (who, what, where, when, and why), you can reduce any URL to three Ws (who, what, and where) and an H (how). So, the basic form of any URL ends up looking like this:

How://Who/Where/What

Hmm. I'm definitely talking serious weirdness here, so let's see what the heck I mean by all that:

♦ **How.** The first part of the URL specifies how the data is going to be transferred across Net lines. This is called the *protocol* and, luckily, mere mortals like you and I don't need to concern ourselves with the guts of this stuff. All you need to know is which protocol each resource uses, which is easy. For example, the World Wide Web uses something called HTTP (I tell you which protocols other resources use later in this chapter). So, the "how" part of the URL is the protocol, followed by a colon (:) and two slashes (//). (I told you this stuff was arcane; it makes alchemy look like *The Cat in the Hat*.) So, a web page URL always starts like this (lowercase letters are the norm, but they're not necessary): http://.

◆ **Who.** Calling the next part the "who" of the URL is, I admit, a bit of a misnomer because there's no person involved. Instead, it's the name of the computer where the resource is located—in geek circles, this is called the *host name*. (This is the part of an Internet address that has all those dots you're always hearing, such as ncsa.uiuc.edu or www.yahoo.com.) For example, this book's home page is located on a computer named www.mcfedries.com. You just tack this "who" part onto the end of the "how" part, as shown here: http://www.mcfedries.com.

◆ **Where.** The next part of the address specifies where the resource is located on the computer. This generally means the directory in which the resource is stored; the directory might be something like /pages or /pub/junk/software. This book's home page is in its own directory, which is /creatingawebpage/. (To get your own directory, you need to sign up with a company that puts pages on the web; see Chapter 7 for details.) So now you just staple the directory onto the URL and then add another slash on the end, for good measure: http://www.mcfedries.com/creatingawebpage/.

◆ **What.** Almost there. The "what" part is just the name of the file you want to see. For a web page, you use the name of the document that contains the HTML codes and text. The file containing this book's home page is called index.html, so here's the full URL: http://www.mcfedries.com/creatingawebpage/index.html.

CAUTION   Page Pitfalls

I mentioned earlier that you can use uppercase or lowercase letters (the latter are normally used) for the "how" part of the URL. The same is true for the "who" part, but case is often crucial when entering the directory and file name. With most (but not all) websites, if you enter even a single letter of a directory or file name in the wrong case, you may not get to where you want to go. (Technical aside: Web servers that run the Unix operating system are finicky about case, while those that run Windows are not.) That's why I always tell people to use nothing but lowercase letters for directory and file names; it just keeps things simpler (and saves wear and tear on your typing fingers by not having to stretch over to the Shift key).

Okay, Mr. Smartypants writer, lemme ask you this: I visit your website all the time, but to get there, I only have to enter http://www.mcfedries.com/creatingawebpage/. How come I can get away without entering a file name?

Ah, that's because most web servers have something they call a *default file name*. This means that if the user doesn't specify a file name, the server just assumes they want the default file. On most servers, the default file is named index.html, so if you enter this: http://www.mcfedries.com/creatingawebpage/, what you really get is this: http://www. mcfedries.com/creatingawebpage/index.html. When you sign up with a web host, you need to find out what the default file name is and then be sure to use that name for your main page. (Otherwise, your site visitors will just see an ugly list of all the files in your directory or, even worse, an error message.)

Got all that? Yeah, I know—it's as clear as mud. Well, have no fear. If you can keep the "how, who, where, and what" idea in your head, it'll all sink in eventually.

Getting Hyper: Creating Links in HTML

Okay, with that drivel out of the way, it's time to put your newfound know-how to work (assuming, that is, I haven't scarred you for life!). To wit, this section shows you how to use HTML to add links to your web page or blog.

The HTML tags that do the link thing are <A> and </A>. (Why "A"? Well, as you'll find out later on—see the section "Anchors Aweigh: Internal Links"—you can create special links called *anchors* that send your readers to other parts of the same document instead of sending them to a different document.) The <A> tag is a little different from the other tags you've seen (you just knew it would be). Specifically, you don't use it by itself but, instead, you shoehorn the URL of your link into it. Here's how it works:

```
<A HREF="URL">
```

Here, HREF stands for *HyperText Reference*. Just replace *URL* with the actual URL of the web page you want to use for the link (and, yes, you have to enclose the address in quotation marks). Here's an example:

```
<A HREF="http://www.mcfedries.com/creatingawebpage/index.html">
```

Now you can see why I made you suffer through all that URL poppycock earlier: It's crucial for getting the <A> tag to work properly.

You're not done yet, though, not by a long shot (insert groan of disappointment here). What are you missing? Right, you have to give the reader some descriptive link text to click. Happily, that's easier done than said because all you do is insert the text between the <A> and </A> tags, like this:

```
<A HREF="URL">Link text goes here</A>
```

Need an example? You got it (see the file link.htm on the CD in this book):

```
Why not head to this book's
<A HREF="http://www.mcfedries.com/creatingawebpage/index.html">home page</A>?
```

Figure 5.1 shows how it looks in a web browser. Notice how the browser highlights and underlines the link text and when I point my mouse at the link, the URL I specified appears in the browser's status bar.

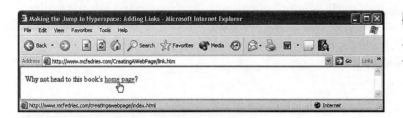

Figure 5.1

How the link appears in Internet Explorer.

Site Organization: Dealing with Directories

You may be aware that a *directory* is a file storage area that's been carved out of a hard disk. If you use Windows or a Mac, you may be more familiar with the term *folder,* which means the same thing. However, the word "directory" is more often used in web page publishing circles, so that's what I use throughout this book. Before continuing with the link lesson, let's take a short side trip to understand how directories work in the web world.

When you sign up with a company that will "host" your web pages, that company will supply you with your very own directory on its server. If you're only putting together a few pages, that directory should be more than adequate. If you're constructing a larger site, however, you should give some thought to how you organize your files. Why? Well, think of your own computer. It's unlikely that you have everything crammed into a single directory. Instead, you probably have separate directories for the different programs you use and other directories for your data files.

There's no reason why you can't cook up a similar scheme in your web home. On my site, to give you an example, I have separate directories for many of my books (such as this book's creatingawebpage directory), a directory called "ramblings" that stores miscellaneous writings, another called "toys" that has a few online applications, a "graphics" directory to store all my image files, and so on.

With this type of multidirectory setup, how you reference files in other directories can be a bit tricky. As an example, consider a website that has three directories:

```
/ (this is the main directory)
things/
stuff/
```

Here, "things" and "stuff" are subdirectories of the main directory. There are three scenarios to watch out for:

◆ **Referencing a file in the same directory.** This is the easiest because you don't have to include any directory information. Suppose that the HTML file you're working on is in the "stuff" directory and that you want to reference a page named tirade.html that's also in that directory. In this case, you just use the name of the file, like this:

```
<A HREF="tirade.html">
```

◆ **Referencing a file in a subdirectory from the main directory.** This is a common scenario because your home page (which is almost certainly in the main directory) is likely to have links to files in subdirectories. For example, suppose you want to link to a page named "doggerel.html" in the "things" subdirectory from your home page. Then your <A HREF> tag takes the following form:

```
<A HREF="things/doggerel.html">
```

◆ **Referencing a file in a subdirectory from a different subdirectory.** This is the trickiest scenario. For example, suppose you have a page in the "things" subdirectory and you want to link to a page named "duh.html" in the "stuff" subdirectory. Here's the <A HREF> tag:

```
<A HREF="../stuff/duh.html">
```

Weird, eh? The ".." thing represents what's called the *parent* directory (that is, the one that contains the current directory). It essentially says, "From here, go up to the parent directory, and then go down into the stuff subdirectory."

Anchors Aweigh: Internal Links

When a surfer clicks a standard link, the page loads and the browser displays the top part of the page. However, it's possible to set up a special kind of link that will force the browser to initially display some other part of the page, such as a section in the middle of the page. For these special links, I use the term *internal links*, because they take the reader directly to some inner part of the page.

When would you ever use such a link? Most of your HTML pages will probably be short and sweet, and the web surfers who drop by will have no trouble navigating their way around. But if, like me, you suffer from a bad case of terminal verbosity combined with bouts of extreme long-windedness, you'll end up with web pages that are lengthy, to say the least. Rather than force your readers to scroll through your tomelike creations, you can set up links to various sections of the document. For example, you could then assemble these links at the top of the page to form a sort of "hypertable of contents."

Blog On

Internal links are also used quite often in the blog world, where the main page is composed of several (possibly dozens of) individual entries. If you want someone to read a specific entry rather than forcing him to scroll through the entire blog, you'd be better off setting up an internal link so he can surf directly to the relevant blog entry. And internal links are a must if you set up an archive for your blog. See Chapter 16 for details.

Internal links actually link to a special version of the <A> tag—called an *anchor*—that you've inserted somewhere in the same page. To understand how anchors work, think of how you might mark a spot in a book you're reading. You might dog-ear the page, attach a note, or place something between the pages, such as a bookmark or your cat's tail.

An anchor performs the same function: It "marks" a particular spot in a web page, and you can then use a regular <A> tag to link to that spot.

I think an example is in order. Suppose I want to create a hypertext version of this chapter. (As a matter of fact, I did! Look for the file named chapter5.htm on this book's CD.) To make it easy to navigate, I want to include a table of contents at the top of the page that includes links to all the section headings. My first chore is to add anchor tags to each heading. Here's the general format for an anchor:

```
<A NAME="Name"></A>
```

As you can see, an anchor tag looks a lot like a regular link tag. The major difference is that the HREF attribute is replaced by NAME="*Name*"; *Name* is the name you want to give the anchor. You can use whatever you like for the name, but most people choose relatively short names to save typing. Notice, too, that you don't need any text between the <A NAME> tag and the </A> end tag.

Where do you put this tag? The best place is immediately before the start of the section you want to link to. For example, this chapter's first section is titled "The URL of Net: A Cyberspace Address Primer." If I want to give this section the uninspired name Section1, I use the following anchor:

```
<A NAME="Section1"></A>
<H2>The URL of Net: A Cyberspace Address Primer</H2>
```

Now, when I set up my table of contents, I can create a link to this section by using a regular <A> tag (with the HREF thing) that points to the section's name. And, just so a web browser doesn't confuse the anchor name with the name of another document, I preface the anchor name with a number sign (#). Here's how it looks:

```
<A HREF="#Section1">The URL of Net: A Cyberspace Address Primer</A>
```

Just so you get the big picture, here's an excerpt from the HTML file for this chapter (Figure 5.2 shows how it looks in a browser):

```
<H3>Hypertable of Contents:</H3>
<DL>
<DD><A HREF="#Section1">The URL of Net: A Cyberspace Address Primer</A>
<DD><A HREF="#Section2">Getting Hyper: Creating Links in HTML</A>
<DL>
<DD><A HREF="#Section2a">Site Organization: Dealing with Directories</A>
<DD><A HREF="#Section2b">Anchors Aweigh: Internal Links</A>
</DL>
<DD><A HREF="#Section3">Creating an E-mail Link</A>
<DD><A HREF="#Section4">The Least You Need to Know</A>
</DL>
<HR>
  [Rambling introduction goes here]
<A NAME="Section1"><H2>The URL of Net: A Cyberspace Address Primer</H2>_</A>
```

Figure 5.2

The hypertext version of this chapter.

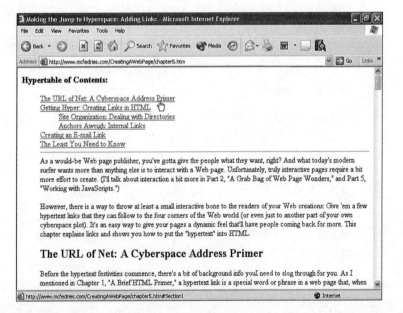

Although you'll mostly use anchors to link to sections of the same web page, there's no law against using them to link to specific sections of other pages. All you do is add the appropriate anchor to the other page and then link to it by adding the anchor's name (preceded, as usual, by #) to the end of the page's file name. For example, suppose you want to put a link in a page and you want that link to whisk the reader immediately to the "Getting Hyper: Creating Links in HTML" section of chapter5.htm. I gave that section the anchor name Section2, so here's a tag that sets up a link to it:

```
<A HREF="chapter5.htm#Section2">How to Create a Link</A>
```

Creating an E-mail Link

As I mentioned earlier, there's no reason a link has to lead to a web page. In fact, all you have to do is alter the "how" part of the URL, and you can connect to most other Internet services, including FTP and Usenet.

CAUTION

Page Pitfalls

Setting up an e-mail link may not work properly if the user has a web-based e-mail service such as Yahoo!. That's because when the user clicks the e-mail link, the browser attempts to launch the user's e-mail software. But that software isn't used for web e-mail, so the browser will have no way of sending the message. Note, however, that recent versions of Outlook Express do allow you to connect to a Hotmail account, which is a step in the right direction.

In this section, however, I'll concentrate on the most common type of nonweb link: e-mail. In this case, someone clicking an e-mail link is presented with a window he or she can use to send a message to your e-mail address. Now that's interactive!

This type of link is called a *mailto link* because you include the word *mailto* in the <A> tag. Here's the general form:

```
<A HREF="mailto:YourEmailAddress">The link text goes here</A>
```

Here, *YourEmailAddress* is your Internet e-mail address. For example, the president of the United States' e-mail address is president@whitehouse.gov. To include an e-mail link for this address in one of your web pages, you'd set up the link as follows:

```
You can write to the president of the United States at this
<A HREF="mailto:president@whitehouse.gov">e-mail address.</A>
```

CAUTION

Page Pitfalls _____

Putting your (or someone else's) address on a web page can be problematic because spammers have programs that automatically "harvest" such addresses. You can "munge" (as the hackers say) the address by altering it in such a way that will fool the spammer program but not a human (such as president(at)DELETETHISPARTwhitehouse. gov).

Figure 5.3 shows how it looks in Netscape 4. Note that when you point at the link with your mouse, the mailto address appears in the browser's status bar.

Figure 5.3

A web page with an e-mail link.

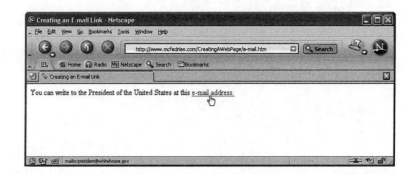

Webmaster Wisdom _____

If you want to try your hand at linking to FTP sites or Usenet newsgroups, here's a rundown of the types of URLs to use:

Resource	URL
FTP (directory)	ftp://Who/Where/
FTP (file)	ftp://Who/Where/What
Usenet	news:newsgroup.name

Note that **Who, Where,** and **What** are the same as I defined them earlier in this chapter. Also, **newsgroup.name** is just the name of the newsgroup that has articles you want to see.

The Least You Need to Know

◆ To make URLs easier to figure out, you can break them down into four sections: *How://Who/Where/What. How* is the protocol (such as http); *Who* is the host name (such as www.mcfedries.com); *Where* is the directory (such as /creatingawebpage/); and *What* is the file name (such as index.html).

◆ Here's the basic structure of an HTML link:

```
<A HREF="URL">Link text</A>
```

◆ If the page you're linking to is in the same directory as the current document, you can get away with specifying only the file name in the link's URL.

◆ To create an anchor, use the following variation on the <A> tag theme:

```
<A NAME="Name"></A>
```

◆ To set up a link to an anchor, use this tag:

```
<A HREF="#Name">Link text</A>
```

◆ E-mail links use the *mailto* form of the <A> tag:

```
<A HREF="mailto:E-mailAddress">Link Text</A>
```

Chapter 6

A Picture Is Worth a Thousand Clicks: Working with Images

In This Chapter

- ♦ A quick look at some image basics
- ♦ Using the <IMG> tag to insert an image on your web page or blog
- ♦ How to make text and images get along
- ♦ Using an image as the page background
- ♦ Using a "pixel shim" for precise positioning
- ♦ Adding the finishing touches to your web page with icons, bullets, buttons, and other graphical glad rags

You've probably seen those TV ads proclaiming in no uncertain terms (true hipsters are never uncertain about their hipness) that "image is everything." You know they couldn't put it on TV if it wasn't true (!), so you need to think about what kind of image your web page presents to the outside world.

You've seen how tossing a few text tags, a list or two, and a liberal dose of links can do wonders for drab, lifeless pages. But face it: Anybody can do that kind of stuff. If you're looking to make your web abode really stand out from the crowd, you need to go graphical with a few well-chosen images. To that end, this chapter gives you the ins and outs of images, including some background info on the various graphics formats, tags for inserting images, and lots more. (You can even use images as links. I'll show you how it's done in Chapter 9.)

Images: Some Semi-Important Background Info

Before you get down to brass tacks and start trudging through the HTML tags that plop pictures onto your pages, there are a few things I need to discuss. Not to worry, though; it's nothing overly technical. (That, of course, would be contrary to *The Complete Idiot's Guide* bylaw 4.17c: "Thou shalt not cause the eyes of thy readers to glaze over with interminable technical claptrap.") Instead, I just look at a few things that help you choose and work with images, and that should help make all this stuff a bit clearer.

No, Images Aren't Text, But That's Okay.

First off, let me answer the main question that's probably running through your mind even now about this entire graphics rumpus:

If the innards of a web page are really just text and HTML tags, then how in the name of h-e-double-hockey-sticks am I supposed to get an image in there?

Hey, that's a darn good question. Here's the easy answer: You don't.

Huh?

Yeah. As you see later on (in the section "The Nitty-Gritty at Last: The <IMG> Tag"), all you're really doing is, for each image you want to use, adding a tag to the document that says, in effect, "Yo! Mr. Browser! Insert image here." That tag specifies the name of the graphics file, so the browser just opens the file and displays the image within the web page. In other words, you have two files: your HTML file and a separate graphics file. It's the browser's job to combine them into your beautiful web page.

Graphics Formats: Can't We All Just Get Along?

Some computer wag once said that the nice thing about standards is that there are so many of them! Graphics files are no exception. It seems that every geek who ever gawked at a graphic has invented his own format for storing them on disk. And talk about alphabet soup! Why, there are images in GIF, JPEG, BMP, PCX, TIFF, DIB,

EPS, and TGA formats, and those are just off the top of my head. How's a budding web page architect supposed to make sense of all this acronymic anarchy?

Well, my would-be web welders, I bring tidings of great joy. You can toss most of that graphic traffic into the digital scrap heap, because the web has standardized on just two formats—GIF and JPEG—that account for 99 percent of all web imagery. Oh, happy day! Here's a quick look at them:

◆ **GIF.** This was the original web graphics format. It's limited to 256 colors, so it's best for simple images: line art, clip art, text, and so on. GIFs are also useful for setting up images with transparent backgrounds (see "Giving a GIF a Transparent Background," later in this chapter) and for creating simple animations (see Chapter 11).

Webmaster Wisdom

When you work with graphics files, bear in mind that GIF files use the .gif extension, while JPEG files use the .jpg or .jpeg extensions.

◆ **JPEG.** This format (which gets its name from the Joint Photographic Experts Group that invented it; gee, don't *they* sound like a fun bunch of guys to hang out with?) supports complex images that have many millions of colors. The main advantage of JPEG files is that, given the same image, they're smaller than GIFs, so they take less time to download. This doesn't matter much with simple images, but digitized photographs and other high-quality images tend to be huge; the JPEG format *compresses* these images so they're easier to manage.

Page Pitfalls

If you use Windows, then you're probably familiar with the BMP (bitmap) images that you can create with the Paint program. Although Internet Explorer is willing to work with these types of images, Netscape isn't. Therefore, I suggest that you avoid them and use only GIFs and JPEGs. (Even if you know all your users run Internet Explorer, you should still avoid BMPs because they tend to be huge compared to the equivalent GIF or JPEG file.)

How Do I Get Graphics?

The text part of a web page is, at least from a production standpoint, a piece of cake for most folks. After all, even the most pathetic typist can peck out at least a few words a minute. Graphics, on the other hand, are another kettle of digital fish entirely. Creating a snazzy logo or eye-catching illustration requires a modicum of artistic talent, which is a bit harder to come by than basic typing skills.

However, if you have such talent, you're laughing: Just create the image in your favorite graphics program and save it in GIF or JPEG format. (If your program gives you several GIF options, use GIF87 or, even better, GIF89, if possible. If your software doesn't know GIF from a hole in the ground, see the next section, where I show you how to convert the file.)

The nonartists in the crowd have to obtain their graphics goodies from some other source. Fortunately, there's no shortage of images floating around. Here are some ideas:

♦ Many software packages (including Microsoft Office and most paint and illustration programs) come with clip art libraries. *Clip art* is professional-quality artwork that you can freely incorporate in your own designs. If you don't have a program that comes with its own clip art, most software stores have CDs for sale that are chock-full of clip art images.

♦ Grab an image from a web page. When your browser displays a web page with an image, the corresponding graphics file is stored temporarily on your computer's hard disk. Most browsers have a command that lets you save that file permanently. (Although see my note about copyright concerns, below.) Here are some examples:

Internet Explorer: Right-click the graphic and then click **Save Picture As** from the shortcut menu.

Netscape: Right-click the graphic and click **Save Image As** from the menu that appears.

♦ Take advantage of the many graphics archives on the Internet. There are sites all over the Net that store hundreds, even thousands, of images. Go to Google (google.com) and run a search on the phrase "graphics archive" and you'll find quite a few sites to get you started.

♦ If you have access to a scanner, you can use it to digitize photos, illustrations, doodles, or whatever.

♦ If you have a digital camera, you can hook it up to your computer and transfer the photos to your machine.

♦ Use the images that come with this book. I've included hundreds of GIF and JPEG images on this book's CD that I hope will come in handy.

Page Pitfalls

Don't forget that many images are the property of the individuals who created them in the first place. Unless you're absolutely sure the picture is in the public domain, you need to get permission from the artist before using it. Note, however, that all the graphics that come on this book's CD are public domain, so you can use them at will.

Converting Graphics to GIF or JPEG

What do you do if you've got the perfect image for your web page, but it's not in GIF or JPEG format? You need to get your hands on a graphics program that's capable of converting images into different formats. Here are some that are commonly used by web graphics gurus:

- **Paint Shop Pro.** An excellent all-around graphics program that's great not only for converting graphics, but also for manipulating existing images and for creating new images. Best of all, there's no download required because a trial version of this program is available on this book's CD. See www.jasc.com.

- **GraphX.** This is a neat little program that's happy to convert a whack of graphics formats into GIF or JPEG. See www.group42.com.

- **ACDSee32.** This is a simple program that works best as a graphics viewer. However, it can also convert many different graphics formats into JPEG (but not GIF, unfortunately). A trial version of this program is available on this book's CD, as well. See www.acdsystems.com.

- **LView Pro.** The latest versions can perform lots of image manipulation tricks, but it's still best as a graphics converter. See www.lview.com.

- **PolyView.** A good converter with some interesting graphics features (such as the ability to create a web page from a set of images). See www.polybytes.com.

- **Graphic Workshop.** This program has a bit of a clunky interface, but it does a good job of converting graphics. See www.mindworkshop.com/alchemy/gwspro.html.

- **IrfanView.** This powerful program can not only convert your images to all the major formats, but it's free, too! See www.irfanview.com.

Webmaster Wisdom

Unfortunately, the programs on the CD are all Windows versions. However, Mac users have several graphics conversion programs to play with, including GraphicConverter (see www.lemkesoft.de/en) and GIFConverter (see www.kamit.com/gifconverter).

For most of these programs, you use the same steps to convert an image from one format to another:

1. In the program, select the **File, Open** command and use the Open dialog box to open the image file you want to convert.

2. Select the **File, Save As** command. The Save As dialog box drops by.

3. In the **Save as type** list, choose either JPEG or GIF. (In some programs, the latter is called CompuServe Graphics Interchange format.)

4. Click **Save**.

The Nitty-Gritty at Last: The ‹IMG› Tag

Okay, enough of all that. Let's get the lead out and start squeezing some images onto our web pages. As I mentioned earlier, there's an HTML code that tells a browser to display an image: the <IMG> tag. Here's how it works:

```
<IMG SRC="filename">
```

Here, SRC is short for "source" and *filename* is the name of the graphics file you want to display. For example, suppose you have an image named logo.gif. To add it to your page, you use the following line:

```
<IMG SRC="logo.gif">
```

Webmaster Wisdom

Your HTML file and your image file don't *have* to be in the same directory. Many webmasters create a subdirectory just for images, which keeps things neat and tidy. If you plan on doing this, make sure you study my instructions for using directories and subdirectories in Chapter 5.

In effect, this tag says to the browser, "Excuse me? Would you be so kind as to go out and grab the image file named logo.gif and insert it in the page right here where the <IMG> tag is?" Dutifully, the browser loads the image and displays it in the page.

For this simple example to work, bear in mind that your HTML file and your graphics file need to be sitting in the same directory on your computer, assuming you're just testing things at home. (When you put your page online [see the next chapter], you have to send the image file to your web host and make sure it's in the same directory as your HTML file.)

Let's check out an example. Most folks are constantly tinkering with their website—modifying existing pages, pruning dead wood (I know I do a lot of that!), and adding new stuff. Until the new pages are ready, however, you don't want to subject your visitors to them. Instead, you can just display a generic page (I call it a "Procrastination Page") that tells people the new module isn't quite ready for prime time just yet.

If you'd like something similar for your web pages, here's some HTML code that does the job (look for the file "undercon.htm" on this book's CD):

```
<HTML>
<HEAD>
<TITLE>Detour!</TITLE>
</HEAD>
<BODY>
<IMG SRC="constru1.gif">
<FONT SIZE="+2"><B>Web Work In Progress!</B></FONT>
<HR>
Sorry for all the mess, but I haven't quite gotten around to
implementing this section yet. I'm hoping to have everything
up and running real soon.
<P>
<A HREF="index.html">Go back to the home page.</A>
</P>
</BODY>
</HTML>
```

To emphasize the work-in-progress feel, this page includes a small graphic (constru1. gif) that says "Contents Under Construction" and shows a construction worker in action (see Figure 6.1). Note, too, that the page includes a link that gives the reader an easy way to get back to your home page. (In the <A> tag, make sure you change "index.html" to the appropriate name of your home page. Refer to Chapter 5 if you need a refresher course on this link stuff.)

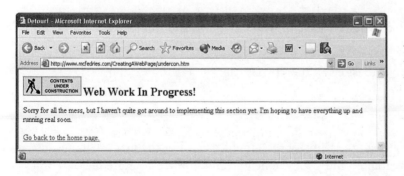

Figure 6.1

A web page to use as a substitute for pages you're still slaving away at.

Help! The #%@*&! Browser Won't Display My Images!

After adding your <IMG> tag, you might be dismayed to find that the browser refuses to display the image. Instead, it just shows a little "X" icon where the image should be. Grrrr. Here are some possible solutions to this all too common problem:

♦ If you're viewing your page on your home machine, the HTML file and the image files might be sitting in separate directories on your computer. Try moving your image file into the directory that holds your HTML file.

♦ If you're viewing your page on the web, perhaps you didn't send the image file to your server.

♦ Make sure you have the correct match for uppercase and lowercase letters. If an image is on your server and it's named "image.gif", and your IMG tag refers to "IMAGE.GIF", your image may not show up. In this case, you'd have to edit your IMG tag so that it refers to "image.gif".

♦ If you're using Netscape to view the page, make sure there are no spaces in the image's file name. Remember, too, that Netscape doesn't understand BMP graphics.

♦ Make sure you're not missing a quotation mark in the <IMG> tag's SRC attribute.

Specifying Image Height and Width

When surfing websites that contain graphics, have you ever wondered why it sometimes takes quite a while before anything appears on the screen? Well, one of the biggest delays is that most browsers won't display the entire page until they've calculated the height and width of all the images. The ever-intrepid browser programmers realized this, of course, and decided to do something about it. "What if," they asked themselves, "there was some way to tell the browser the size of each image in advance? That way, the browser wouldn't have to worry about it, and things would show up onscreen much faster."

Thus were born two extensions to the <IMG> tag: the HEIGHT and WIDTH attributes:

```
<IMG SRC="filename" WIDTH="x" HEIGHT="y">
```

Here, *filename* is, as usual, the name of the graphics file. For the new attributes, use x for the width of the graphic and y for the height. Both dimensions are measured in *pixels* (short for *picture elements*), which are the tiny dots that make up any computer screen image. Any good graphics program tells you the dimensions of an image.

Alternatively, you can express the width and height as percentages of the browser window. For example, the following line displays the image bluebar.gif so its width always takes up 90 percent of the screen:

```
<IMG SRC="bluebar.gif" WIDTH="90%">
```

The advantage here is that, no matter what size screen someone is using, the graphic always takes up the same amount of room across the screen. As proof, check out the next two figures showing the bluebar.gif image with WIDTH set to 90 percent. As you can see in Figures 6.2 and 6.3, the image always usurps 90 percent of the available width, no matter how big the Internet Explorer window. (Note, too, that because I didn't specify the HEIGHT, Internet Explorer adjusts the height in proportion to the increase or decrease of the width.)

Figure 6.2

The bluebar.gif image in a relatively narrow window.

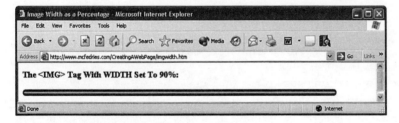

Figure 6.3

The same image in a wider window.

Aligning Text and Images

As you saw earlier in the Work-In-Progress example, you can display images and text on the same line. You set this up by inserting the <IMG> tag inside the page text.

This is all very reasonable, but you might run into problems with tall images, because the bottom of the image is aligned with the bottom of the line of text. If you prefer your text to appear at the top or the middle of the image, or if you want text to wrap around the image, the <IMG> tag has an extra ALIGN attribute that you can use. Here's how it works:

```
<IMG SRC="filename" ALIGN="value">
```

Here, the *value* can be any one of the following:

◆ **Top.** Text is aligned with the top of the image.

◆ **Middle.** Text is aligned with the middle of the image.

◆ **Bottom.** Text is aligned with the bottom of the image.

◆ **Left.** The image appears on the left side of the browser window, and text wraps around the image on the right.

◆ **Right.** The image appears on the right side of the browser window, and text wraps around the image on the left.

The following HTML listing (align.htm) gives you a demo (Figure 6.4 shows the results):

```
<HTML>
<HEAD>
<TITLE>Aligning Text and Images</TITLE>
</HEAD>
<BODY>
<IMG SRC="constru1.gif" ALIGN="TOP"> This text appears at the top of the image.
<P>
<IMG SRC="constru1.gif" ALIGN="MIDDLE"> This text appears in the middle of the
image.
</P>
<P>
<IMG SRC="constru1.gif" ALIGN="BOTTOM"> This text appears at the bottom of the
image.
</P>
<P>
<IMG SRC="constru1.gif" ALIGN="LEFT">
As you saw earlier in the Work-In-Progress example, you can display images and
text on the same line. You set this up by inserting the &lt;IMG&gt; tag inside
the page text.
<IMG SRC="constru1.gif" ALIGN="RIGHT">
This is all very reasonable, but you might run into problems with tall images,
because the bottom of the image is aligned with the bottom of the line. If you
prefer your text to appear at the top or the middle of the image, or if you
want text to wrap around the image, the &lt;IMG&gt; tag has an extra ALIGN
attribute that you can use.
</P>
</BODY>
</HTML>
```

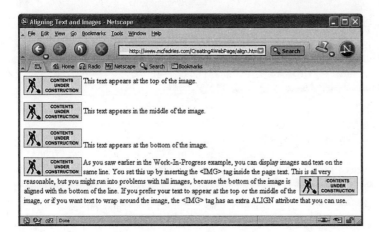

Figure 6.4

The <IMG> tag's ALIGN options.

Webmaster Wisdom

What happens if you're using ALIGN="LEFT" or ALIGN="RIGHT" to wrap text around an image, but then you want to start a new line or a new paragraph *after* the image? The solution here is to toss in a
 (line break) tag that uses the CLEAR attribute. There are three different CLEAR values you can use:

```
<BR CLEAR="LEFT">
<BR CLEAR="RIGHT">
<BR CLEAR="ALL">
```

Use CLEAR="LEFT" to start the next line when the left margin is clear; use CLEAR="RIGHT" to start the next line when the right margin is clear; use CLEAR="ALL" to start the next line when both margins are clear.

Handling Browsers with Graphics Turned Off

Most browsers come with a feature that enables you to turn off the display of images. This feature is a favorite among people with slow Internet connections because it means that most web pages load considerably faster. In this case, the user sees only an icon where the image would normally appear.

If you want to help out these users, you can provide a description of each of your images. To do this, the <IMG> tag offers an extra ALT attribute you can throw in to provide alternative text that appears in place of the image. Here's the general format:

```
<IMG SRC="filename" ALT="alternative text">
```

Here, *alternative text* is whatever text you want to use instead of the graphic. For example, if you have a picture of your hometown in your page, you can display the words *A lovely pic of my hometown* with the following line:

```
<IMG SRC="hometown.gif" ALT="A lovely pic of my hometown">
```

Webmaster Wisdom

Another excellent reason to include the ALT attribute in all your <IMG> tags is that it helps visually impaired surfers to navigate your page because they depend upon the ALT text to "see" what an image is all about.

Note, too, that even if a surfer does have graphics turned on, using ALT is still a good idea because many modern browsers (particularly Internet Explorer) display the ALT text in a banner when the user hovers his mouse pointer over the image.

Separating Text and Images

If you surround your images with text, you'll find that the text often bumps up against the image borders. To create a margin between the image and the surrounding text, add the HSPACE and VSPACE attributes to the <IMG> tag:

```
<IMG SRC="filename" HSPACE="h" VSPACE="v">
```

HSPACE—the "H" stands for horizontal—creates a margin between the image and the text to its left and right (where *h* is the size of the margin, in pixels). VSPACE—the "V" stands for vertical—creates a margin between the image and the text above and below (where *v* is the size of the margin, in pixels).

Good Uses for Images on Your Web Page

Images are endlessly useful, and they're an easy way to give your page a professional look and feel. Although I'm sure you can think of all kinds of ways to put pictures to work, here are a few suggestions:

◆ A company logo on a business-related page

◆ Graphics from an ad

◆ Drawings done by the kids in a paint program

◆ Charts and graphs

- ◆ Fancy-schmancy fonts
- ◆ Your signature
- ◆ Using a graphic line in place of the <HR> tag
- ◆ Using graphic bullets to create a better bulleted list

You might be wondering how to do that last item. Well, there are a number of ways to go about it, but the one I use for short lists is to create a definition list (see Chapter 4) and precede each item in the list with a graphic bullet. For example, the following code uses a file called redball.gif:

```
<DL>
<DD><IMG SRC="redball.gif">First item</DD>
<DD><IMG SRC="redball.gif">Second item</DD>
<DD><IMG SRC="redball.gif">Third item</DD>
</DL>
```

If the text in one or more of the bullets is quite long, a better approach is to create a table. I show you how to do this in Chapter 10.

Words from the Web

A **Jpig** is a web page that takes forever to load because it's either jammed to the hilt with graphics, or because it contains one or two really large images. Also, a **vanity plate** is an annoyingly large image that serves no useful purpose.

Page Pitfalls

Although graphics have a thousand and one uses, that doesn't mean you should include a thousand and one images in each page. Bear in mind that many of your readers are accessing your site from a slow modem link, so graphics take forever to load. If you have too many images, most folks give up and head somewhere else.

Changing the Page Background

Depending on the browser you use, web page text and graphics often float in a sea of dull, drab gray or plain white. It's about as exciting as a yawning festival. To give things a little pep, you can change the background color your page appears on to whatever suits your style. You can also specify an image to appear as the background.

Using a Color as the Background

The guts of your page appear within the body, so it makes sense that you change the background by tweaking the <BODY> tag. The simplest method is specifying a new background color:

```
<BODY BGCOLOR="#rrggbb">
```

Page Pitfalls

If the user tries to print your page, note most browsers don't include the background color (that is, they print using a white background). So, white or light text (such as the text shown in Figure 6.5) won't show up in the printout.

Yes, you're right: The rrggbb part is the same color code that I talked about back in Chapter 3. Figure 6.5 shows an example page that uses a black background (see blakback.htm on this book's CD). Note, too, that I had to use white for the page text so the surfer can read the page (which is kind of important).

Figure 6.5

A page that uses a black background and white text.

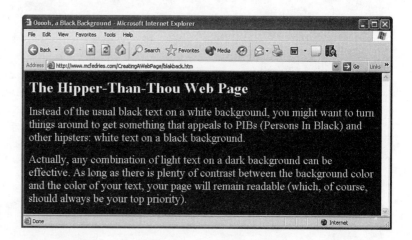

Using an Image as the Background

Instead of a color, you can specify an image to use as the background (similar to the way Windows and the Mac let you cover the desktop with wallpaper). This doesn't have to be (nor should it be) a large image. The browser takes smaller graphics and *tiles* them so they fill up the entire window. The secret to background images is the <BODY> tag's BACKGROUND attribute:

Webmaster Wisdom

One of the most popular styles of web page backgrounds these days is the margined background, which features a colored strip down the left (and sometimes also the right) side of the page. I show you how to create this attractive background style in Chapter 10.

```
<BODY BACKGROUND="filename">
```

Here, *filename* is the name of the graphics file you want to use.

In general, I recommend sticking with just a different background color. Tiled background images take longer to load, and they can make text devilishly difficult to read. If you really want to use a background image, then I suggest you also use the BGCOLOR attribute and set it equal to a color that more or less approximates the background color of the image. This will make your page look a bit nicer while it's loading.

A Special Image: The Pixel Shim (spacer.gif)

One of the biggest problems faced by web designers is positioning text and images with precision. Regular HTML just doesn't have any way of manipulating the position of any object.

You can get around this limitation by using something called a *pixel shim*. A pixel shim is a transparent GIF that's 1 pixel wide and 1 pixel tall. Because it's transparent, it doesn't show up on the page. However, by manipulating the <IMG> tag's HEIGHT and WIDTH attributes, you can create any amount of blank space that you need, which is great for precise positioning of text and images (I'll show you an example in Chapter 10).

I've put a pixel shim on this book's CD. Look for the file named spacer.gif.

Giving a GIF a Transparent Background

I talked about the page background earlier, but there's also another type of background that you have to worry about: the background of a specific image. For example, if you have an image of a house that's surrounded by black, the black is said to be the image's background color.

One of the features you get with a GIF image is the ability to set the background color to be "transparent." This just means that the browser doesn't show the background when it displays the file. This can make an image look much neater. For example, compare the two images shown in Figure 6.6. See how the one on the right doesn't show the black background?

Figure 6.6

GIF files can have transparent backgrounds.

Here's how you give a GIF file a transparent background in Paint Shop Pro:

1. Load your image into the program.

2. Select the **Colors, Set Palette Transparency** command.

3. If Paint Shop Pro mumbles something about reducing the number of layers and colors, click **Yes** and then click **OK** in the Decrease Color Depth dialog box.

4. In the Set Palette Transparency dialog box, activate the **Set the transparency value to palette entry** option.

5. Move the mouse pointer into the image and then click the color that you want to be transparent.

6. Click **OK**.

7. Activate the **Colors, View Palette Transparency** command. This will show the background color as a checkerboard pattern, which is what Paint Shop Pro uses to indicate transparency.

8. Select **File, Save As** to open the Save As dialog box.

9. In the **Save as type** list, choose **CompuServe Graphics Interchange (*.gif)**.

10. Click **Options**, activate the **Version 89a** option, and click **OK**.

11. Click **Save**.

CAUTION

Page Pitfalls

For this transparency stuff to work, your image must have a solid color background. If you try to use an image that has a shaded or multi-colored background, you won't get a proper transparent effect. Also, the background should be different than any color in the image itself, otherwise those parts of the image that use the same color will also appear transparent.

It's also possible to make a transparent background in Paint Shop Pro when you start an image from scratch. In the New Image dialog box, select **Transparent** in the **Background color** list box. Then select **Colors, Set Palette Transparency**. In the dialog box, activate **Set the transparency value to the current background color** and then click **OK**.

The Least You Need to Know

♦ There are, seemingly, billions and billions of graphics formats floating around, but only two are used extensively on the web: GIF and JPEG.

♦ Other than your own artistic endeavors, graphics are available from clip art libraries, other web pages, Internet archives, via scanner or fax, and on the CD that accompanies this book.

♦ If you have a graphic that isn't GIF or JPEG, convert it using Paint Shop Pro or one of the other graphics programs that comes on the CD in this book.

♦ To add an image to your web page, include the <IMG SRC="*filename*"> tag, where *filename* is the name of the graphics file.

♦ To change the page background, use the <BODY> tag's BGCOLOR attribute to change the color and/or the BACKGROUND attribute to use an image as the background.

♦ The pixel shim (spacer.gif) is a 1 × 1 transparent image. You use it to precisely position text and other graphics by putting spacer.gif in an <IMG> tag and then manipulating the HEIGHT and WIDTH attributes as needed.

Chapter 7

The Host with the Most: Choosing a Web Hosting Provider

In This Chapter

- ♦ Understanding web hosting providers
- ♦ A rundown of the various choices for hosting your page
- ♦ A guide to choosing the host that's right for you
- ♦ A review of some companies that will put your pages on the web
- ♦ Everything you need to know about this web hosting hoo-ha

I've covered a lot of ground in the past few chapters, and no doubt you've worked your fingers to the bone applying the electronic equivalent of spit and polish to buff your web page to an impressive sheen. However, there are still a couple of related tasks you need to perform before you can cross "Make Web Page" off your to-do list:

- ♦ You have to find a web home for your home page.
- ♦ You have to move your files into that new home.

This chapter takes care of the first task by showing you how to look for and choose a spot on the web where friends, family, and even total strangers from far-flung corners of the world can eyeball your creation. Once you've done that, Chapter 8 gives you the details on getting your files from here to there.

What in the Name of Sam Hill Is a Web Hosting Provider?

The third most common question posed by web page–publishing neophytes is "Where the heck do I put my page when I'm done?" (The most common question, in case you're wondering, is "How do I get started?" The second most common question is "Why is Jerry Lewis so popular in France?") If you've asked that question yourself, then you're doing okay, because it means you're clued in to something crucial: Just because you've created a web page and you have an Internet connection doesn't mean your page is automatically a part of the web.

The reasons for this are mind-numbingly technical, but the basic idea is that people on the Net have no way of "getting to" your computer and, even if they did, your computer isn't set up to hand out documents (such as web pages) to visitors who ask for them.

Computers that can do this are called *servers* (because they "serve" stuff out to the Net), and computers that specialize in distributing web pages are called *web servers*. So, to get to the point at long last, your web page isn't on the web until you store it on a web server. Because this computer is, in effect, playing "host" to your pages, such machines are also called *web hosts*. Companies that run these web hosts are called *web hosting providers*.

> **Blog On**
>
> Don't confuse a web hosting provider with a *blog hosting provider*. The latter is a service that is specifically designed for blogs and it comes with tools and features that enable you to set up and maintain your blog. See Chapter 18 to learn more.

Okay, that's all more or less reasonable. Now, just how does one go about finding one of these web server thingamajigs? Well, the answer to that depends on a bunch of factors, including the type of page you have, how you got connected to the Internet in the first place, and how much money (if any) you're willing to shell out for the privilege. In the end, you have three choices:

- Use your existing Internet provider.

- Try to find a free hosting provider.

- Sign up with a commercial hosting provider.

Use Your Existing Internet Provider

If you access the Internet via a corporate or educational network, your institution might have its own web server that you can use. If you get your Net jollies through an Internet service provider (ISP), phone or e-mail its customer service department to ask whether the company has a web server available. Many providers provide space so that their customers can put up personal pages free of charge. (This is particularly true of the big online service providers such as AOL.)

Try to Find a Free Hosting Provider

If cash is in short supply, or if you just have a naturally thrifty nature, there are a few hosting providers that will bring your web pages in from the cold out of the goodness of their hearts. In some cases these services are open only to specific groups, such as students, artists, nonprofit organizations, less fortunate members of the Partridge Family, and so on. However, there are plenty of providers that put up personal home pages free of charge. What's the catch? Well, there are almost always restrictions both on how much data you can store and on the type of data you can store (no ads, no dirty pictures, and so on). You'll probably also be required to display on your pages some kind of "banner" advertisement for the hosting provider.

Later in this chapter, I supply you with a collection of sites that offer lists of free web hosts. See the section titled "Lists of Free Web Hosts."

Sign Up with a Commercial Hosting Provider

For personal and business-related web pages, many web artisans end up renting a chunk of a web server from a commercial hosting provider. You normally fork over a setup fee to get your account going, and then you're looking at a monthly fee.

Why fork out all those shekels when there are so many free sites lying around? Because, as with most things in life, you get what you pay for. By paying for your host, you generally get more features, better service, and fewer annoyances (such as the ads that most free sites have to display).

Again, later in this chapter I take you through a bunch of sites that provide lists of commercial web hosts. See the section titled "Lists of Commercial Web Hosts."

A Buyer's Guide to Web Hosting

Unfortunately, choosing a web host isn't as straightforward as you might like it to be. For one thing, there are hundreds of hosts out there clamoring for your business; for another, the pitches and come-ons employed by your average web host are strewn with jargon and technical terms. I can't help reduce the number of web hosts, but I can help you to understand what the heck those hosts are yammering on about. Here's a list of the terms that you're most likely to come across when researching web hosts:

♦ **Storage space.** This refers to the amount of room allotted to you on the host's web server to store your files. The amount of acreage you get determines the amount of data you can store. For example, if you get a 1MB (one megabyte) limit, you can't store more than 1MB worth of files on the server. HTML files don't take up much real estate, but large graphics sure do, so you need to watch your limit. Generally speaking, the more you pay for a host, the more storage space you get.

♦ **Bandwidth.** This is a measure of how much of your data the server serves. For example, suppose the HTML file for your page is 1KB (one kilobyte) and the graphics associated with the page consume 9KB. If someone accesses your page, the server ships out a total of 10KB; if 10 people access the page (either at the same time or over a period of time), the total bandwidth is 100KB. Most hosts give you a bandwidth limit (or "cap"), which is most often a certain number of megabytes or gigabytes per month. (A gigabyte is equal to about 1,000 mega-bytes.) Again, the more you pay, the greater the bandwidth you get.

♦ **Domain name.** A domain name is a general Internet address such as mcfedries.com or whitehouse.gov. They tend to be easier to remember than the long-winded addresses that most web hosts supply you by default, so they're a popular feature. There are two types of domain names available:

Page Pitfalls

If you exceed your bandwidth limit, users will still be able to get to your pages. However, almost all web hosts charge you an extra fee for exceeding your bandwidth, so check this out before signing up. The usual penalty is a set fee per every megabyte or gigabyte over your cap.

A regular domain name (yourdomain.com or yourdomain.org). To get one of these domains, you either need to contact Network Solutions (networksolutions.com) directly, or you can use one of the many other registration services (such as register.com). A more convenient route is to choose a web hosting provider that will do this for you. Either way, it will usually cost you U.S. $35 per year. (Although some hosts offer cheap domains as a "loss leader" and recoup their costs with hosting fees.) If you go the direct route, you have to find a web host who is willing to host your domain.

A subdomain name (yourdomain. webhostdomain.com). In this case, "webhostdomain.com" is the domain name of the web hosting company, and they simply tack on whatever name you want to the beginning. There are many web hosts who will provide you with this type of domain, often for free.

◆ **E-mail mailboxes.** Most hosts offer you an e-mail mailbox along with your web space. The more you pay, the more mailboxes you get.

Page Pitfalls

If you decide to get your own domain name, make sure that it is *you* who owns the domain, not the web host. Also, make sure that your name is listed as the domain's "administrative" contact and that the web host is listed only as the "technical" contact.

◆ **E-mail forwarding.** This service enables you to have messages that are sent to your web host address rerouted to some other e-mail address.

◆ **Shared server.** If the host offers this type of server (it's also called a *virtual server*), it means that you'll be sharing the server with other websites (there could be dozens or even hundreds of them). The web host takes care of all the highly technical server management chores, so all you have to do is maintain your site. This is by far the best (and cheapest) choice for individuals or small business types.

◆ **Dedicated server.** This type of server means that you get your very own server computer on the host. That may sound like a good thing, but it's usually up to you to manage the server, which can be a dauntingly technical task. Also, dedicated servers are hideously expensive (they usually start at a few hundred dollars a month).

◆ **Operating system.** This refers to the operating system on the web server. You usually have two choices: Unix (or Linux) and Windows (NT, 2000, or 2003). Unix systems have the reputation of being very reliable and fast, even under heavy traffic loads, so they're usually the best choice for a shared server. Windows systems are a better choice for dedicated servers because they're easier to administer than their Unix brethren. Note, too, that Unix servers are case sensitive in terms of file and directory names, while Windows servers are not.

◆ **Ad requirements.** Almost all free web hosts require you to display some type of advertising on your pages. This could be a banner ad across the top of the page, a "pop-up" ad that appears each time a person accesses your pages, or a "watermark" ad, usually a semitransparent logo that "hovers" over your page. Escaping these annoying ads is the number one reason, by far, that webmasters switch to a commercial host.

Webmaster Wisdom

People often ask me if I can supply them with a script or some other means to disable or hide the ads displayed by their free web host. My answer is always an emphatic "No!" because those ads are how the host makes its money. If enough people circumvent the ads, the host will eventually lose money and will no longer be able to offer free hosting.

◆ **Uptime.** This refers to the percentage of time that the host's server is up and serving. There's no such thing as 100 percent uptime because all servers require maintenance and upgrades at some point. However, the best hosts will have uptime numbers over 99 percent. (If a host doesn't advertise its uptime, it's probably because it's very low. Be sure to ask before committing yourself.)

◆ **Tech support.** If you have problems setting up or accessing your site, you want to know that help is just around the corner. Therefore, the best hosts offer 24/7 tech support, which means that you can contact the company—either by phone or e-mail—24 hours a day, seven days a week.

◆ **cgi-bin.** This is a special directory that is meant to store CGI "scripts" that perform behind-the-scenes tasks. The most common use for these scripts is to process form data, as described in Chapter 12. If you want to use any of the pre-fab scripts available on the web, or if you want to create your own, then you'll need a cgi-bin directory in which to store them. You should also check to see if the cgi-bin is shared with other sites or if you have your own. In general, the host will place greater restrictions on a shared cgi-bin than on a personal one.

◆ **Scripts.** Speaking of scripts, most good hosts will also offer you a selection of ready-to-run scripts for things such as guest books and e-mailing form data.

◆ **FTP access.** As you'll see in Chapter 8, you'll usually use the Internet's FTP service to transfer your files from your computer to the web host. If a host offers FTP access (some hosts have their own method for transferring files), make sure that you can use it any time you like and that there are no restrictions on the amount of data you can transfer at one time.

◆ **Anonymous FTP.** This variation on the FTP theme enables you to set up your own FTP server where other people can log in and download files from or upload files to your site. The more you pay for your site, the more likely you are to get this feature.

◆ **FrontPage support.** This means that you can use a program called Microsoft FrontPage to manage your website from the comfort of your computer.

◆ **Website statistics.** These stats tell you things such as how many people have visited your site, which pages are the most popular, how much bandwidth you're consuming, which browsers and browser versions surfers are using, and more.

Most decent hosts will offer a ready-made stats package, but the best ones will also give you access to the "raw" log files so that you can play with the data yourself.

◆ **E-commerce.** Some hosts offer a service that lets you set up a web "store" so that you can sell stuff on your site. That service usually includes a "shopping script," access to credit card authorization and other payment systems, and the ability to set up a secure connection. You usually get this only in the more expensive hosting packages, and you'll most often have to pay a setup fee to get your store built.

◆ **Scalability.** This buzzword means that the host is able to modify your site's features as required. For example, if your site becomes very popular, you might need to increase your bandwidth limit. If the host is scalable, then it can easily change your limit (or any other feature of your site).

A List of Lists: Sites That Offer Lists of Web Hosts

Now that you understand some of the lingo and concepts that surround this web hosting business, you're ready to start researching the hosts to find one that suits your web style. As I mentioned earlier, there are hundreds of hosts, so how is a body supposed to whittle them down to some kind of short list? Here are a few pointers:

◆ **Ask your friends and colleagues.** The best way to find a good host is that old standby, word of mouth. If someone you trust says a host is good, chances are you won't be disappointed. (This is assuming that you and your pal have similar hosting needs. If you want a full-blown e-commerce site, don't solicit recommendations from someone who has only a humble home-page.)

◆ **Solicit host reviews from experts.** Ask existing webmasters and other people "in the know" about which hosts they recommend or have heard good things about. Sites such as Epinions.com are also good sources of host reviews.

> **Webmaster Wisdom**
>
> For your shopping convenience, I've gathered the links shown here and in the next section and dropped them into a web page. It's called hostlist.htm, and you'll find it on this book's CD. To check out a list, open the page in your favorite browser, click the link, and you're there!

- ◆ **Contact web host customers.** Visit sites that use a particular web host and send an e-mail message to the webmaster asking what he or she thinks of the host's service.

- ◆ **Peruse the lists of web hosts.** There are a number of sites out there that track and compare web hosts, so they're an easy way to get in a lot of research.

The next couple of sections provide you with capsule reviews and addresses of these host lists.

Lists of Free Web Hosts

During the height of the dot-com frenzy, free web hosts seemed to sprout with a weed-like intensity. When the alleged "new economy" became old news and the dot-commers went down in flames, a lot of the free hosts went sneakers up, as well. Of the survivors, many converted themselves into commercial hosts to survive. There are still lots of free hosts left, however, and you can find most of them via the following sites that review or compare these hosts:

- ◆ **www.100best-free-web-space.com.** This top-quality site gives you a summary of the features of each free host, ranks the host on a scale of one to five, and offers a short review of the host.

- ◆ **www.freewebsiteproviders.com.** This comprehensive site lists hundreds of free hosts divided into various categories, including Personal, Business, Nonprofit, and Special Interest. The site provides you with a chart showing the features offered by each host and there are also reviews of some hosts.

- ◆ **www.freewebspace411.com.** One of the nice features about this site is that it includes a large number of capsule reviews for various free web hosts. One of the not-so-nice features is the ridiculous number of pop-up ads that the site foists upon a visitor. Annoying!

- ◆ **www.freewebspace.net.** A useful feature of this site is that it includes a large number of user reviews for various free web hosts. There are also discussion areas, news stories about hosts, and much more.

- ◆ **dir.yahoo.com/Business_and_Economy/Business_to_Business/ Communications_and_Networking/Internet_and_World_Wide_Web/ Network_Service_Providers/Hosting/Web_Site_Hosting/Free_Hosting.** As usual, Yahoo! is one of the best places to go for information. In this case, it offers an extensive index of free web hosting providers. And, as usual, the URL is finger-numbingly long.

Lists of Commercial Web Hosts

The world's capitalists—efficient free-market types that they are—smelled plenty of money to be had after the explosive growth of the web became apparent. This means there's certainly no shortage of commercial web hosting providers available. In fact, there are hundreds of the darn things. Once again, here are some sites that can supply you with lists of such providers.

◆ **www.cnet.com/internet.** This excellent site divides hosts into various categories and it also offers a "Most Popular" list so you can see who's using whom.

◆ **www.findahost.com.** This site lets you search for a web host by selecting the features you need.

◆ **www.hostfinders.com.** As the name implies, this site also offers a search feature for finding a web host that has what you want.

◆ **www.hostindex.com.** This site offers a large index of web hosts. However, its best feature is a monthly ranking of web hosts based on user feedback, features, pricing, and more.

◆ **www.thelist.internet.com.** This is *the* site for listings of Internet Service Providers. For our purposes, it also tells you whether or not the providers host web pages.

◆ **www.tophosts.com.** This impressively comprehensive site lists hosts in various categories, offers a "HostMatch" service to help you find a host that's right for you, has news articles and information related to hosting, and much more.

◆ **www.webhostdir.com.** Make sure you have plenty of time to spare when you visit this site. It not only lists hosts in a wide range of categories, but it also offers a quotation service, a search service, news and how-to articles, discussion forums, host awards, and more.

◆ **dir.yahoo.com/Business_and_Economy/Business_to_Business/ _Communications_and_Networking/Internet_and_World_Wide_Web/ _Network_Service_Providers/Hosting/Web_Site_Hosting/Directories.** Yahoo! maintains a list of web hosting directories at this address.

The Least You Need to Know

◆ A web host is a company that runs a web server and supplies you with a chunk of hard disk real estate on that server so that other people can enjoy your pages.

◆ If you don't want to spend any money to host your site, either ask your ISP if it does web hosting, or try out one of the free web hosts.

◆ The two most important things to bear in mind when shopping for a web host are storage (how much room you have on the server to store your files) and bandwidth (how much of your data can be served up to surfers).

◆ If you want to get your very own domain name, either you can ask your web host to register one for you or you can find a host who'll create a subdomain.

◆ To help you choose from the hundreds of hosts out there, ask people you know to recommend a host, look for expert reviews, contact a web host's customers, and use the lists of hosts that I provide in this chapter.

Chapter 8

Publish or Perish: Putting Your Page or Blog on the Web

In This Chapter

- ◆ A look inside your new web home
- ◆ How to get your pages to the provider
- ◆ Getting your site on the search engines
- ◆ A blow-by-blow description of the whole page-publishing thing

In the same way that (some say) a tree falling in the forest makes no sound if no one is around to hear it, a web page makes no impact if no one else can see it. In philosophical circles, this conundrum is known as the Use-It-Or-Lose-It Theory. What it really means is that all your efforts of the past few chapters will have been wasted if you don't take that final step, your biggest and boldest one yet: publishing your pages to the web.

This chapter shows you how to help your web pages emigrate from their native land (your hard disk) to the New World (the web). I show you how to best prepare them for the journey, how to select a mode of transportation, and how to settle your pages when they've arrived.

What Does Your Web Home Look Like?

After you sign up with a web hosting provider and your account is established, the web administrator creates two things for you: a directory on the server computer that you can use to store your web page files, and your very own web address. (This is also true if you're using a web server associated with your corporate or school network.)

The directory usually takes one of the following forms:

```
/yourname/
/usr/yourname/
/usr/yourname/www-docs/
```

In each case, *yourname* is the login name (or user name) that the provider assigns to you, or it may be your domain name (minus the .com part). Remember, this is a slice of the host's web server and this slice is yours to monkey around with as you see fit. This usually means you can do all or most of the following:

- Add files to the directory
- Add subdirectories to the directory
- Move or copy files from one directory to another
- Rename files or directories
- Delete files from the directory

Your web address will normally take one of the following shapes:

http://*provider*/*yourname*/

http://*yourname*.*provider*/

http://www.*yourname*/

Here, *provider* is the host name of your provider (for example, www.angelfire.com or just angelfire.com) and *yourname* is your login name or domain name. Here are some examples:

http://www.geocities.com/paulmcfedries/

http://mcfedries.150m.com/

http://www.mcfedries.com/

The Relationship Between Your Directory and Your Web Address

There's a direct and important relationship between your server directory and your address. That is, your address actually "points to" your directory and it enables other people to view the files that you store in that directory. For example, suppose I decide to store a file named thingamajig.html in my directory and that my main address is http://mcfedries.150m.com/. This means that someone else can view that file by typing the following URL into his browser:

http://mcfedries.150m.com/thingamajig.html

Similarly, suppose I create a subdirectory named CreatingAWebPage and I use it to store a file named index.html. This means that a surfer can view that file by convincing her browser to head for the following URL:

http://mcfedries.150m.com/creatingawebpage/index.html

In other words, folks can surf to your files and directories just by strategically tacking on the appropriate file names and directory names after your main web address.

Making Your Hard Disk and Your Web Home Mirror Images of Each Other

For largish sites, I mentioned in Chapter 5 that you should divide your stuff into separate subdirectories to keep things organized. (If you have a small site and are planning to keep all your files in a single directory, feel free to leap right over this section without penalty or embarrassment.) If you're going to go this route, then you can make your *uploading* duties immeasurably easier if you set up your own computer to have the same directory setup as the one you plan to use at your website. You can go about this in a number of ways, but here's the simplest:

Words from the Web

Moving a file from your computer to a remote location (such as your web host's server) is known in the file transfer trade as **uploading**.

◆ Create a *folder* on your computer that acts as the "home base" for all your HTML files. This is the equivalent of your main *directory* at your web hosting provider. Note that you can name this folder whatever you like (for example, HTML Stuff or My Web Weavings).

Webmaster Wisdom

To help reduce the confusion, in this chapter when I use the word **folder**, I'm referring to a directory on your computer; when I use the term **directory**, I'm referring to a directory on your web host's server.

◆ Create your subfolders under this home base folder. In this case, the subfolders you create must have the same names as the ones you want to use on your website.

To see why this is so useful, suppose you set up a subfolder on your computer named *graphics* that you use to store your image files. To insert into your page a file named mydog.jpg from that folder, you'd use the following tag:

```
<IMG SRC="graphics/mydog.jpg">
```

When you send your HTML file to the server and you then display the file in a browser, it will look for mydog.jpg in the graphics subdirectory. If you don't have such a subdirectory—either you didn't create it or you used a different name, such as images—the browser won't find mydog.jpg and your image won't show. In other words, if you match the subdirectories on your web server with the subfolders on your computer, your page will work properly without modifications both at home and on the web.

CAUTION **Page Pitfalls**

One common faux pas that beginning HTMLers make is to include the drive and all the folder names when referencing a file. Here's an example:

```
<IMG SRC="C:\My Documents\HTML Stuff\graphics\mydog.jpg">
```

This image will show up just fine when it's viewed from your computer, but it will fail miserably when you upload it to the server and view it on the web. That's because the "C:\My Documents\HTML Stuff\" part exists only on your computer.

Figure 8.1 shows a folder structure that I'll use as an example in this chapter. The main folder is called HTML Stuff, there's a subfolder called graphics for image files, and there are four subfolders that store related HTML files: books (which has its own subfolders), links, tirades, and wordplay.

Figure 8.1

The folder structure I'll use as an example.

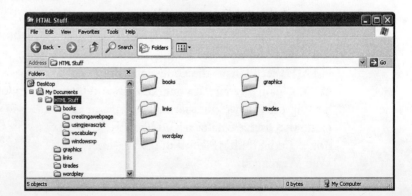

A Pre-Trip Checklist

After you decide on a hosting provider and a directory structure, you're just about ready to transfer your files to your directory on your hosting provider's server. Before you do that, however, you need to do the look-before-you-leap thing. That is, you need to give your files the once-over to make sure everything's on the up-and-up. Here's a short checklist to run through:

♦ HTML isn't hard, but it's fussy, persnickety stuff. If you miss even the smallest part of a single tag, your entire page could look like a real dog's breakfast (or not show up at all). To avoid this, recheck your tags to make sure they look right. In particular, make sure that each tag's opening angle bracket (<) has a corresponding closing angle bracket (>). Also, make sure that links and <IMG> tags have both opening and closing quotation marks (" "), and that tags such as <B>, <I>, <U>, <H1>, <OL>, <DL>, and <A> have their appropriate closing tags (</B>, </I>, and so on).

♦ If you want to give your page a thorough HTML check, there are resources on the web that do the dirty work for you. These so-called HTML "analyzers" check your page for improper tags, mismatched brackets, missing quotation marks, and more. Here are some to check out:

   ♦ **W3C HTML Validation Service.** This validation service is courtesy of the World Wide Web Consortium (W3C); they are the people who create and maintain the HTML standard (among others), so you can be sure they know what they're talking about. See validator.w3.org.

   ♦ **NetMechanic's HTML Toolbox.** This service not only checks your page for HTML errors, but it also tells you if your page contains broken links and the approximate load time for the page. See www.netmechanic.com/toolbox/html-code.htm.

   ♦ **NetMechanic's Browser Photo.** This unique service sends you "photos" that show you how your page looks in various browsers, browser versions, operating systems, and screen sizes. See www.netmechanic.com/browser-index.htm.

   ♦ **Bobby.** This service is a bit different from the others in this list. Bobby's job is to scan your page and then tell you if people with disabilities (such as impaired eyesight) might have problems viewing or reading it. If any problems are found, Bobby offers suggestions for improving the page's accessibility. See www.cast.org/bobby.

◆ URLs are easy to mistype, so double-check all your links. The best way to do this is to load the page into a browser and then try clicking the links.

◆ Different browsers have different ways of interpreting your HTML codes. To make sure your web page looks good to a large percentage of your readers, load the page into as many different browsers as you can. Note that Netscape Navigator and Internet Explorer together control about 98 percent of the browser market, so you should always run your page through some version of these two programs. At the very least, you should try out the page using Internet Explorer 5.x or 6.x and Netscape Navigator 4.x and 7.x.

◆ Pages can also look radically different depending on the screen resolution. If your video card supports them, make sure you view your page using the following resolutions: 640 × 480, 800 × 600, and 1024 × 768. (To change the resolution in Windows, right-click the desktop, click **Properties,** and then select the **Settings** tab. For the Mac, pull down the Apple menu and then select **Control Panels, Monitors.**)

◆ One of the advantages of using a word processor to create HTML files is that you usually have access to a spell checker. If so, make sure you use it to look for spelling gaffes in your page. You might want to add all the HTML tags to your custom dictionary so they don't constantly trip up the spell checker. In any case, you should always reread your text to make sure things make sense and are at least semigrammatical.

◆ Make backup copies of all your files before beginning the transfer. If anything untoward should happen while you're sending your files, you'll be able to recover gracefully.

Okay, Ship It!

Now, at long last, you're ready to get your page on the web. If the web server is on your company or school network, you send the files over the network to the directory set up by your system administrator. Otherwise, you send the files to the directory created for you on the hosting provider's web server.

In the latter case, you probably need to use the Internet's FTP (File Transfer Protocol) service. (Note, however, that AOL and some web hosts offer their own file upload services.) For this portion of the show, you have a number of ways to proceed:

◆ Use the demo version of CuteFTP that comes on the CD with this book. This is a Windows FTP program that makes it easy to send files from your computer to the web server. The next couple of sections show how to configure and use CuteFTP to get the job done.

◆ If you're an America Online user, you can use AOL's FTP service to ship your files to your "My Place" home directory.

◆ Mac users have a number of FTP programs to try out, including the most popular one, which is called Fetch. You can get them via TUCOWS (www.tucows.com). Click the **Macintosh** link.

> **Blog On**
>
> If you're building a blog and decide to use a blog hosting service, the service will have some mechanism to enable you to automatically upload and edit your pages. Check out Chapter 18 for details.

Adding Your Web Host's FTP Site

Before you can send anything to the web server, you have to tell CuteFTP how to find it and how to log on. Thankfully, you have to do this only once, and you're set for life (or at least until you move to another web host). Before you begin, you need three pieces of data, which your web host should have given to you when you signed up:

◆ The address of the host's FTP site. (This most often takes the form ftp.myhost.com, but in many cases you use the address of the web host, such as www.myhost.com.)

◆ Your FTP user name (which is usually the same as your website user name).

◆ Your FTP password (which, again, is usually the same as your website password).

With that info in hand, here's how it's done:

1. Start CuteFTP. The Site Manager dialog box appears.

2. Click the **New site** button. CuteFTP then prompts you to enter the settings for the new site.

3. In the **Label for site** text box, enter a name for this site (something like "My Web Home" or the name of the web host is just fine).

4. In the **FTP Host Address** text box, enter the address of the host's FTP site.

5. Enter your FTP user name in the FTP **site User Name** text box.

6. Enter your FTP password in the FTP **site Password** text box. (Note that, for security reasons, the password appears as asterisks.)

7. Click the **Edit** button to come face to face with the Site Properties dialog box.

8. Use the **Default Local Directory** text box to enter the drive and folder on your computer that contain your web page files. (If you're not sure, click the folder icon to the right of this box to pick out the folder using a dialog box.)

9. Click **OK** to close the Site Settings dialog box. Figure 8.2 shows this dialog box with the settings filled in for an example site.

10. Click **Exit** to store your settings.

Figure 8.2

An example of a completed FTP Site Settings dialog box.

Sending the Files via FTP

With CuteFTP ready for action, you can get down to it. Here are the basic steps to follow when sending your files to the web server via FTP:

1. If you haven't done so already, establish a connection with your regular Internet Service Provider.

2. Select **File, Site Manager** (or press **F4**) to get reacquainted with the Site Manager.

3. Make sure the site you just added is highlighted and then click the **Connect** button. After you're logged in to the server, CuteFTPmight display a Login Messages dialog box.

4. If so, click **OK.** You're now at the main CuteFTP window. As you can see in Figure 8.3, this window shows your computer's files on the left and your web server files on the right. (The latter, not surprisingly, will be empty right now since you haven't sent anything to the server yet.)

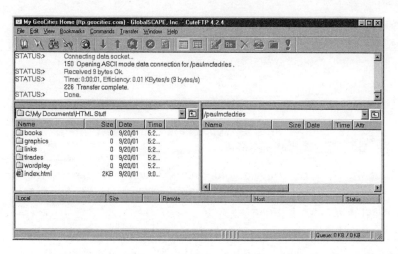

Figure 8.3

CuteFTP shows your computer's files on the left and your web server files on the right.

5. Select all the files on your computer that you want to send. The easiest way to do this is to hold down the **Ctrl** key, move your mouse into the left box, and then click each file that you're sending. When you finish selecting the files, release the **Ctrl** key.

6. Pull down the **Transfer** menu and select **Upload** (or press **Ctrl+Page Up**). CuteFTP sends the files one by one to the web server.

7. After the files have arrived safely, pull down the **FTP** menu and select **Disconnect** (or press **Shift+F4**) to shut down the connection.

Webmaster Wisdom

A quick way to send files to the server is to use your mouse to drag the highlighted files from the left pane and drop them on the right pane. When CuteFTP asks you to confirm, click **Yes.**

CAUTION

Page Pitfalls

I mentioned back in Chapter 5 that the Unix computers that play host to the vast majority of web servers are downright finicky when it comes to the uppercase and lowercase letters used in file and directory names.

Therefore, it's crucial that you check your <A> tags and <IMG> tags to make sure that the file and directory names you use match the combination of uppercase and lowercase letters used on your server. For example, suppose you have a graphics file on your server that's named vacation.gif. If your <IMG> tag points to, say, VACATION.GIF, the image won't appear. To help prevent problems, you can tell CuteFTP to force all your file names to lowercase letters. In the Site Manager, highlight your FTP site, click **Edit,** and then display the **Advanced** tab. In the **Filenames** group, activate the **Force Lowercase** option and then click **OK.**

To make sure everything's working okay, plug your web address into your browser and give your page a test surf. If all goes well, then congratulations are in order, because you've officially earned your webmeister stripes!

Creating a New Directory

If you need to create separate subdirectories for your graphics or HTML files, CuteFTP makes it easy. You have two choices:

◆ If you already have the corresponding subfolder on your computer, upload the entire folder to the server. (That is, highlight the folder in CuteFTP's left file pane and then select **Transfer, Upload.**)

◆ To create a new subdirectory on the server, first open the server directory you want to work (or just click anywhere inside the right file pane to activate it). Then select the **Commands, Directory, Make new directory** command (or press **Ctrl+M**). In the dialog box that appears, enter the name of the new directory and then click **OK.**

Again, remember that your goal is to end up with exactly the same directory structure on both your own computer and on the server. Figure 8.4 shows an example.

Figure 8.4

When you're finished, the list of files and directories on the web server (right) should be identical to the list of files and folders on your computer (left).

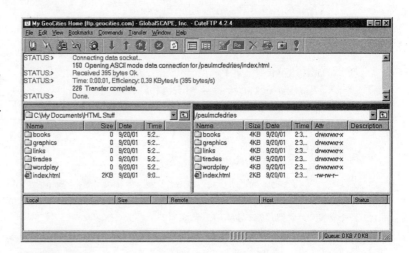

Making Changes to Your Web Files

What happens if you send an HTML file to your web provider and then realize you've made a typing gaffe? Or what if you have more information to add to one of your web pages? How do you make changes to the files that you've already sent?

Well, here's the short answer: You don't. That's right, after you've sent your files, you never have to bother with them again. That doesn't mean you can never update your site, however. Instead, you make your changes to the HTML files that reside on your computer and then send these revised files to your web provider. These files replace the old files, and your site is updated with no questions asked.

Page Pitfalls

Make sure you send the updated file to the correct directory on the server. Otherwise, you may overwrite a file that happens to have the same name in some other directory.

"Hey, I'm over Here!" Getting Your Site on the Search Engines

If you build it, they will come, right? Unfortunately, the answer to that is, "not necessarily." The web is a massive place that boasts billions (yes, I said *billions*) of pages. So even though your magnificent and hard-won work is on the web, all you've really done at this point is add your own needle to the web's digital haystack.

How are people supposed to know that your new cyberhome is up and running and ready for visitors? Well, people won't beat a path to your door unless you tell them how to get there. For starters, you can spread the news via word of mouth, e-mail notes to friends and colleagues, and by handing out your shiny, new business cards that have your home page address plastered all over them. Also, it's worth checking to see if your hosting provider has a section devoted to announcing new customer pages.

However, if you want to count your visitors in the hundreds or even the thousands, you need to cast a wider net. That is, you need to get your site listed in the web's major search engines so that other people can find you when they search for sites that have content similar to yours. The rest of this chapter takes you through the fine art of getting on the search engines and getting good rankings once you're there.

Submitting Your Site

The most straightforward way to get your site listed on a search engine is to stick the search engine's nose in it, so to speak. All search engines have a page that you can use to submit the particulars of your site. Here are the addresses of the submission pages for a dozen of the top search engines (see engines.htm on this book's CD):

AllTheWeb. www.alltheweb.com/add_url.php

AltaVista. www.altavista.com/sites/search/addurl

AOL Search. search.aol.com/add.adp

Google. www.google.com/intl/en_extra/addurl.html

HotBot. hotbot.lycos.com/addurl.asp

InfoSpace. www.infospace.com/submit.html

MSN. submit.looksmart.com/info.jhtml?synd=zdd&chan=zddhome

Webcrawler. www.webcrawler.com/info/add_url/

Yahoo! docs.yahoo.com/info/suggest/

Bear in mind, however, that your page won't necessarily show up on a search engine immediately after you make your submission. Some search engines are remarkably fast at updating their databases, but others can take weeks or even *months*, so patience is the key.

Webmaster Wisdom

Rather than submitting your site to the search engines by hand, there are services out there that will perform this drudgery for you. Although some will charge you a fee, there are many free services available, although most of the freebies will submit your site to only a limited number of search engines. Here are two of the more popular ones:

Submit It. www.submit-it.com

Add Me. www.addme.com

See also the Yahoo! Promotion index: yahoo.com/Business_and_Economy/ Business_to_Business/Marketing_and_Advertising/Internet/Promotion/

Also, don't submit *all* of your pages to the search engine; your main page is enough. The search engine's crawler will visit your main page and then follow your links to get to your other pages.

Using the ‹META› Tag to Make Search Engines Notice Your Site

The big search engines such as Google and AltaVista scour the web for new and updated sites. If you haven't submitted your site by hand, chances are they'll stumble upon your humble home one of these days and add your pages to their massive data-bases. Either way, is it possible to ensure that your pages will come out near the top if someone runs a search for topics related to your site? Well, no, there isn't any way to guarantee a good placement. However, you can help things along tremendously by adding a couple of special <META> tags that you insert between the <HEAD> and </HEAD> tags.

The first of these tags defines a description of your site:

```
<META NAME="Description" CONTENT="Your description goes here">
```

Most search engines use this description when they display your page in the results of a web search.

The second <META> tag defines one or more keywords that correspond to the key topics in the page. The search engines use these keywords to match your page with keywords entered by users when they perform a web search. Here's the syntax:

```
<META NAME="Keywords" CONTENT="keyword1, keyword2, etc.">
```

Here's an example:

```
<HTML>
<HEAD>
<TITLE>Tickle Me Elmomentum</TITLE>
<META NAME="Description"
CONTENT="This page examines the Tickle Me Elmo
phenomenon and attempts to understand its social ramifications.">
<META NAME="Keywords" CONTENT="tickle me elmo, toy, doll, giggle,
frenzy, fad, parental pressure">
</HEAD>
<BODY>
etc.
```

Tips for Composing Search Engine–Friendly ‹META› Tags

The mere fact that you're conscientious enough to add <META> tags to your pages is no guarantee that you'll get excellent positions within search results. Instead, you need to take a bit of extra time to craft your <META> tags for maximum effect. Here are some pointers:

◆ **Watch the length of your <META> content.** Most search engines have a limit on the length of the <META> tag Content values. For the Description tag, don't go longer than about 200 characters; for the Keywords tag, a maximum of 1,000 characters will keep you in good stead.

◆ **Use lowercase keywords.** To ensure compatibility with most search engines, you should put all of your keywords in lowercase.

- **Spread your keywords around.** Search engines rank sites based not only on the words in the Keywords <META> tag, but also on those found in the <TITLE> and in the page text, especially the first few lines.

- **Don't go keyword crazy.** You might think you could conjure yourself up a better search result placement by repeating some of your keywords a large number of times. Don't do it! Search engines *hate* this (they call it *spamdexing*) and they'll usually disqualify your site if they think you're trying to pull the web wool over their eyes. Use a word no more than six or seven times max.

Words from the Web

Including a keyword an excessive number of times is called **spamdexing**.

- **You can't fool them.** Over the years, webmasters have tried all kinds of tricks to fool search engine rankings. For example, they've included important keywords numerous times in the body of the page, but changed the text color to match the background so the user doesn't see the repeated words. Search engines are hip to this and other tricks.

- **Okay, you can fool them a little ....** One way to get around the keyword limitation is to include the keyword in appropriate phrases, like this:

```
<META NAME="Keywords" CONTENT="rutabaga, rutabaga recipes, rutabaga
biology, rutabaga quotations, rutabaga philosophy, rutabaga
worship, rutabaga news, rutabaga heroes">
```

- **Include keyword variations.** Include different parts of speech for important keywords (for example, play, plays, and playing). Also, you might want to allow for the different spelling used by American and Canadian or British users (for example, color and colour).

- **Crucial keywords go first.** Search engines tend to prioritize keywords in the order they appear. Therefore, if you have one or more important keywords, put them at the beginning of the <META> tag.

Perhaps the best advice I can give you is to try and get your head inside the searcher. If it were *you* who were searching for data similar to what's on *your* page, what keywords and phrases would *you* use?

The Least You Need to Know

♦ Your main web address points to your main directory on the host's web server. This means that any files or subdirectories you add can be viewed by adding the appropriate file and directory names to the address.

♦ Make sure that the folder structure you use on your computer is identical to the directory structure you set up on the host.

♦ Before sending your page to the host, check for things such as missing angle brackets, quotation marks, and end tags, and mistyped link addresses. Also, be sure to check your page in different browsers and at different screen resolutions.

♦ Use the pages provided by most search engines to tell them about your new site.

♦ For search engines to properly index your site, and for surfers to find it, include both a Description and a Keywords <META> tag on all of your pages.

Part 2

A Grab Bag of Web Page and Blog Wonders

The HTML hoops I made you jump through in Part 1 will stand you in good stead for the majority of your web page projects. In fact, you now have enough HTML trivia crammed into your brain to keep you going strong for the rest of your career as a web author. But that doesn't mean you should rip out the rest of this book and turn it into confetti. Heck no. You still have quite a few nuggets of HTML gold to mine, and that's just what you do here in Part 2. Think of the next few chapters as page-bound piñatas, stuffed full of various HTML candies and toys. You only have to whack each one with a stick (metaphorically speaking, of course) to spill out things like using images as links, adding sounds, and creating tables, forms, and frames.

Chapter 9

Images Can Be Links, Too

In This Chapter

♦ How to set up an image as a hypertext link

♦ Some handy ideas for using image links

♦ A few image pitfalls to watch out for

♦ How to create your own image maps—without programming!

♦ Nifty techniques for turning image *lead* into link *gold*

You might think that web page images are all show and no go, but I assure you they can "go" with the best of them. Specifically, I mean you can use them as links, just like regular text. The reader just clicks the image, and then goes off to whatever corner of the web you specify. This chapter shows you not only how to set up an image as a link but also how to create *image maps*—graphics that contain multiple links.

Turning an Image into a Link

Recall from Chapter 5 that you use the <A> tag to build a link into a web page:

```
<A HREF="URL">The link text goes here</A>
```

The *URL* part is the Internet address of the web page (or whatever) to which you want to link.

Designating an image as a link is not a whole lot different from using text. You use the same <A> tag, but you insert an <IMG> tag between the <A> and </A> tags, like this:

```
<A HREF="URL"><IMG SRC="filename"></A>
```

Again, *URL* is the address of the linked page, and *filename* is the name of the graphics file that you want to appear in the page and that you want the surfer to click.

For example, it's often a good idea to include a link from all your other web pages back to your home page. This makes it easy for your readers to start over again. Here's a document (backhome.htm on this book's CD) that sets up an image of a house as the link back to the home page:

```
<HTML>
<HEAD>
<TITLE>Images Can Be Links, Too</TITLE>
</HEAD>
<BODY>
Click this house <A HREF="index.htm"><IMG
SRC="house.gif"></A>
to return to my home page.
</BODY>
</HTML>
```

Figure 9.1 shows what it looks like. Notice how the browser displays a border around the image to identify it as a link.

Page Pitfalls

Always keep the <IMG> tag and the </A> end tag on the same line in your HTML file. In other words, don't do this:

```
<A HREF="URL"><IMG
SRC="filename">
</A>
```

If you do, you'll see a tiny (yet very annoying) line protruding from the bottom-right corner of your image.

Webmaster Wisdom

The link border that appears around an image link isn't usually very flattering to the image. To keep your images looking good, get rid of the border by adding BORDER="0" to your <IMG> tag:

```
<IMG SRC="house.gif"
BORDER="0">
```

Figure 9.1

An image masquerading as a link.

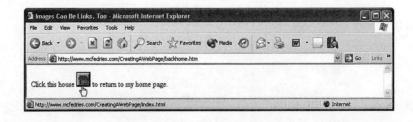

Why Should I Use an Image as a Link?

That's a good question, and I can answer it with two simple words: eye candy. You already know that adding images is a great way to liven up a dull-as-dishwater web page. So if it's your goal to encourage people to surf your site and see what you have to offer, it's just more tempting for would-be surfers to click interesting-looking images.

That's not to say you have to turn every last one of your links into an image (or vice versa). As always, prudence is the order of the day, and a page with just a few image links is more effective than a page that's covered in them. So, for example, you might want to add links to get people back to your home page, to enable visitors to send you an e-mail message, or for important areas of your site. The next three sections also take you through three common uses for image links: toolbars, navigation buttons, and thumbnails.

Example 1: A Web Page Toolbar

Most modern programs have toolbars with various buttons that give you one-click access to the program's most-used commands and features. You can use image links to provide similar convenience to the folks who trudge through your site.

The basic process for setting this up involves three steps:

1. Use your favorite graphics program to create button-like images that represent important sections of your website (your home page, your guest book, your list of links to Ozzy Osbourne sites, and so on).

2. Create <IMG> tags to set up these buttons as image links that point to the appropriate pages.

3. Insert these <IMG> tags consecutively (that is, on a *single* line in the text file) at the top and/or bottom of each page. The consecutive <IMG> tags cause the images to appear side by side. Presto: instant web toolbar!

The design of your buttons is entirely up to you, but most web toolbars use some combination of image and text. Personally, I don't have an artistic bone in my body, so I prefer to use "text-only" images, as shown in Figure 9.2. This toolbar is just six linked images displayed on a single line.

Webmaster Wisdom

Every good graphics program has some kind of "Text" tool that enables you to add text to an image.

Here's the HTML code that I used to create this toolbar:

```
<HTML>
<HEAD>
<TITLE>A Web Page Toolbar</TITLE>
</HEAD>
<BODY>
<A HREF="/Books/index.html">
➥<IMG SRC="books.gif" BORDER=0></A>
➥<A HREF="/Ramblings/index.html">
➥<IMG SRC="ramblings.gif" BORDER=0></A>
➥<A HREF="/Toys/index.html">
➥<IMG SRC="toys.gif" BORDER=0></A>
➥<A HREF="/guestbook.html">
➥<IMG SRC="guestbk.gif" BORDER=0></A>
➥<A HREF="/search.html">
➥<IMG SRC="search.gif" BORDER=0></A>
➥<A HREF="/index.html">
➥<IMG SRC="homepage.gif" BORDER=0></A>
</BODY>
</HTML>
```

To make sure the buttons are smushed together, be sure to type out all the <A> tags and <IMG> tags on a single line.

Figure 9.2

Cram consecutive image links together for a handy web page toolbar.

Example 2: Navigation Buttons

Some websites contain material that could (or should) be read serially. That is, you read one page and then the next page, and so on. In these situations, it's convenient to give the reader an easy method for navigating back and forth through these pages. The solution that many sites use is to set up VCR-style buttons on the page. These are usually arrows that point forward or backward, as well as a "rewind" button that takes the reader to the first page in the series.

For example, Figure 9.3 shows a page from my website. This page is part of a primer on Internet e-mail and the buttons near the top of each page enable you to navigate to the next installment (the Next button), the previous installment (the Prev button), the first installment (the Top button), or to the home page for this section of my site (the Index button).

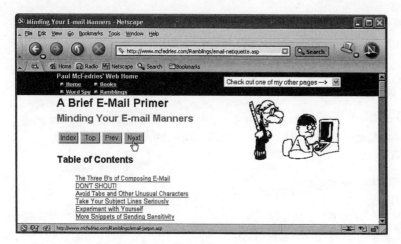

Figure 9.3

An example of a web page that uses image links as navigation buttons.

Example 3: Creating Image Thumbnails

Painters, photographers, and other artistic types often turn their websites into online galleries to show off their work. Unfortunately, the image files associated with this kind of work are often huge, so putting even a couple of them on a single page can lead surfers to seek their highbrow entertainment elsewhere.

A better approach is to create a smaller version—called a *thumbnail*, in the trade—of each large image and display those scaled-down copies on your "gallery" page or pages. You then set up each thumbnail to link directly to the larger version of the image.

To create a thumbnail, you first load the full-size image into your favorite graphics program. You then use the program's **Resize** command to chop the image down to size. Here's how you do this with Paint Shop Pro:

1. Select the **Image, Resize** command. The Resize dialog box check box is activated.

2. Make sure the **Maintain aspect ratio of** check box is activated.

3. Use either the **Width** or the **Height** text box to enter the thumbnail's width or height. (Note that you need to adjust only one of these values because Paint Shop Pro will adjust the other value automatically to compensate.)

4. Click **OK**.

Webmaster Wisdom

If you have a lot of images, you might want to avoid the drudgery of converting them all to thumbnails. Here are three programs that can automate the thumbnail process:

Easy Thumbnails. www.fookes.com/ezthumbs

Irfanview. www.irfanview.com

AllThumbs. www.slideshow-refinery.com

5. Select the **File, Save As** command, give the thumbnail a name that's different from the original file, and then click **Save**.

That last step is important because you don't want to change anything about the original file, so you save your changes to a new file.

With the thumbnail created, you then do the linking part. For example, suppose your original image is named photo.jpg and your thumbnail is named photo-thumb.jpg. Here's the code you'd use:

```
<A HREF="photo.jpg"><IMG SRC="photo-thumb.jpg"></A>
```

The Ins and Outs of Image Links

If you plan on using images and links on your web pages, here are a few tidbits to bear in mind when designing these links:

- **Don't use massive images for your links.** It's frustrating enough waiting for a humungous image to load if you have a slow Internet connection. However, it's doubly frustrating if that image is an important part of the site's navigation system. In this case, most folks simply take their surfing business elsewhere. As a general rule, it shouldn't take more than a few seconds for surfers with slow connections to download your image.

- **Try to use images that have at least some connection to the link.** For example, suppose you want to set up a link back to your home page. You might have some kind of personal logo or symbol that might seem appropriate, but how many of your surfers will know what this means? A simple icon of a house would probably be more effective.

- **Unless your image is ridiculously obvious, you should always accompany the graphic with explanatory text.** A simple line such as "Click the mailbox icon to send me a message" does wonders for making your site easier to figure out.

- **Consider turning the explanatory text itself into a link that points to the same page as the image.** That way, if the surfer is using a text-only browser or a graphical browser with images turned off, he or she can still navigate your site. Figure 9.4 shows an example where I've augmented the toolbar with the equivalent text links.

Webmaster Wisdom

Remember that most modern browsers display the <IMG> tag's ALT text as a banner when the user hovers the mouse over an image. With an image link, you can use the ALT text to tell the surfer where the link takes him or her.

Figure 9.4

It's often useful to supple-ment your image links with the equivalent text links.

Images Can Be Maps, Too

An *image map* is a graphic with several defined *hot spots*. Click one area and a particu-lar web page loads; click a different area and a different page loads. In other words, each of these areas is just a special kind of link. Image maps give you much more flex-ibility than simple image links because you have more freedom to arrange the links and you can use more elaborate graphics (but not *too* elaborate; remember those poor surfers with slow modem connections).

Originally, setting up an image map was a complicated affair in which you actually had to write a program that would decipher clicks on the image and tell the web server which page to load. Although gluttons for punishment can still take that road, the rest of us now have an easier method. The tall-forehead types call this method *client-side image maps*, but a better name would probably be *browser-based image maps*. In other words, in contrast to the old method that required the intervention of a pro-gram and a web server, this new method has everything built right into the browser. You also get the following extra benefits:

◆ Browser-based image maps are faster because the web server doesn't have to process any image map info.

◆ The browser shows the actual URL of each image map link. With server-based image maps, all you get are the coordi-nates of the map.

◆ You can test out your map on your own computer before you load everything onto the web.

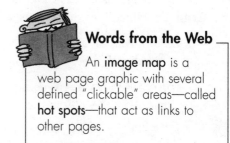

Words from the Web

An **image map** is a web page graphic with several defined "clickable" areas—called **hot spots**—that act as links to other pages.

For your image map to work correctly, you have to perform three steps:

1. Decide which distinct image regions you want to use and then determine the coordinates of each region.

2. Use the <MAP> and <AREA> tags to assign a link to each of these regions.

3. Add a special version of the <IMG> tag to your web page.

The next few sections take you through each of these steps to show you how to create your own browser-based image maps.

Step 1: Determine the Map Coordinates

All the information that you see on your computer screen is divided into tiny little points of light called *pixels*. Suppose you went insane one day and decided you wanted to invent a way to specify any particular pixel on the screen. Well, because a typical screen arranges these pixels in 800 columns by 600 rows, you might do this:

◆ Number the columns from left to right starting with 0 as the first column (remember, you're insane) and 799 as the last column.

◆ Number the rows from top to bottom starting with 0 as the first row and 599 as the last row.

So far, so good(!). Now you can pinpoint any pixel just by giving its column number followed by its row number. For example, pixel 10,15 is the teensy bit of light in the 11th column and 16th row. And, because your insanity has math-geek overtones, you call the column value "X" and the row value "Y."

This "coordinate system" that you've so cleverly developed is exactly what you use to divide an image map, where the top-left corner of the image is 0,0. For example, check out the image displayed in Figure 9.5. This image is 600 pixels wide and 100 pixels high, and it's divided into three areas, each of which is 200 pixels wide and 100 pixels high:

◆ **Area A.** This area is defined by coordinate 0,0 in the upper-left corner and coordinate 199,99 in the lower-right corner.

◆ **Area B.** This area is defined by coordinate 199,0 in the upper-left corner and coordinate 399,99 in the lower-right corner.

◆ **Area C.** This area is defined by coordinate 399,0 in the upper-left corner and coordinate 599,99 in the lower-right corner.

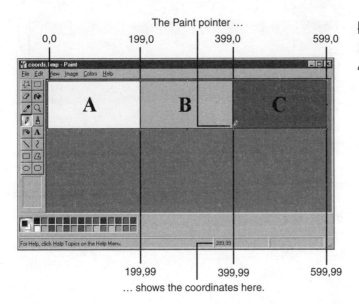

Figure 9.5

Use a coordinate system to divide your image.

Why bother with all this coordinate malarkey? Well, it's how you let the browser know what to do when the user clicks the image. For example, suppose you want to load a page named a.htm when the surfer clicks inside area A in the preceding image. Then you'd tell the browser (this is explained in the next section) that if the mouse pointer is within the rectangle bounded by the coordinates 0,0 and 199,99, load a.htm.

That's all well and good, but how the heck are you supposed to figure out these coordinates? One way would be to load the image into a graphics program. Paint, for example, shows the current coordinates in the status bar when you slide the mouse around inside the image (as shown in Figure 9.5).

If you don't have a graphics program that does this, there's a method you can use to display the coordinates within the browser. (Note, however, that this works only in Windows; Mac browsers aren't hip to this trick.) What you have to do is set up an HTML file with a link that uses the following format:

```
<A HREF="whatever"><IMG SRC="YourImageMap" ISMAP></A>
```

Here, replace *YourImageMap* with the name of the image file you want to use for your map. The ISMAP attribute fools the browser into thinking this is a server-based image map. So what? So this: Now load this HTML file into a browser, move your mouse pointer over the image and—voilà!—the image coordinates of the current mouse position appear in the status bar! As shown in Figure 9.6, you just point at the corners that define the image areas and record the coordinates that appear.

Figure 9.6

To determine coordinates, set up your image as a link with the ISMAP attribute, and the browser does all the hard work for you.

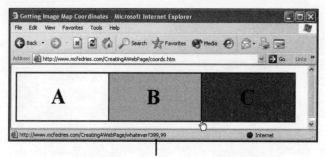

Jot down the coordinates for each image area.

Step 2: Use ‹MAP› to Define the Image Map

With your image coordinates now scribbled on a piece of paper, you can set about defining the image map. To do this, you start with the <MAP> tag, which uses the following general form:

```
<MAP NAME="MapName">
</MAP>
```

The *MapName* part is a name that you assign to this map definition. Next, you have to specify the clickable areas on the image. You do this by using the <AREA> tag:

```
<AREA SHAPE="Shape" COORDS="Coords" HREF="URL">
```

Looks pretty ugly, doesn't it? Well, it's not too bad. The SHAPE attribute determines the shape of the area, the COORDS attribute defines the area's coordinates, and the HREF attribute specifies the web page that loads when the user clicks this area.

The COORDS attribute depends on what value you use for the SHAPE attribute. Most image map areas are rectangles, so you specify RECT as the SHAPE and set the COORDS attribute equal to the coordinates of the area's upper-left corner and lower-right corner. For example, here's an <AREA> tag for area A in the example we've been using:

```
<AREA SHAPE="RECT" COORDS="0, 0, 199, 99" HREF="a.htm">
```

You then stuff all your <AREA> tags between the <MAP> and </MAP> tags, like this:

```
<MAP NAME="TestMap">
<AREA SHAPE="RECT" COORDS="0, 0, 199, 99" HREF="a.htm">
<AREA SHAPE="RECT" COORDS="199, 0, 399, 99" HREF="b.htm">
<AREA SHAPE="RECT" COORDS="399, 0, 599, 99" HREF="c.htm">
</MAP>
```

Webmaster Wisdom

The <AREA> tag's SHAPE attribute also accepts the values CIRCLE (for, duh, a circle) and POLY (for a polygon).

For a circle, the COORDS attribute takes three values: the x coordinate of the circle's center point, the y coordinate of the center point, and the radius of the circle.

For a polygon, the COORDS attribute takes three or more sets of coordinates. The browser determines the area by joining a line from one coordinate to the other.

Step 3: Add the Image Map to Your Web Page

Okay, it's all over but the shouting, as they say. To put all that coordinate stuff to good use, you just toss a special version of the <IMG> tag into your web page:

```
<IMG SRC="YourImageMap" USEMAP="#MapName">
```

As before, you replace *YourImageMap* with the name of the image map file. The key, though, is the USEMAP attribute. By setting this attribute equal to the name of the map you just created (with an extra # tacked on the front), the browser treats the graphic as an image map. For example, here's an <IMG> tag that sets up an image map for the example we've been using:

```
<IMG SRC="coords.gif"
USEMAP="#TestMap">
```

Figure 9.7 shows you that this stuff actually works. Notice that when I point to area A, the name of the linked page (a.htm, in this case) appears in the status bar.

Webmaster Wisdom

There are also programs available that can automate most of this image map malarkey (now I tell you!). See Appendix A for the addresses of some image map software.

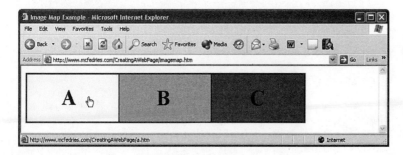

Figure 9.7

The image map is now ready for prime time.

The Least You Need to Know

◆ To set up an image as a link, shoehorn the appropriate <IMG> tag between <A> and </A>:

```
<A HREF="URL"><IMG SRC="filename"></A>
```

◆ Use small images that have some connection with the link, and add explanatory text so that people know exactly what they're clicking.

◆ Image maps, Step 1: Determine the coordinates of the various clickable areas on your map. A graphics program is the best way to do this, but you can also use the ISMAP trick:

```
<A HREF="whatever"><IMG SRC="YourImageMap" ISMAP></A>
```

◆ Image maps, Step 2: Use the <MAP> tag to name the map (for example, <MAP NAME="MyMap"> and then use the <AREA> tag to define the clickable areas of the image map:

```
<AREA SHAPE="Shape" COORDS="Coords" HREF="URL">
```

◆ Image maps, Step 3: Tell the browser about the image map by adding the USEMAP attribute to the <IMG> tag:

```
<IMG SRC="YourImageMap" USEMAP="#MapName">
```

Chapter 10

Table Talk: Adding Tables to Your Page

In This Chapter

- ◆ What are tables, and why are they useful?
- ◆ Creating simple tables
- ◆ Ever-so-slightly advanced tables
- ◆ Using tables to create a page with a margin
- ◆ Tons of table tips and techniques

In this chapter, you learn a bit of computer carpentry as I show you how to build and work with *tables*. Don't worry if you can't tell a hammer from a hacksaw; the tables you'll be dealing with are purely electronic. An HTML table is a rectangular grid of rows and columns on a web page, into which you can enter all kinds of info, including text, numbers, links, and even images. This chapter tells you everything you need to know to build your own table specimens.

What Is a Table?

Despite the name, HTML tables aren't really analogous to the big wooden thing you eat on every night. Instead, as I've said, a table is a rectangular arrangement of rows and columns on your screen. Figure 10.1 shows an example table.

Figure 10.1

An HTML table in a web document.

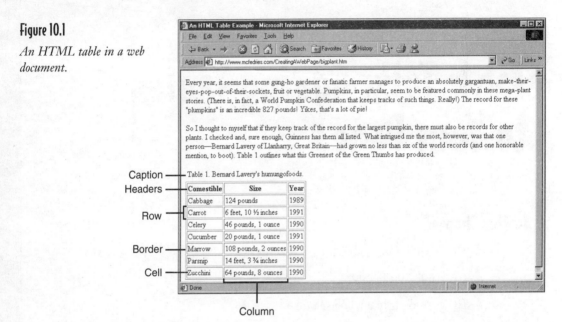

To make sure you understand what's going on (that *is* my job, after all), let's check out a bit of table lingo:

- ◆ **Row.** A single "line" of data that runs across the table. In the example table shown in Figure 10.1, there are eight rows in all.

- ◆ **Column.** A single vertical section of data. In the Figure 10.1 table, there are three columns.

- ◆ **Cell.** The intersection of a row and column. The cells are where you enter the data that appears in the table.

- ◆ **Caption.** This is text that appears (usually) above the table and is used to describe the contents of the table.

- ◆ **Headers.** The first row of the table. The headers are optional, but many people use them to label each column.

- ◆ **Borders.** These are the lines that surround the table and each cell.

Nothing too rocket science-y there.

Wait a minute. Way back in Chapter 3, you showed me how to use the <PRE> tag to make text line up all nice and neat. So why use a table when <PRE> can do a similar job?

Good question. Here are just a few advantages that tables bring to the, uh, table:

♦ Getting text to line up using <PRE> is frustrating at best, and a hair-pulling, head-pounding, curse-the-very-existence-of-the-@#$%&!-World-Wide-Web chore at worst. With tables, though, you can get your text to line up like boot camp recruits with very little effort.

♦ Each table cell is self-contained. You can edit and format the contents of a cell without disturbing the arrangement of the other table elements.

♦ The text "wraps" inside each cell, making it a snap to create multiple-line entries.

♦ Tables can include not only text, but images and links as well (even other tables!).

♦ Most text tags (such as <B>, <I>, <H1>, and so on) are fair game inside a table, so you can format the table to suit your needs (with some cautions, as you'll see a bit later).

Web Woodworking: How to Build a Table

Okay, it's time to put the table pedal to the HTML metal and start cranking out some of these table things. The next few sections take you through the basic steps. As an example, I'll show you how I created the table in Figure 10.1.

The Simplest Case: A One-Row Table

Tables always use the following basic container:

```
<TABLE>
</TABLE>
```

All the other table tags fit between these two tags. There are two things you need to know about the <TABLE> tag:

♦ If you want your table to show a border, use the <TABLE BORDER="*n*"> tag instead of <TABLE>, where *n* is the border width you want.

♦ If you don't want a border, use just <TABLE>.

Webmaster Wisdom

I can't tell you how many table troubles I've solved just by turning on the border to get a good look at the table structure. Therefore, I highly recommend using a border while constructing your table. You can always get rid of

After completing the previous steps, most of your remaining table chores involve the following four-step process:

1. Add a row.

2. Divide the row into the number of columns you want.

3. Insert data into each cell.

4. Repeat Steps 1 through 3 until done.

To add a row, you toss a <TR> (table row) tag and a </TR> tag (its corresponding end tag) between <TABLE> and </TABLE>:

```
<TABLE BORDER="1">
<TR>
</TR>
</TABLE>
```

Now you divide that row into columns by placing the <TD> (table data) and </TD> tags between <TR> and </TR>. Each <TD></TD> combination represents one column (or, more specifically, an individual cell in the row), so if you want a three-column table (with a border), you do this:

```
<TABLE BORDER="1">
<TR>
<TD></TD>
<TD></TD>
<TD></TD>
</TR>
</TABLE>
```

Now you enter the row's cell data by typing text between each <TD> tag and its </TD> end tag:

```
<TABLE BORDER="1">
<TR>
<TD>Cabbage</TD>
<TD>124 pounds</TD>
<TD>1989</TD>
</TR>
</TABLE>
```

Remember that you can put any of the following within the <TD> and </TD> tags:

- Text
- HTML text-formatting tags (such as <B> and <I>)
- Links
- Lists
- Images

Page Pitfalls

Text-formatting tags will work within only a *single* cell at a time. For example, you can't surround a table with the <FONT> and </FONT> tags in an effort to format, say, the font color for all the text in the table.

Adding More Rows

When your first row is firmly in place, you repeat the procedure for the other rows in the table. For our example table, here's the HTML that includes the data for all the rows:

```
<TABLE BORDER="1">
<TR>
<TD>Cabbage</TD><TD>124 pounds</TD><TD>1989</TD>
</TR>
<TR>
<TD>Carrot</TD><TD>6 feet, 10 &#189; inches</TD><TD>1991</TD>
</TR>
<TR>
<TD>Celery</TD><TD>46 pounds, 1 ounce</TD><TD>1990</TD>
</TR>
<TR>
<TD>Cucumber</TD><TD>20 pounds, 1 ounce</TD><TD>1991</TD>
</TR>
<TR>
<TD>Marrow</TD><TD>108 pounds, 2 ounces</TD><TD>1990</TD>
</TR>
<TR>
<TD>Parsnip</TD><TD>14 feet, 3 &#190; inches</TD><TD>1990</TD>
</TR>
<TR>
<TD>Zucchini</TD><TD>64 pounds, 8 ounces</TD><TD>1990</TD>
</TR>
</TABLE>
```

Creating a Row of Headers

If your table displays stats, data, or other info, you can make your readers' lives easier by including at the top of each column labels that define what's in the column. (You don't need a long-winded explanation; in most cases, a word or two should do the job.) To define a header, use the <TH> and </TH> tags within a row, like this:

```
<TR>
<TH>First Column Header</TH>
<TH>Second Column Header</TH>
<TH>And So On, Ad Nauseum</TH>
</TR>
```

As you can see, the <TH> tag is a lot like the <TD> tag. The difference is that the browser displays text that appears between the <TH> and </TH> tags as bold and centered within the cell. This helps the reader differentiate the header from the rest of the table data. Remember, though, that headers are optional; you can bypass them if your table doesn't need them.

Here's how I added the headers for the example you saw at the beginning of the chapter:

```
<TABLE BORDER="1">
<TR>
<TH>Comestible</TH><TH>Size</TH><TH>Year</TH>
</TR>
etc.
</TABLE>
```

Including a Caption

The last basic table element is the caption. A *caption* is a short description (a sentence or two) that tells the reader the purpose of the table. You define the caption with the <CAPTION> tag:

```
<CAPTION ALIGN="where">Caption text goes here.</CAPTION>
```

Here, *where* is either TOP or BOTTOM; if you use TOP, the caption appears above the table; if you use BOTTOM, the caption appears—you guessed it—below the table. Here's the <CAPTION> tag from the example (for the complete document, look for bigplant.htm on this book's CD):

```
<TABLE BORDER>
<CAPTION ALIGN="TOP">Table 1. Bernard Lavery's humungofoods.</CAPTION>
etc.
</TABLE>
```

Table Refinishing—More Table Tidbits

The tags we've eyeballed so far are enough to enable you to build tables that are sturdy, if not altogether flashy. If that's all you need, you can safely ignore the rest of the flapdoodle in this chapter. However, if you'd like a tad more control over the layout of your tables, the next few sections take you through a few refinements that can give your tables that certain *je ne sais quoi*.

Aligning Text Within Cells

The standard-issue alignment for table cells is left-aligned for data (<TD>) cells and centered for header (<TH>) cells. Not good enough? No sweat. Just shoehorn an ALIGN attribute inside the <TD> or <TH> tag and you can specify the text to be left-aligned, centered, or right-aligned. Here's how it works:

```
<TD ALIGN="alignment">
<TH ALIGN="alignment">
```

In both cases, *alignment* can be LEFT, CENTER, or RIGHT. That's not bad, but there's even more alignment fun to be had. You can also align your text vertically within a cell. This comes in handy if one cell is quite large (because it contains either a truck-load of text or a relatively large image), and you'd like to adjust the vertical position of the other cells in the same row. In this case, you use the VALIGN (vertical alignment) attribute with <TD> or <TH>:

```
<TD VALIGN="vertical">
<TH VALIGN="vertical">
```

Here, *vertical* can be TOP, MIDDLE (the default alignment), or BOTTOM. Here's an example document (tblalign.htm on this book's CD) that demonstrates each of these alignment options:

```
<HTML>
<HEAD>
<TITLE>Table Alignment</TITLE>
</HEAD>
<BODY>
<TABLE BORDER>
<CAPTION>Aligning Text Within Cells:</CAPTION>
<TR>
<TD></TD>
<TD ALIGN="LEFT">Left</TD>
<TD ALIGN="CENTER">Center</TD>
<TD ALIGN="RIGHT">Right</TD>
</TR>
```

```
<TR>
<TD><IMG SRC="constru1.gif">
<TD VALIGN="TOP">Top o' the cell</TD>
<TD VALIGN="MIDDLE">Middle o' the cell</TD>
<TD VALIGN="BOTTOM">Bottom o' the cell</TD>
</TR>
</TABLE>
</BODY>
</HTML>
```

Figure 10.2 shows how the table looks in the browser.

Figure 10.2

The various and sundry cell alignment options.

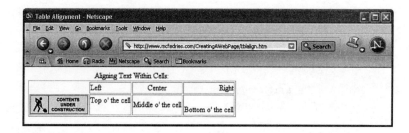

Webmaster Wisdom _____

In Figure 10.2, did you notice that the cell in the top-left corner of the table is empty? I did this by placing a <TD> tag and </TD> end tag side by side, with nothing in between. Note that, in the browser, the cell appears "filled in." If you want a truly empty cell, insert a nonbreaking space, like this: <TD> </TD>.

Spanning Text Across Multiple Rows or Columns

The data we've entered into our table cells so far has been decidedly monogamous. That is, each hunk of data has shacked up with only one cell. But it's possible (and perfectly legal) for data to be bigamous (take up two cells) or even polygamous (take up three or more cells). Such cells are said to *span* multiple rows or columns, which can come in quite handy for headers and graphics.

Let's start with spanning multiple columns. To do this, you need to interpose the COLSPAN (column span) attribute into the <TD> or <TH> tag:

```
<TD COLSPAN="cols">
<TH COLSPAN="cols">
```

In this case, *cols* is the number of columns you want the cell to span. Here's a simple example (tblspan1.htm on this book's CD) that shows a cell spanning two columns:

```
<HTML>
<HEAD>
<TITLE>Spanning Text Across Multiple Columns</TITLE>
</HEAD>
<BODY>
<TABLE BORDER="1">
<CAPTION>The Spanning Thing -- Example #1 (COLSPAN)</CAPTION>

<TR>
<TD COLSPAN="2">This item spans two columns</TD>
<TD>This one doesn't</TD>
</TR>

<TR>
<TD>The 1st Column</TD>
<TD>The 2nd Column</TD>
<TD>The 3rd Column</TD>
</TR>

</TABLE>
</BODY>
</HTML>
```

Figure 10.3 shows how the table looks in Internet Explorer.

Figure 10.3

A cell that spans two columns.

Spanning multiple rows is similar, except that you substitute ROWSPAN for COLSPAN in <TD> or <TH>:

```
<TD ROWSPAN="rows">
<TH ROWSPAN="rows">
```

The *rows* value is the number of rows you want the cell to span. Here's an example (tblspan2.htm on this book's CD) that shows a cell spanning two rows:

```
<HTML>
<HEAD>
<TITLE>Spanning Text Across Multiple Rows</TITLE>
</HEAD>
```

```
<BODY>
<TABLE BORDER="1">
<CAPTION>The Spanning Thing -- Example #2 (ROWSPAN)</CAPTION>

<TR>
<TD ROWSPAN="2">This here item spans two whole rows</TD>
<TD>The 1st Row</TD>
</TR>

<TR>
<TD>The 2nd Row</TD>
</TR>

<TR>
<TD>This one doesn't</TD>
<TD>The 3rd row</TD>
</TR>

</TABLE>
</BODY>
</HTML>
```

Figure 10.4 shows the result.

Figure 10.4

A cell that spans two rows.

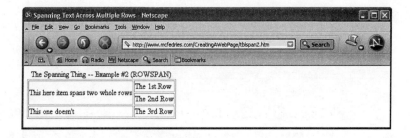

More Table Attributes

For our next table trick, we pull a few more table attributes out of our HTML hat. There are all kinds of wild extras, but the following are the most useful ones:

- ◆ **The background color.** You learned in Chapter 6 that you can adjust the background color of your entire web page. However, you can also assign a custom color to just the background of a table or even an individual cell. To do this, you add the BGCOLOR="#*rrggbb*" attribute to the <TABLE> tag or the <TD> tag, where *rrggbb* is a value that specifies the color you want (see Chapter 3). For example, the following tag gives your table a light gray background:

```
<TABLE BGCOLOR="#CCCCCC">
```

◆ **A background image.** Another thing you can do is set a background image instead of just a background color for a table or cell. This is just like setting a background image for a web page. In this case, you toss the BACKGROUND attribute inside the <TABLE> or <TD> tag and set the attribute equal to the name of the image file you want to use, as in this example:

```
<TABLE BACKGROUND="tablebg.gif">
```

◆ **The border size.** To change the thickness of the table border, you can assign a value to the <TABLE> tag's BORDER attribute. (Note that this applies only to the part of the border that surrounds the outside of the table; the inner borders aren't affected.) For example, to display your table with a border that's five units thick, you use the following:

Webmaster Wisdom

You can also use the HEIGHT attribute to set the overall height of the table, although this is rarely done. The most common use is to set HEIGHT to "100%" so that the table always spans the height of the

```
<TABLE BORDER="5">
```

◆ **The width of the table.** The browser usually does a pretty good job of adjusting the width of a table to accommodate the current window size. If you need your table to be a particular width, however, use the WIDTH attribute for the <TABLE> tag. You can either specify a value in pixels or, more likely, a percentage of the available window width. For example, to make sure your table always usurps 75 percent of the window width, you use this version of the <TABLE> tag:

```
<TABLE WIDTH="75%">
```

◆ **The width of a cell.** You can also specify the width of an individual cell by adding the WIDTH attribute to a <TD> or <TH> tag. Again, you can either specify a value in pixels or a percentage of the entire table. (Note that all the cells in the column will adopt the same width.) In this example, the cell takes up 50 percent of the table's width:

```
<TD WIDTH="50%">
```

◆ **The amount of space between cells.** By default, browsers allow just two pixels of space between each cell (vertically and horizontally). To bump that up, use the CELLSPACING attribute for the <TABLE> tag. Here's an example that increases the cell spacing to 10:

```
<TABLE CELLSPACING="10">
```

◆ **The amount of space between a cell's contents and its border.** Browsers like to cram data into a cell as tightly as possible. To that end, they leave a mere one pixel of space between the contents of the cell and the cell border. (This space is called the *cell padding*.) To give your table data more room to breathe, use the <TABLE> tag's CELLPADDING attribute. For example, the following line tells the browser to reserve a full 10 pixels of padding above, below, left, and right of the content in each cell:

```
<TABLE CELLPADDING="10">
```

Here's a web page that shows you an example for most of these attributes (see tblattr.htm on this book's CD):

```
<HTML>
<HEAD>
<TITLE>Some Table Extensions</TITLE>
</HEAD>
<BODY>
<B>&lt;TABLE BGCOLOR="#CCCCCC"&gt;</B>
<TABLE BORDER="1" BGCOLOR="#CCCCCC">
<TR>
<TD>Dumb</TD>
<TD>Dumber</TD>
<TD>Dumbest</TD>
</TR>
</TABLE>

<P>
<B>&lt;TABLE BORDER="5"&gt;</B>
</P>
<TABLE BORDER="5">
<TR>
<TD>One</TD>
<TD>Two</TD>
<TD>Buckle my shoe</TD>
</TR>
</TABLE>

<P>
<B>&lt;TABLE WIDTH="75%"&gt;</B>
</P>
<TABLE BORDER WIDTH="75%">
<TR>
<TD>Three</TD>
```

```
<TD>Four</TD>
<TD>Shut the door</TD>
</TR>
</TABLE>

<P>
<B>&lt;TD WIDTH="50%"&gt;</B>
</P>
<TABLE BORDER>
<TR>
<TD WIDTH="50%">WIDTH="50%"</TD>
<TD>Normal width</TD>
<TD>Normal width</TD>
</TR>
</TABLE>

<P>
<B>&lt;TABLE CELLSPACING="10"&gt;</B>
</P>
<TABLE BORDER CELLSPACING="10">
<TR>
<TD>Eeny</TD>
<TD>Meeny</TD>
<TD>Miney</TD>
<TD>Mo</TD>
</TR>
</TABLE>

<P>
<B>&lt;TABLE CELLPADDING="10"&gt;</B>
</P>
<TABLE BORDER CELLPADDING="10">
<TR>
<TD>Veni</TD>
<TD>Vidi</TD>
<TD>Vici</TD>
</TR>
</TABLE>

</BODY>
</HTML>
```

When you load this file into Internet Explorer, you see the tables shown in Figure 10.5.

Figure 10.5

Examples of some useful table attributes.

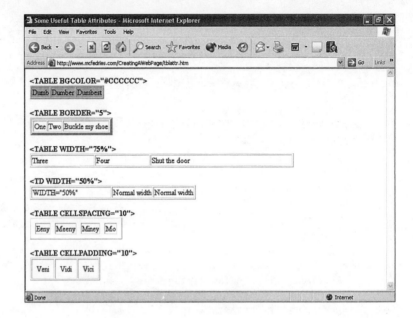

Using a Table to Set Up a Page with a Margin

Many websites and blogs set up their pages with a "margin" down the left side. This margin can be an image or, more likely, a color that's different from the page background color. These margins can be either purely decorative or they can contain links and other info.

Blog On

Margins are pretty much standard in the blog scheme of things because the traditional blog layout requires various "modules," which are usually tidbits of information or collections of links or other lists (Chapter 16 discusses modules in more depth). And by far the easiest way to display such modules is within a page margin (or, often, within two margins—one on the left and one on the right).

The good news is that it's easy to create such a margin by using a table that has the following characteristics:

- Set the table's height to 100 percent using the <TABLE> tag's HEIGHT attribute.

- The first column is the margin. Use the BACKGROUND or BGCOLOR attribute to define the image or color you want to use as the margin pattern.

Also, set the WIDTH attribute equal to the width of the margin you want. (Note, too, that you need *something* inside the column or Netscape won't display the margin. I use a nonbreaking space: .)

♦ The second column is where you put all your regular web page text and graphics.

Here's the basic layout for the web page (see margin1.htm on this book's CD):

```
<HTML>
<HEAD>
<TITLE>A Page with a Left-Hand Margin</TITLE>
</HEAD>
<BODY LEFTMARGIN="0" TOPMARGIN="0" MARGINWIDTH="0" MARGINHEIGHT="0">

<TABLE HEIGHT="100%">
<TR>

<TD BACKGROUND="grn2.gif" WIDTH="100"> </TD>

<TD VALIGN="TOP">
The rest of your web page stuff goes here.
</TD>

</TR>
</TABLE>

</BODY>
</HTML>
```

Figure 10.6 shows the page in the browser. As you can see, the left side of the page (that is, the left column of the table) displays an image that serves as the page margin.

Webmaster Wisdom

Notice how the <BODY> tag includes four new attributes: LEFTMARGIN, TOPMARGIN, MARGINWIDTH, and MARGINHEIGHT. Setting all of these to 0 ensures that you don't end up with extra space above

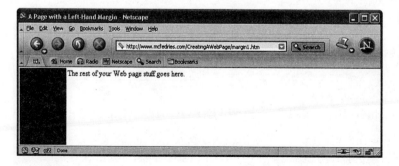

Figure 10.6

This page features a margin down the side.

Web designers commonly use the margin to insert text, links, images, and other stuff. Here's some sample code that does this (see margin2.htm on this book's CD):

```
<HTML>
<HEAD>
<TITLE>Populating the Margin with Text and Links</TITLE>
</HEAD>
<BODY LEFTMARGIN="0" TOPMARGIN="0" MARGINWIDTH="0" MARGINHEIGHT="0">

<TABLE HEIGHT="100%">
<TR>

<TD BGCOLOR="#FFFF00" WIDTH="200" VALIGN="TOP">
<B>The Complete Idiot's Guide to Creating a Web Page</B>
<P>
Here are some links for your surfing pleasure:
</P>
<A HREF="index.html">Home</A><BR>
<A HREF="about.html">About the Book</A><BR>
<A HREF="links.html">Links to Reader Pages</A><BR>
<A HREF="faq.html">Frequently Asked Questions</A><BR>
<A HREF="mailing-list.html">The CIGHTML Mailing List</A>
</TD>

<TD VALIGN="TOP">
The rest of your web page stuff goes here.
</TD>

</TR>
</TABLE>

</BODY>
</HTML>
```

Figure 10.7 shows what it looks like.

Figure 10.7

This page crams some text and links inside the margin.

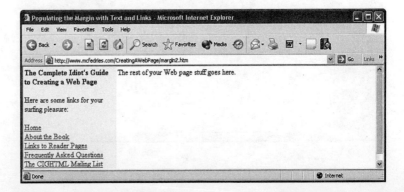

The Least You Need to Know

♦ The <TABLE> tag defines the table as a whole. Use the WIDTH and HEIGHT attributes to define the size of the table; use the BORDER attribute to define the size of the table border; use the BACKGROUND or BGCOLOR attributes to set a background image or color.

♦ The <TR> tag defines a row inside the table.

♦ The <TD> tag defines a column in the table (or, more precisely, it defines a cell inside the current row). Use the ALIGN attribute to align the cell data horizontally; use the VALIGN attribute to align the cell data vertically.

♦ To create a page with a margin, set up a table with two columns: The left column is the margin (a background image or color) and the right column contains the regular page data.

Making Your Web Pages Dance and Sing

In This Chapter

◆ Adding beeps, boops, burps, and other sounds to your web page

◆ Combining multiple images into a single, animated GIF

◆ Animating text with the <MARQUEE> tag

◆ How to turn a web page into a full-fledged entertainment center

Web pages are no longer restricted to static displays of text and graphics; now they're dynamic, kinetic, and truly interactive environments. Instead of mere documents to read and look at, pages have become programs that you can manipulate and play with. We've moved away from the simple type-it-and-send-it world of forms to a world in which pages have started performing the web equivalent of singing and dancing.

This chapter shows you a few techniques for enhancing your own pages with this kind of HTML technology. You learn how to turn your website into a multimedia marvel that includes sounds, animated GIF images, moving text, and more.

Sound Advice: Adding Sounds to Your Page

The web is alive with the sounds of—well, you name it! There's music, poetry, special effects, and sound snippets of every stripe. So now that you've labored long and hard to make your web page pleasing to the eye, perhaps you'd like to add a few extras to appeal to your visitors' ears, as well. It's actually pretty easy to do, and you hear all about it in this section.

First, Some Mumbo Jumbo About Sound Formats

If you read Chapter 6, you were no doubt traumatized by all those graphic formats and their incomprehensible TLAs (three-letter acronyms). The bad news is that the world's audio geeks (yes, these are the same guys who were the audio/visual nerds back in high school) also derive great pleasure in creating a constant stream of new sound formats. However, like graphic formats, the good news is that there are just a few audio formats that the web has ordained as standards:

- **AU.** This is a common format in the web soundscape. It's supported by both Netscape Navigator and Internet Explorer.

- **WAV.** This is the standard format used with Windows, which means it's becoming the standard format on the web. It's supported by all versions of Internet Explorer and by Netscape Navigator 3.0 and up.

- **MP3.** This is an incredibly popular format for digital music. The latest versions of Internet Explorer and Netscape use the Windows Media Player as the helper application for playing MP3 files. You can also get MP3 players from the MP3.com site (www.mp3.com).

- **RA.** This is the RealAudio format, which is used to "stream" large audio files. This means that you don't wait for the entire file to download. Instead, the browser grabs the first part of the file and starts playing it while the rest of the file downloads in the background.

- **MIDI.** This is the Musical Instrument Digital Interface format, and it's used to represent electronic music created with a MIDI synthesizer. This format is supported by Internet Explorer and Netscape Navigator 4.0 (for Navigator 3.0, you need the appropriate helper application setup).

Webmaster Wisdom

If you don't have a ready supply of audio material on hand, here are some sites that will get you started:

- ◆ **The Daily .WAV.** This site posts a new WAV file each weekday. It also has an extensive archive of WAV and MIDI files. See www.dailywav.com.
- ◆ **EarthStation1.** This site claims to be "The Internet's #1 Audio/Visual Archive," and judging by the massive number of sound and video clips they have on hand, I am not going to doubt them. See www.earthstation1.com.
- ◆ **FindSounds.** You won't find any sound files archived on this site. Instead, you use it to search the web for a particular sound effect. You can specify the sound format you want, the quality of the recording, and more. See www.findsounds.com.
- ◆ **SoundAmerica.** This site has thousands of sound clips from all walks of life, including cartoons, movies, TV, and more. It also has a nice collection of MIDI music. See www.soundamerica.com.
- ◆ **Yahoo!'s Audio Index.** This site has many links to audio and music sites, including those that offer audio archives. See www.yahoo.com/ Computers_and_Internet/Multimedia/Audio.

Sounding Off with Sound Links

After you have your mitts on a sound file, adding the sound to your web page is a no-brainer. All you have to do is copy the file to your website and then set up a link that points to that file, like this:

```
<A HREF="burp.wav">Click here for a special greeting!</A>
```

Assuming the viewer's browser is set up to handle the sound format you're using, the sound file downloads and then plays without further fuss.

Embedding Sound Files

If you want to add MIDI music or other sound files to your pages, one way to go is the <EMBED> tag, which is supported by both Netscape Navigator and Internet Explorer. At its simplest, you use the SRC attribute to specify the name of the sound file, like this:

```
<EMBED SRC="playme.mid">
```

Here's an example page (see midi.htm on this book's CD), and Figure 11.1 shows the Internet Explorer interpretation.

```
<HTML>
<HEAD>
<TITLE>A MIDI Example</TITLE>
</HEAD>
<BODY>
Click the Play button to hear some cool jazz music:<BR>
<EMBED SRC="jazz.mid">
</BODY>
</HTML>
```

Webmaster Wisdom

If you load midi.htm into Netscape, the program might tell you that it needs a "plug-in" in order to play the MIDI file. You should see a window with a "Get the Plug-In" link. If you don't see that link, use the following address: wp.netscape. com/plugins/index. html. Since this might also happen to some of your visitors, consider putting in a link to this address on the same page as your embedded sound file.

Figure 11.1

The <EMBED> tag adds a "player" to the web page.

The <EMBED> tag also supports the following extras:

- **AUTOSTART="FALSE".** If you add this attribute, the browser doesn't play the sound file automatically when the user surfs to your page.

- **LOOP="*Value*".** The LOOP attribute tells the browser how many times to play the sound. If you set *Value* to 2, for example, the browser runs through the sound twice. If you really want to drive your visitors away, set *Value* to INFINITE to tell the browser to play the sound indefinitely.

- **HIDDEN="TRUE".** If you add this attribute, the browser hides the controls. (If you use this, don't use AUTOSTART="FALSE" or the user will have no way of launching the sound file.)

Another Way to Add a Background Sound

With Internet Explorer, the <EMBED> tag isn't the only way to wire your site for sound. Specifically, Internet Explorer supports the <BGSOUND> tag that enables you to specify a sound that plays automatically when someone surfs to your site. (Much like the <EMBED> tag's AUTOSTART=TRUE attribute.) Here's the generic format:

```
<BGSOUND SRC="Filename" LOOP="Times">
```

The *Filename* part is the name of the sound file that you want to play (you can use AU, WAV, or MIDI files). The *Times* part tells the browser how many times to play the sound. You can either enter some positive number or use LOOP="INFINITE" to play the sound until the surfer puts their fist through the screen. (Note that you can put this tag anywhere you like in the page.) Here's an example:

```
<BGSOUND SRC="newagetouchyfeely.mid" LOOP="1">
```

Do-It-Yourself Disney: Animated GIF Images

In Chapter 6, I talked about how you can spruce up an otherwise drab web page by adding an image or two. However, if you *really* want to catch the eye of a busy web surfer, why not go one step further and add an animation to your page?

Sound impossible? It's actually a lot easier than you might think thanks to an interesting variation on the GIF file theme: an *animated GIF*. This format actually incorporates several GIF images into a single package. By using a special program, you can specify that these images be displayed sequentially, thus creating an animation! And the really great news is that the Windows program you need—it's called GIF Animator—resides right on this book's CD, so you don't have to bother hunting it down and suffering through an endless download. (Please note that GIF Animator is shareware. If you plan on using it regularly, be sure to fork over the U.S. $49.95 it costs to register the program.)

Webmaster Wisdom

Mac users can also get in on the GIF animation fun. Just check out a nifty (and free!) program called GIFBuilder, which is available from apple.com: http://www.apple.com/downloads/macosx/imaging_3d/gifbuilder.html. To use it, you create a series of images in a separate graphics program, import the images into GIFBuilder, and then set up the animation (the time between each image, the number of loops, and so on).

To get started, first use Paint, Paint Shop Pro, or some other drawing program to create the individual image files that will make up your animation. (It doesn't matter which format you use to save the files; GIF Animator can use most graphic formats, including the BMP files created by Paint. There is one caveat, though: To ensure a smooth animation, make each image the same size.) Figure 11.2 shows the images I'm using as an example. (These images are on this book's CD as well. They're named aninew1.gif through aninew5.gif. The resulting animated GIF is called aninew.gif.) As you can see, all I've done is change the coloring of the letters from image to image. For your own animations, you can change colors, shapes, text, or whatever else you need to create the effect you're looking for.

Figure 11.2

These images can be combined into a single animated GIF.

Launch GIF Animator and you eventually see the Startup Wizard dialog box. Now follow these steps:

1. In the Startup Wizard dialog box, click the **Animation Wizard** button to launch the Animation Wizard. (If you closed the Startup Wizard, select the **File, Animation Wizard** command, instead.)

2. Enter the **Width** and **Height** of the animation. This should be the same as the width and height of the GIF files you'll be incorporating into the animation. In my example, the width is 75 and the height is 47. Click **Next.**

3. Click **Add Image** to get to the Open dialog box, and then open the folder that contains the image or images you want to use.

4. You now have two ways to proceed:

   ◆ If all the image files you need for the animation are in the folder, hold down the **Ctrl** key and click each file name. Click **Open** when you're done.

   ◆ If you need only a single image from the folder, click it to highlight it and then click **Open.** You need to repeat steps 4 and 5 until you've selected all the image files for the animation.

5. Drag the files up and down to put them in the proper order, and then click **Next.** The wizard now asks for the amount of time to display each image (this is called the *delay*).

6. To set the delay, use the **Delay time** spinner to enter a value in 100ths of a second. (You might need to experiment with this value to get your animation just right. A value of 25 is a good place to start.) Alternatively, use the **Specify by frame rate** spin box to set the number of images you want displayed per second. Click **Next.**

7. In the final wizard dialog box, click **Finish.**

8. Select the **File** menu's **Save** command, enter a name for the new GIF file, and then click **Save.**

9. To check out your animation, click the **Preview** tab, or select **View, Play Animation.**

That's it! Your animated GIF is ready for action. Now you can add it to a web page by setting up a regular <IMG> tag where the SRC attribute points to the GIF file that you just created.

Page Pitfalls

GIF Animator makes it a breeze to create your own animations. There's also no shortage of ready-to-roll animated GIFs on the web, and I've even included a few on this book's CD. So this is probably as good a place as any to caution you against using too many animated images on your pages. One or two animations can add a nice touch to a page, but any more than that is distracting at best, and downright annoying at worst.

Creating a Marquee

Internet Explorer offers webmeisters an easy way to insert a chunk of animated text on a page. Specifically, you can display a word or phrase that enters the browser screen on the right, scrolls all the way across the screen, and then exits on the left. You can repeat this any number of times and even change the direction of the text. Because this is somewhat reminiscent of text on a theater marquee, the tag you use to control is called the < MARQUEE> tag. In its basic, no-frills guise, this tag has the following structure:

```
<MARQUEE>Put your scrolling text here.</MARQUEE>
```

The text you cram between the <MARQUEE> and </MARQUEE> tags is what scrolls across the screen. To gain a little more control over the scrolling, the <MARQUEE> tag supports quite a few attributes. Here are the most useful ones:

Webmaster Wisdom

Only Internet Explorer supports the <MARQUEE> tag, so it doesn't work in Netscape or any other browser. If you want scrolling text that works in most browsers, you can use JavaScript, as described in Chapter 24.

- ◆ **ALIGN=***"Alignment"*. Determines how the surrounding text is aligned vertically with the marquee. For *Alignment*, use either TOP or BOTTOM.

- ◆ **BEHAVIOR=***"Type"*. Determines how the text behaves within the marquee. For *Type*, use SCROLL to get the standard scroll-across movement; use SLIDE to make the text scroll in and then stop when it reaches the opposite side; use ALTERNATE to make the text "bounce" back and forth within the marquee.

- ◆ **BGCOLOR=***"Color"*. Sets the color of the marquee background.

- ◆ **DIRECTION=***"WhichWay"*. This attribute tells the browser which way to scroll the text. *WhichWay* can be either LEFT or RIGHT.

- ◆ **LOOP=***"Times"*. This attribute specifies the number of times you want the text to scroll. If you set *Times* to INFINITE or –1, the text will scroll until kingdom come.

- ◆ **SCROLLDELAY=***"Time"*. This attribute sets the delay in milliseconds between each loop.

- ◆ **SCROLLAMOUNT=***"Pixels"*. This attribute determines how many pixels the text jumps with each iteration. The higher the value for *Pixels*, the faster the text scrolls.

- ◆ **HEIGHT=***"Value"*. Specifies the marquee height either in pixels or as a percentage of the screen.

- ◆ **WIDTH=***"Value"*. Specifies the marquee width either in pixels or as a percentage of the screen.

Here's an HTML file (look for marquee.htm on this book's CD) that uses several of these attributes. Figure 11.3 shows how it looks in Internet Explorer. (When Netscape users view this page, they see all of the text between <MARQUEE> and </MARQUEE> at once.)

```
<HTML>
<HEAD>
<TITLE>Marquee Malarkey</TITLE>
</HEAD>
```

```
<BODY>
Welcome Web<MARQUEE ALIGN="BOTTOM" BGCOLOR="SILVER" WIDTH="50" SCROLLAMOUNT="4">
maker.........master.........meister.........
spinner.........weaver.........welder.........
</MARQUEE>!
</BODY>
</HTML>
```

Figure 11.3

Only Internet Explorer supports the <MARQUEE> tag.

Redirecting Browsers with Client Pull

If you move your site—or if you rename a page—it's best (when possible) to create a page in the old location that includes a link to the new site or page. Surfers can then click the link to get where you want them to go.

However, you can also use a nifty feature called *client pull* to send visitors to your new page automatically. To see an example, dial the following address into your browser: www.mcfedries.com/books/cightml/index.html.

This is the old address of this book's home page. When you go there, the page loads and—magic!—two seconds later you're whisked automatically to the book's current home page. Here's the header for the page you loaded:

```
<HTML>
<HEAD>
<TITLE>This page has moved!</TITLE>

<META
   NAME="REFRESH"
   CONTENT="2; URL=http://www.mcfedries.com/CreatingAWebPage/">

</HEAD>
```

The secret is the extra <META> tag in the header. The guts of the tag is the CONTENT attribute, which uses the following format:

```
CONTENT="seconds; URL=NewPage"
```

Here, *seconds* is the number of seconds the browser waits before loading the page specified with the URL value.

The Least You Need to Know

♦ There are five standard sound formats on the web: AU, WAV, MP3, RA, and MIDI.

♦ The easiest way to add sound to your site is to set up the sound file as a link using the <A HREF> tag:

```
<A HREF="burp.wav">Click here for a special greeting!</A>
```

♦ To place the sound file right in the page, use the <EMBED> tag:

```
<EMBED SRC="playme.mid">
```

♦ Remember that the <BGSOUND> and <MARQUEE> tags only work with Internet Explorer.

♦ To automatically redirect a browser to another page, use this form of the <META> tag:

```
<META
    NAME="REFRESH"
    CONTENT="seconds; URL=NewPage">
```

Chapter 12

Need Feedback?
Create a Form!

In This Chapter

♦ An introduction to forms

♦ Populating your form with buttons, boxes, and other bangles

♦ Where to find the programs that make your form run

♦ Almost everything you need to know to create great forms

In Chapter 5 and Chapter 9, I showed you how to use hypertext links to add a semblance of interactivity to your pages. However, beyond this basic level of interaction lies a whole genre of web pages called *forms*. This chapter tells you what forms are all about and takes you step-by-step through the creation of a basic form. I even point out a few resources that you can turn to for processing forms (including a special resource designed just for readers of this book).

What Is a Form, Anyway?

Most modern programs toss a dialog box in your face if they need to extract some information from you. For example, selecting a program's

Print command most likely results in some kind of Print dialog box showing up. The purpose of this dialog box is to pester you for information, such as the number of copies you want, the pages you want to print, and so on.

A form is essentially the web page equivalent of a dialog box. It's a page populated with text boxes, drop-down lists, and command buttons to get information from the user. For example, Figure 12.1 shows a form from my website. This is a search form that people can use to search the archives of my Word Spy site. As you can see, it's possible to create forms that look just like dialog boxes.

Figure 12.1

A form used for searching.

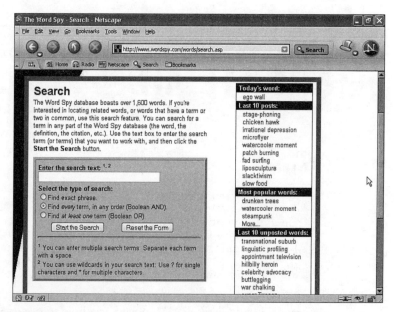

Blog On

Most blogs enable visitors to post comments about the blog entries, and they always use a form to record these comments. Chapter 17 discusses the details of setting up a comment system.

Of course, there are many possible uses for forms. If you put out a newsletter or magazine, you can use forms to gather information from subscribers. If your website includes pages with restricted access, you can use a form to get a person's user name and password for verification. If you have information in a database, you can use a form to have people specify what type of information they want to access.

Creating a Form

You create forms using special HTML tags, and it's pretty easy to set up a form. To get started, enter the <FORM> and </FORM> tags. These tags can be inserted anywhere inside the body of the page. You place all the other form-related tags (which I show you in the rest of this chapter) between <FORM> and </FORM>.

⚠ Page Pitfalls _____

Creating a form is fairly easy, but getting your mitts on the information that the reader types into the form is another matter. The problem is that this requires some programming, so it's well beyond the scope of a humble book such as this. So what's a poor, programming-challenged web wizard to do? Check out the section titled "Oh say, can you CGI?" later in this chapter.

The <FORM> tag always includes a couple of extra goodies that tell the web server how to process the form. Here's the general format:

```
<FORM ACTION="url" METHOD="METHOD">
</FORM>
```

Here, the ACTION attribute tells the browser where to send the form's data. This is almost always a program (or *script*, as they're often called) that processes the data and then performs some kind of action (hence the name). The *url* is the address of the script file that contains the program.

The METHOD attribute tells the browser how to send the form's data to the URL specified with ACTION. You have two choices here for *METHOD:* POST and GET. The method you use depends on the script, but POST is the most common method.

Let's bring all this gobbledygook down to earth with a concrete example. You can test your forms by using a special script that I host on my server. Here's how to use it:

```
<FORM ACTION="http://www.mcfedries.com/scripts/formtest.asp" METHOD="POST">
```

What this script does is return a page that shows you the data that you entered into the form. You can try this out after you build a working form. The next few sections take you through the basic form elements.

Making It Go: The Submit Button

Most dialog boxes, as you probably know from hard-won experience, have an OK command button. Clicking this button says, in effect, "All right, I've made my choices. Now go put everything into effect." Forms also have command buttons, and they come in two flavors: submit buttons and reset buttons.

A *submit button* (I talk about the reset button in the next section) is the form equivalent of an OK dialog box button. When the reader clicks the submit button, the form data is shipped out to the program specified by the <FORM> tag's ACTION attribute. Here's the simplest format for the submit button:

```
<INPUT TYPE="SUBMIT">
```

As you'll see, most form elements use some variation on the <INPUT> tag and, as I said before, you place all these tags between <FORM> and </FORM>. In this case, the TYPE="SUBMIT" attribute tells the browser to display a command button labeled Submit Query (or, on some browsers, Submit or Send). Note that each form can have just one submit button.

If the standard Submit Query label is a bit too stuffy for your needs, you can make up your own label, as follows:

```
<INPUT TYPE="SUBMIT" VALUE="Label">
```

Here, *Label* is the label that appears on the button. In the following example (submit.htm on this book's CD), I've inserted a submit button with the label Make It So!, and Figure 12.2 shows how it looks in a browser.

```
<HTML>
<HEAD>
<TITLE>Submit Button Custom Label Example</TITLE>
</HEAD>
<BODY>
<H3>An example of a custom label for a submit button:</H3>

<FORM ACTION="http://www.mcfedries.com/scripts/formtest.asp" METHOD="POST">
<INPUT TYPE="SUBMIT" VALUE="Make It So!">
</FORM>

</BODY>
</HTML>
```

Figure 12.2

A submit button with a custom label.

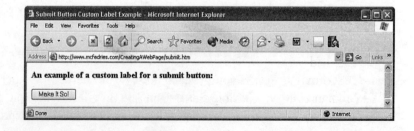

Webmaster Wisdom

Rather than using a boring command button to submit a form, you might prefer to have the user click an image. That's no sweat. What you need to do is add TYPE="IMAGE" to the <INPUT> tag, and add a SRC attribute that specifies the name of the graphics file (much like you do with the <IMG> tag). Here's an example:

```
<INPUT TYPE="IMAGE" SRC="go.gif">
```

You should know, too, that when you use an image as a submit button, the test script returns two extra values named "x" and "y." These give you the coordinates of the spot on the image that the user clicked. They can be safely ignored.

Starting Over: The Reset Button

If you plan on creating fairly large forms, you can do your readers a big favor by including a *reset button* somewhere on the form. A reset button clears all the data from the form's fields and reenters any default values that you specified in the fields. (I explain how to set up default values for each type of field as we go along.) Here's the tag you use to include a reset button:

```
<INPUT TYPE="RESET">
```

This creates a command button labeled Reset. Yes, you can create a custom label by tossing the VALUE attribute into the <INPUT> tag, as in the following example:

```
<INPUT TYPE="RESET" VALUE="Start From Scratch">
```

Using Text Boxes for Single-Line Text

For simple text entries, such as a person's name or favorite Beatle, use text boxes. These are just rectangles within which the reader can type whatever he likes. Here's the basic format for a text box:

```
<INPUT TYPE="TEXT" NAME="Field Name">
```

In this case, *Field Name* is a name you assign to the field that's unique among the other fields in the form. For example, to create a text box the reader can use to enter his first name (let's call it First), you'd enter the following:

```
<INPUT TYPE="TEXT" NAME="First">
```

Page Pitfalls

It's crucial to remember that every form control (button, text box, and so on) must have a unique name. The only exception to this is that a group of related radio buttons (discussed a bit later) must have the same name.

For clarity, you also want to precede each text box with a label that tells the reader what kind of information to type in. For example, the following line precedes a text box with First Name: so the reader knows to type in his first name:

```
First Name: <INPUT TYPE="TEXT" NAME="First">
```

Here's some HTML code (textbox.htm on this book's CD) that utilizes a few text boxes to gather some information from the reader:

```
<HTML>
<HEAD>
<TITLE>Text Box Example</TITLE>
</HEAD>
<BODY>
<H3>Please tell me about yourself:</H3>

<FORM ACTION="http://www.mcfedries.com/scripts/formtest.asp" METHOD="POST">
<P>
First Name: <INPUT TYPE="TEXT" NAME="First">
</P>
<P>
Last Name: <INPUT TYPE="TEXT" NAME="Last">
</P>
<P>
Nickname: <INPUT TYPE="TEXT" NAME="Nick">
</P>
<P>
<INPUT TYPE="SUBMIT" VALUE="Just Do It!">
<INPUT TYPE="RESET" VALUE="Just Reset It!">
</P>
</FORM>

</BODY>
</HTML>
```

Figure 12.3 shows how it looks in Internet Explorer.

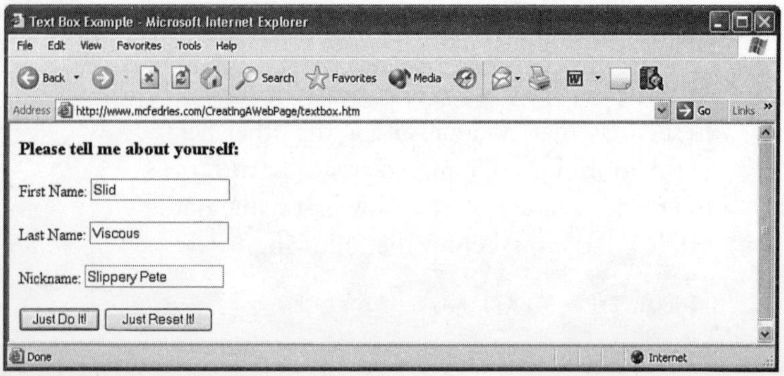

Figure 12.3

A form with a few text boxes.

If you run this form (that is, if you click the Just Do It! button), the data is sent to my test script. Why? Because I included the following line:

```
<FORM ACTION="http://www.mcfedries.com/scripts/formtest.asp" METHOD="POST">
```

You'd normally replace this ACTION attribute with one that points to a script that does something useful to the data. You don't have such a script right now, so it's safe just to use my script for testing purposes. Remember that this script doesn't do much of anything except send your data back to you. If everything comes back okay (that is, there are no error messages), then you know your form is working properly. Just so you know what to expect, Figure 12.4 shows an example of the page that gets returned to the browser. Notice how the page shows the names of the fields followed by the value the user entered.

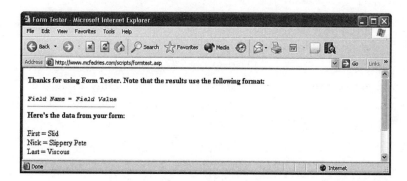

Figure 12.4

An example of the page that's returned when you send the form data to my text script.

Text boxes also come with the following bells and whistles:

◆ **Setting the default value.** If you'd like to put some prefab text into the field, include the VALUE attribute in the <INPUT> tag. For example, suppose you want to know the address of the user's home page. To include *http://* in the field (because most addresses begin with this), you'd use the following tag:

```
<INPUT TYPE=TEXT NAME="URL" VALUE="http://">
```

◆ **Setting the size of the box.** To determine the length of the text box, use the SIZE attribute. (Note that this attribute affects only the size of the box and not the length of the entry; for the latter, see the MAXLENGTH attribute in the following paragraph.) For example, the following tag displays a text box that's 40 characters long:

```
<INPUT TYPE=TEXT NAME="Address" SIZE="40">
```

◆ **Limiting the length of the text.** In a standard text box, the reader can type away until her fingers are numb. If you'd prefer to restrict the length of the entry, use the MAXLENGTH attribute. For example, the following text box is used to enter a person's age and sensibly restricts the length of the entry to three characters:

```
<INPUT TYPE=TEXT NAME="Age" MAXLENGTH="3">
```

Using Text Areas for Multiline Text

If you want to give your readers lots of room to type their hearts out, or if you need multiline entries (such as an address), you're better off using a *text area* than a text box. A text area is also a rectangle that accepts text input, but text areas can display two or more lines at once. Here's how they work:

```
<TEXTAREA NAME="Field Name" ROWS="Total Rows" COLS="Total Columns" WRAP>
</TEXTAREA>
```

Here, *Field Name* is a unique name for the field, *Total Rows* specifies the total number of lines displayed, and *Total Columns* specifies the total number of columns displayed. The optional WRAP attribute tells the browser to wrap the text onto the next line whenever the user's typing hits the right edge of the text area.

Note, too, that the <TEXTAREA> tag requires the </TEXTAREA> end tag. If you want to include default values in the text area, just enter them—on separate lines, if necessary—between <TEXTAREA> and </TEXTAREA>.

The following HTML tags (textarea.htm on this book's CD) show a text area in action, and Figure 12.5 shows how it looks in a browser.

```
<HTML>
<HEAD>
<TITLE>Text Area Example</TITLE>
</HEAD>
<BODY>
<H3>Today's Burning Question</H3>

<FORM ACTION="http://www.mcfedries.com/scripts/formtest.asp" METHOD="POST">
<P>
First Name: <INPUT TYPE="TEXT" NAME="First">
</P>
<P>
Last Name: <INPUT TYPE="TEXT" NAME="Last">
</P>
```

```
<P>
Today's <I>Burning Question</I>: <B>How did the fool and his money get
together in the first place?</B>
</P>
<P>
Please enter your answer in the text area below:
<BR>
<TEXTAREA NAME="Answer" ROWS="10" COLS="60" WRAP>
</TEXTAREA>
</P>
<P>
<INPUT TYPE="SUBMIT" VALUE="I Know!">
<INPUT TYPE="RESET">
</P>
</FORM>

</BODY>
</HTML>
```

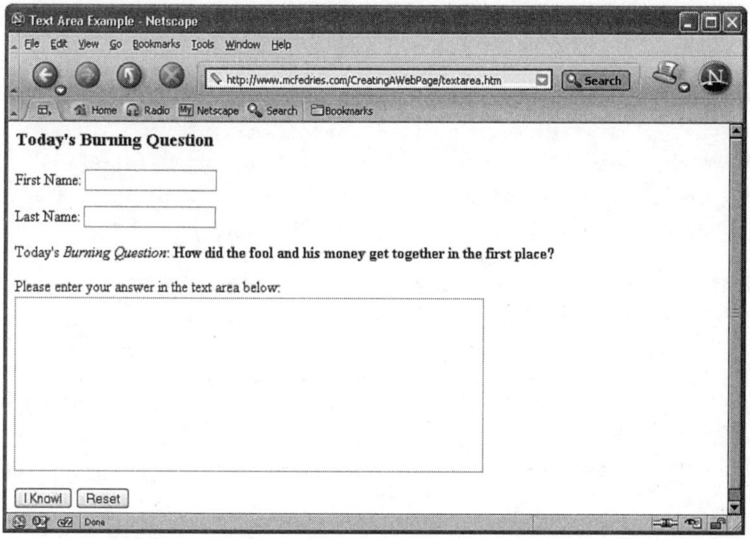

Figure 12.5

An example of a text area.

Toggling an Option On and Off with Check Boxes

If you want to elicit yes/no or true/false information from your readers, use check boxes because it's a lot easier to check a box than it is to type in the required data. Here's the general format for an HTML check box:

```
<INPUT TYPE="CHECKBOX" NAME="Field Name">
```

As usual, *Field Name* is a unique name for the field. You can also add the CHECKED attribute to the <INPUT> tag, which tells the browser to display the check box "prechecked." Here's an example:

```
<INPUT TYPE="CHECKBOX" NAME="Species" CHECKED>Human
```

Notice in the preceding example that I placed some text beside the <INPUT> tag. This text is used as a label that tells the reader what the check box represents. Here's a longer example (checkbox.htm on this book's CD) that uses several check boxes:

```
<HTML>
<HEAD>
<TITLE>Check Box Example</TITLE>
</HEAD>
<BODY>
<H3>Welcome to Hooked On Phobics!</H3>
<HR>

<FORM ACTION="http://www.mcfedries.com/scripts/formtest.asp" METHOD="POST">
<P>
What's <I>your</I> phobia? (Please check all that apply):
</P>
<P>
<INPUT TYPE="CHECKBOX" NAME="Ants">Myrmecophobia (Fear of ants)<BR>
<INPUT TYPE="CHECKBOX" NAME="Bald">Peladophobia (Fear of becoming bald)<BR>
<INPUT TYPE="CHECKBOX" NAME="Beards" CHECKED>Pogonophobia (Fear of beards)<BR>
<INPUT TYPE="CHECKBOX" NAME="Bed">Clinophobia (Fear of going to bed)<BR>
<INPUT TYPE="CHECKBOX" NAME="Chins" CHECKED>Geniophobia (Fear of chins)<BR>
<INPUT TYPE="CHECKBOX" NAME="Flowers">Anthophobia (Fear of flowers)<BR>
<INPUT TYPE="CHECKBOX" NAME="Flying">Aviatophobia (Fear of flying)<BR>
<INPUT TYPE="CHECKBOX" NAME="Purple">Porphyrophobia (Fear of purple)<BR>
<INPUT TYPE="CHECKBOX" NAME="Teeth" CHECKED>Odontophobia (Fear of teeth)<BR>
<INPUT TYPE="CHECKBOX" NAME="Thinking">Phronemophobia (Fear of thinking)<BR>
<INPUT TYPE="CHECKBOX" NAME="Vegetables">Lachanophobia (Fear of vegetables)<BR>
<INPUT TYPE="CHECKBOX" NAME="Fear" CHECKED>Phobophobia (Fear of fear)<BR>
<INPUT TYPE="CHECKBOX" NAME="Everything">Pantophobia (Fear of everything)<BR>
</P>
<P>
<INPUT TYPE="SUBMIT" VALUE="Submit">
<INPUT TYPE="RESET">
</P>
</FORM>
</BODY>
</HTML>
```

Figure 12.6 shows how it looks (I've checked a few of the boxes so you can see how they appear).

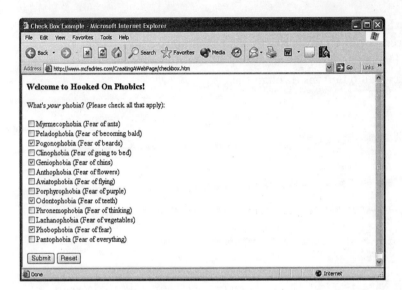

Figure 12.6
Some check box examples.

Webmaster Wisdom

When you submit a form with a check box, the data returned by the test script is a bit different from the data returned by the other controls. For one thing, the script returns only the values for check boxes that were activated; for another, the value returned for these checked check boxes is "on." For example, in the checkbox.htm file, if the check box named "Beards" is activated when the form is submitted, the following line will appear in the results:

```
Beards = on
```

Multiple Choice Options: Radio Buttons

Instead of yes/no choices, you might want your readers to have a choice between three or four options. In this case, *radio buttons* are your best bet. With radio buttons, the user gets two or more options, but they can pick only one at a time.

Here's the general format:

```
<INPUT TYPE="RADIO" NAME="Field Name"
VALUE="Value">
```

Field Name is the usual unique field name, except in this case you supply the same name to *all* the radio buttons that you want grouped together. (More on this in a sec.)

Words from the Web

In a rare burst of nerd whimsy, the HTML powers-that-be named **radio buttons** after the old car radio buttons that you had to push to select a station.

Value is a unique text string that specifies the value of the option when it's selected. In addition, you can also add CHECKED to one of the buttons to have the browser activate the option by default. The following HTML document (radiobtn.htm on this book's CD) puts a few radio buttons through their paces.

```
<HTML>
<HEAD>
<TITLE>Radio Button Example</TITLE>
</HEAD>
<BODY>
<H3>Survey</H3>

<FORM ACTION="http://www.mcfedries.com/scripts/formtest.asp" METHOD="POST">
<P>
Which of the following best describes your current salary level:
</P>
<DL><DD>
<INPUT TYPE="RADIO" NAME="Salary" VALUE="Poverty" CHECKED>Below the poverty
➥line<BR>
<INPUT TYPE="RADIO" NAME="Salary" VALUE="Living">Living wage<BR>
<INPUT TYPE="RADIO" NAME="Salary" VALUE="Comfy">Comfy<BR>
<INPUT TYPE="RADIO" NAME="Salary" VALUE="DINK">DINK (Double Income, No
➥Kids)<BR>
<INPUT TYPE="RADIO" NAME="Salary" VALUE="Rockefellerish">Rockefellerish<BR>
</DD></DL>
<P>
Which of the following best describes your political leanings:
</P>
<DL><DD>
<INPUT TYPE="RADIO" NAME="Politics" VALUE="Way Left" CHECKED>So far left, I'm
➥right<BR>
<INPUT TYPE="RADIO" NAME="Politics" VALUE="Yellow Dog">Yellow Dog Democrat<BR>
<INPUT TYPE="RADIO" NAME="Politics" VALUE="Middle">Right down the middle<BR>
<INPUT TYPE="RADIO" NAME="Politics" VALUE="Republican">Country Club
➥Republican<BR>
<INPUT TYPE="RADIO" NAME="Politics" VALUE="Way Right">So far right, I'm
➥left<BR>
</DD></DL>
<P>
<INPUT TYPE="SUBMIT" VALUE="Submit">
<INPUT TYPE="RESET">
</P>
</FORM>

</BODY>
</HTML>
```

Notice that the first five radio buttons all use the name "Salary" and the next five all use the name "Politics." This tells the browser that it's dealing with two separate groups of buttons. This way, the user can select one (and only one) button in the "Salary" group and one (and only one) button in the "Politics" group, as shown in Figure 12.7.

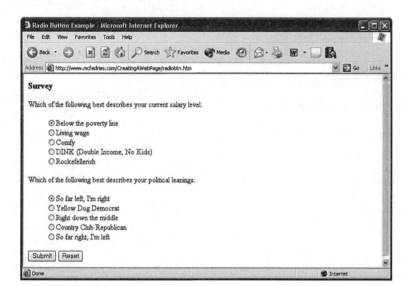

Figure 12.7

A form that uses radio buttons for multiple-choice input.

Selecting from Lists

Radio buttons are a great way to give your readers multiple choices, but they get unwieldy if you have more than about five or six options. For longer sets of options, you're better off using lists, or *selection lists* as they're called in the HTML world. Selection lists are a wee bit more complex than the other form tags we've looked at, but not by much. Here's the general format:

```
<SELECT NAME="Field Name" SIZE="Items">
<OPTION>First item text</OPTION>
<OPTION>Second item text</OPTION>
<OPTION>And so on...</OPTION>
</SELECT>
```

As I'm sure you've guessed by now, *Field Name* is the unique name for the list. For the SIZE attribute, *Items* is the number of items you want the browser to display. If you omit SIZE, the list becomes a drop-down list. If SIZE is two or more, the list becomes a rectangle with scroll bars for navigating the choices. Also, you can insert the MULTIPLE attribute into the <SELECT> tag. This tells the browser to enable the user to select multiple items from the list.

Between the <SELECT> and </SELECT> tags are the <OPTION></OPTION> tags; these define the list items. If you add the SELECTED attribute to one of the items, the browser selects that item by default.

To get some examples on the table, the following document (lists.htm on this book's CD) defines no less than three selection lists:

```
<HTML>
<HEAD>
<TITLE>Selection List Example</TITLE>
</HEAD>
<BODY>
<H3>Putting On Hairs: Reader Survey</H3>

<FORM ACTION="http://www.mcfedries.com/scripts/formtest.asp" METHOD="POST">
<P>
Select your hair color:<BR>
<SELECT NAME="Color">
<OPTION>Black</OPTION>
<OPTION>Blonde</OPTION>
<OPTION SELECTED>Brunette</OPTION>
<OPTION>Red</OPTION>
<OPTION>Something neon</OPTION>
<OPTION>None</OPTION>
</SELECT>
</P>
<P>
Select your hair style:<BR>
<SELECT NAME="Style" SIZE="4">
<OPTION>Bouffant</OPTION>
<OPTION>Mohawk</OPTION>
<OPTION>Page Boy</OPTION>
<OPTION>Permed</OPTION>
<OPTION>Shag</OPTION>
<OPTION SELECTED>Straight</OPTION>
<OPTION>Style? What style?</OPTION>
</SELECT>
</P>
<P>
Hair products used in the last year:<BR>
<SELECT NAME="Products" SIZE="5" MULTIPLE>
<OPTION>Gel</OPTION>
<OPTION>Grecian Formula</OPTION>
```

```
<OPTION>Mousse</OPTION>
<OPTION>Peroxide</OPTION>
<OPTION>Shoe black</OPTION>
</SELECT>
</P>
<P>
<INPUT TYPE="SUBMIT" VALUE="Hair Mail It!">
<INPUT TYPE="RESET">
</P>
</FORM>

</BODY>
</HTML>
```

Figure 12.8 shows what the Netscape 7 browser does with them.

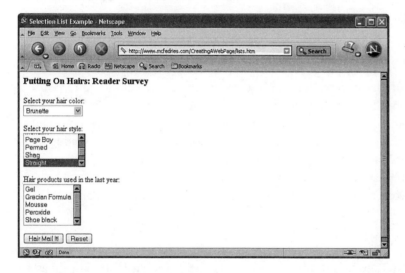

Figure 12.8

A form with a few selection list examples.

Oh Say, Can You CGI?

All this form folderol is fine, but what good is a form if it doesn't really do much of anything? That is, why bother building a fancy form if you have no way to get the data? Unfortunately, as I mentioned earlier, grabbing form data and manipulating it is a programmer's job. Specifically, you have to use something called the *Common Gateway Interface*, or CGI for short. CGI is a method of transferring form data in a manner that makes it relatively easy to incorporate into a program and then massage it all you need. Easy, that is, if you have the requisite nerd skills.

Well, I might not have room to teach you how to program forms, and you might not have the inclination to learn in any case, but that doesn't mean you're totally stuck. The next few sections give you some ideas for getting your forms to do something useful.

A Service Exclusively for Readers

The easy solution to this CGI stuff is to have a helpful author write a program that you can use for submitting your form data. And that's exactly what I've done. I've created a program called MailForm that takes form data and e-mails it to an address you specify.

To use MailForm, you have to register on my website. Here's the place to go: www. mcfedries.com/mailform/register.asp. After you register, you'll receive instructions that tell you how to set up your form to take advantage of what MailForm has to offer.

Ask Your Provider

Many people want to add simple guest books and feedback mechanisms to their sites, but they don't want to have to bother with the programming aspect. So, in response to their customers' needs, most web hosting providers make some simple CGI scripts (programs) available to their customers. For example, one common type of script grabs form data, extracts the field names and values, and sends them to an e-mail address you specify (like my MailForm program). Check with the provider's administrator or webmaster to see if it has any CGI scripts that you can use. And if you haven't settled on a provider yet, you should ask in advance if it has CGI programs available.

The CGI-Joe Route

A more expensive alternative is to hire the services of a CGI wizard (also known as a *CGI-Joe* in web programming circles) to create a custom program for you. Most web hosting providers are only too happy to put together a nice little program tailored to your needs. There's also no shortage of hired guns on the web who create programs to your specifications. As a starting point, check out some of the resources mentioned in the next section.

Check Out the Web's CGI Resources

If your service provider or web hosting provider doesn't have ready-to-run CGI programs that you can use, there's no shortage of sites on the Net that are willing and able to either teach you CGI or supply you with programs. This section runs through a list of some of these sites (see cgisites.htm on this book's CD):

- **Bravenet.** This site offers lots of free scripts and other webmaster goodies. See www.bravenet.com.

- **CGI 101.** As its name implies, this site offers beginner-level training and tutorials for CGI wannabe programmers. It also offers CGI hosting, links to other CGI sites, and much more. See www.cgi101.com.

- **The CGI Directory.** This site is bursting at the seams with great CGI info. There are tutorials, book reviews, an FAQ, links to other CGI sites, and hundreds of scripts. See www.cgidir.com.

- **CGIexpo.com.** This is a nice site with lots of links to scripts, tutorials, mailing lists, books, and much more. See www.cgiexpo.com.

- **CGI For Me.** This site offers what's known in the trade as remote CGI hosting. This means that the scripts run on the CGI For Me server and you link to them from your own page. You don't have to worry about script installation or configuration, and it's perfect if your web host doesn't allow CGI scripts. See www.cgiforme.com.

- **The CGI Resource Index.** If there's a good CGI resource on the web, this site knows about it. It has thousands of links to scripts, tutorials, articles, programmers for hire, and much more. See www.cgi-resources.com.

- **Extropia.** This site is the brainchild of Selena Sol and Gunther Birznieks, and it's one of the best CGI resources on the web. See www.extropia.com/applications.html.

- **Matt's Script Archive.** Matt Wright has written tons of CGI scripts and graciously offers them gratis to the web community. He has scripts for a guest book, random link generator, animation, and lots more. It's a great site and a must for would-be CGI mavens. See www.scriptarchive.com.

- **NCSA—The Common Gateway Interface.** This is *the* place on the web for CGI info. NCSA (the same folks who made the original Mosaic browser) has put together a great collection of tutorials, tips, and sample programs. See hoohoo.ncsa.uiuc.edu/cgi.

- **ScriptSearch.** This site bills itself as "The World's Largest CGI Library," and with thousands of scripts in dozens of categories, I can believe it. See www._scriptsearch.com.

- **comp.infosystems.www.authoring.cgi.** This newsgroup is a useful spot for CGI tips and tricks, and it's just a good place to hang around with fellow web programmers.

◆ **Yahoo's CGI Index.** This is a long list of CGI-related resources. Many of the links have either CGI how-to info or actual programs you can use. See dir.yahoo.com/ Computers_and_Internet/Software/Internet/ World_Wide_Web_Servers/Server_Side_Scripting/ Common_Gateway_Interface_CGI.

Webmaster Wisdom

Note that if you grab a program or two to use, you need to contact your service provider's administrator to get the full lowdown on how to set up the program. In most cases, the administrator will want to examine the program code to make sure it's up to snuff. If it passes muster, it is put in a special directory (usually called a cgi-bin), and then you can refer to the program in your form.

The Least You Need to Know

◆ To create a submit button, use <INPUT TYPE="SUBMIT" VALUE="*Label*">.

◆ To create a reset button, use <INPUT TYPE="RESET" VALUE="*Label*">.

◆ To create a text box, use <INPUT TYPE="TEXT" NAME="*Field Name*">. To create a text area, use <TEXTAREA NAME="*Field Name*" ROWS="*Total Rows*" COLS="*Total Columns*" WRAP></TEXTAREA>.

◆ To create a check box, use <INPUT TYPE="CHECKBOX" NAME="*Field Name*">.

◆ To create a radio button, use <INPUT TYPE="RADIO" NAME="*Field Name*" VALUE="*Value*"> (make sure all related radio buttons use the same name).

◆ To create a selection list, use <SELECT NAME="*Field Name*" SIZE="*Items*"></SELECT> and <OPTION>Item text</OPTION>.

13

Fooling Around with Frames

In This Chapter

◆ What frames are all about

◆ How to get a basic frame layout up and running

◆ Tweaking frames to get them just so

◆ How to handle browsers that don't understand frames

◆ A step-by-step approach with the aim to tame the frame game

Like most guys, I enjoy technology and take every opportunity to ring the bells and blow the whistles on whatever new techtoy comes my way. Take picture-in-picture (PIP), for instance. I think the engineering genius who came up with PIP should be awarded some kind of Nobel Geeks Prize. For my money, it's just insanely great to be able to leave one channel in view while you surf around to see what else is happening.

Whether you're a PIP fan or foe, you'll be interested to know that you can apply the PIP concept to your web pages. That is, you can set up your site so that one page remains in view in part of the browser screen and your visitors can use the rest of the screen to trip the link fantastic. The secret to this seemingly miraculous feat is a concept called *frames*, and you learn all about it in this chapter.

What's with All the Frame Fuss?

The competent web forger always includes a section on each page that enables the user to navigate the important landmarks in her site. This could be a collection of links, a web page "toolbar" (like the ones I showed you how to whip up in Chapter 9) or an image map (again, see Chapter 9). The problem with these navigation sections, though, is that they end up scrolling off the screen whenever the reader moves down the page. (This is assuming the navigation stuff is sitting at the top of the page.) For example, Figure 13.1 shows a page from my site, and Figure 13.2 shows what happens if you scroll down to read more of the text.

Figure 13.1

A page from my site showing my navigation aids at the top.

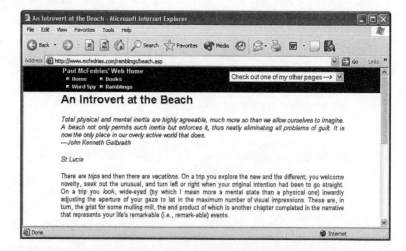

Figure 13.2

Where, oh where, have my links gone?

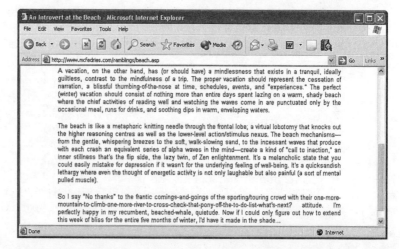

Figure 13.1 shows the various navigation aids that I've plopped onto the top of all the pages on my site. As you can see in Figure 13.2, however, after I scroll down a bit, those navigation doodads are gone like wild geese in winter.

Now have a gander (no pun intended; no, *really*) at Figure 13.3. See how I've scrolled down to the same spot, but the navigation section remains conveniently in view. Weird, huh? The window seems to be divided into two sections: The top section holds the navigation knickknacks, and the bottom section shows the regular page text and graphics. What the heck is happening here?

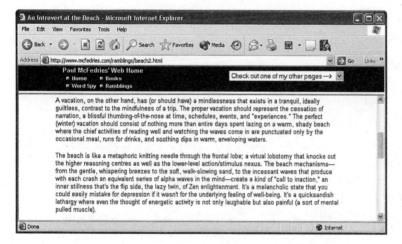

Figure 13.3

This version of the page mysteriously displays the navigation stuff in its own section at the top of the page.

To perform this magic trick, I had to do three things:

♦ I grabbed the HTML tags and text that make up my navigation section, and I put it all into a separate file called header.html.

♦ I grabbed the rest of the page text and put it into another file called beach-f.html.

♦ I created a third page called beach2.html that has a few special tags that serve to divide the browser window into two *frames*. I included in this page the instructions to load the header.html file into the top frame, and the beach-f.html file into the bottom frame.

The big deal is that with this view, surfers can scroll through beach-f.html in the bottom frame until they're blue in the face, and the navigation section remains steadfastly in place. It's even possible to arrange things so that if you click any link, the new page appears in the bottom frame. In other words, the top frame is really the web equivalent of picture-in-picture!

Okay, now that you know what frames are and why you might want to bother with them, let's see how you go about constructing them.

Forging a Frameset Page

The good news about frames is that you can build them using just a few not-too-hard-to-master HTML tags. Unfortunately, most frame neophytes get thrown for a loop right off the bat because the first thing you have to create is a web page that doesn't display anything! *Huh?*

Let me explain. After you enter the frames world, you're faced with not one, but *two* species of web page:

♦ **Content pages.** A content page is just a regular HTML page like the ones you've dealt with throughout this book. That is, they display text, graphics, and whatever other goodies the author packs into the page.

♦ **Frameset pages.** A frameset page has only one mission in life: to divide the browser window into a set of frames, define the size of each frame, and specify which content pages are displayed in each frame. Note that (as you'll soon see) frameset pages have no body section, so you shouldn't populate a frameset page with anything that would normally appear in the body, including regular text and HTML tags such as <B> and <IMG>. If you try, the browser simply ignores your efforts completely and concentrates solely on the frame information.

In other words, the frameset page is really just an empty shell like, say, an ice cube tray. An ice cube tray doesn't do much of anything by itself, and it becomes useful only after you fill in the compartments with water. It's the same with a frameset page: It just divvies up the browser screen into two or more frames, and you have to fill these compartments with separate content pages.

The Basic Frame Tags

Building a frameset page requires two tag types: <FRAMESET> and <FRAME>. The idea is that you begin with <FRAMESET> and between this tag and its corresponding </FRAMESET> end tag, you add one <FRAME> tag for each frame you want to work with. So, to divide the browser window into two frames, you start like this:

```
<HTML>
<HEAD>
<TITLE></TITLE>
</HEAD>
```

```
<FRAMESET>
<FRAME>
<FRAME>
</FRAMESET>

</HTML>
```

Notice two things about the structure of this basic frameset page:

◆ You still use the <HTML> and </HTML> tags, and the head section (the part between <HEAD> and </HEAD>) is exactly the same as in a regular page.

◆ There's no body section (that is, no <BODY> tag).

Now you have to tell the browser whether you want the frames to divide the screen horizontally or vertically.

> **CAUTION**
>
> **Page Pitfalls**
>
> One of most common mistakes that frame rookies make is to include a <BODY> tag somewhere in the frameset page, which usually causes the frames not to work. If you're having trouble seeing your frames, check for a <BODY> tag and delete it if you find one.

Dividing the Screen Horizontally

If you want the frame divider to run horizontally so that the screen is cleaved into a top part and a bottom part, you toss the ROWS attribute inside the <FRAMESET> tag:

```
<FRAMESET ROWS="Size1,Size2,...">
```

Here, *Size1* and *Size2* are numbers that tell the browser how much screen real estate to give to each frame. There are two types of numbers you can use:

◆ **Percentages.** Use percentages to assign a portion of the browser window to each frame. You need to include a percentage value for each frame, and the percentages should add up to 100.

◆ **Pixels.** Use pixels if you know exactly how tall you want a frame to be.

For example, suppose you have two frames and you want the top frame to usurp 25 percent of the screen and the bottom to take the remaining 75 percent. Here's a frameset page (see frame1.htm on this book's CD) that does the job:

```
<HTML>
<HEAD>
<TITLE>Horizontal Frames</TITLE>
</HEAD>

<FRAMESET ROWS="25%,75%">
<FRAME>
<FRAME>
</FRAMESET>

</HTML>
```

If you load this sucker into a browser, you see the rather uninspiring screen shown in Figure 13.4. Now you see what I meant earlier when I said that the frame page is just an empty shell!

Figure 13.4

A frame page that divides the browser screen horizontally.

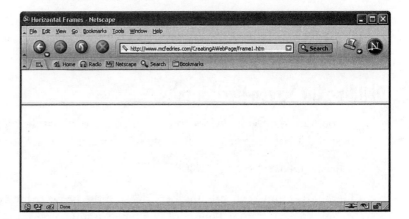

Webmaster Wisdom

It's a common frame scenario to want to give one frame a certain size and to want the second frame to take up whatever room is left in the window. To do the latter, enter an asterisk (*) as the "size" of the second frame. For example, if you want the top frame's height to be 100 pixels and the bottom frame to take up whatever's left, you'd use this tag: `<FRAMESET ROWS="100,*">`.

Dividing the Screen Vertically

If you'd prefer that the frame divider run vertically to cut the screen into left and right sections, you populate the <FRAMESET> tag with the COLS (columns) attribute and some numbers:

```
<FRAMESET COLS="Size1,Size2,...">
```

Again, *Size1* and *Size2* tell the browser how much of the window to parcel out to each frame. Here's another HTML file (frame2.htm on this book's CD) that divides the browser screen into three sections that take up 20 percent, 60 percent, and 20 percent of the screen:

```
<HTML>
<HEAD>
<TITLE>Vertical Frames</TITLE>
</HEAD>

<FRAMESET COLS="20%,60%,20%">
<FRAME>
<FRAME>
<FRAME>
</FRAMESET>

</HTML>
```

Figure 13.5 shows the frames loaded into Internet Explorer.

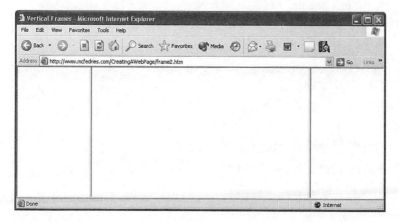

Figure 13.5

This frame page sunders the browser screen into three vertical sections.

Filling the Frames with Content Pages

The nearly naked frame pages you've seen so far aren't too exciting. What happens if you add some regular text or even an <IMG> tag or two? That's an easy one: not a gosh-darned thing! Feel free to type away until your fingers fall off, but you won't get the browser to show anything but the empty frames.

So how do you fill in the frames? You have to specify a separate content page to show in each frame. You do that by adding the SRC attribute into each of the <FRAME> tags. Here's the general format:

```
<FRAME SRC="URL">
```

As you might expect, the *URL* part is the address of the web page you want to display in the frame. Here's an example (frame3.htm on this book's CD):

```
<HTML>
<HEAD>
<TITLE>Horizontal Frames with Content</TITLE>
</HEAD>

<FRAMESET ROWS="25%,75%">
<FRAME SRC="1.htm">
<FRAME SRC="2.htm">
</FRAMESET>

</HTML>
```

Here, 1.htm and 2.htm are just regular HTML web pages. Figure 13.6 shows how things look in the browser. Notice that 1.htm gets displayed in the top frame and 2.htm gets displayed in the bottom frame.

Figure 13.6

To get the frame page to show something useful, specify a separate content page for each frame.

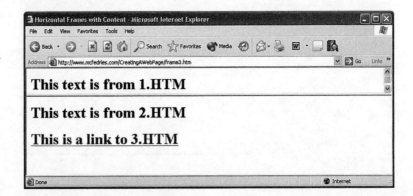

This text is from 1.HTM

This text is from 2.HTM

This is a link to 3.HTM

Teaching Frames and Links to Get Along

What happens if one of your framed content pages contains a link? Well, clicking the link loads the page as usual, but you can't be sure *where* the page appears. In most browsers, the new page appears in the same frame as the page with the link. In other browsers, the new page either takes over the entire window or appears in a separate window. Either way, your carefully laid out frames are history.

To avoid this random behavior, you need to control exactly where the linked pages show up. The trick to doing this is that you first have to assign a name to each frame. After that's done, it becomes an easy matter of modifying your link tags to specify the name of the frame in which you want the page to load.

To assign a name to a frame, you drop the NAME attribute inside the <FRAME> tag, like this:

```
<FRAME SRC="something.htm" NAME="Whatever">
```

For example, here's an updated frame page (frame4.htm on this book's CD) that includes names for the upper and lower frame:

```
<HTML>
<HEAD>
<TITLE>Named Horizontal Frames</TITLE>
</HEAD>

<FRAMESET ROWS="25%,75%">
<FRAME SRC="1.htm" NAME="upper">
<FRAME SRC="2.htm" NAME="lower">
</FRAMESET>

</HTML>
```

With your frames named, you can make any link load inside a particular frame by adding a TARGET attribute to the <A HREF> tag. For example, here's the <A HREF> tag from 2.HTM:

```
<A HREF="3.htm" TARGET="lower">This is a link to 3.HTM</A>
```

As you can see, the TARGET attribute is set to lower, which is the name of the bottom frame. Clicking this link, therefore, loads the new page in this frame, as shown in Figure 13.7.

Figure 13.7

Adding TARGET to a link tag forces the new page to load inside the specified frame.

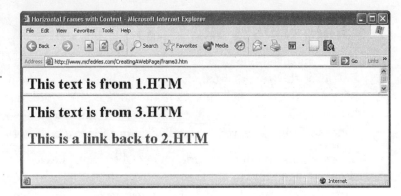

Page Pitfalls

You'll notice in Figure 13.7 that even though I clicked a link to load 2.htm into the bottom frame, Internet Explorer's Address box still shows the same address (that is, the address of the frameset page). That's one of the downsides to frames: The displayed address doesn't change as your readers click from link to link, so the viewers never really know where they are within your site.

Ready-Made Names for Frames

HTML also has three prefab frame names that you can specify with the TARGET attribute:

_self	Loads the new page into the same frame that contains the link.
_top	Loads the new page into the entire window.
_blank	Loads the new page into a new browser window.

Webmaster Wisdom

In frame circles, proper etiquette dictates that links to external sites should either take over the entire screen (TARGET="_top") or be displayed in a separate browser window (TARGET="_blank"). Unfortunately, many framesters don't follow this etiquette and, instead, greedily display *every* link within their frames. Besides cursing their ancestry, what can you do to make sure that *your* page doesn't get jailed within someone else's frames? Include a link on your page that points to the same page, but uses the TARGET="_top" attribute. For example, if your page is named index.html, add a link like this one: `<A HREF="index.html" TARGET="_top">Deframe this page</A>`.

Specifying a Default Target

What do you do if you have a frame that contains tons of links? Do you really have to go through the drudgery of adding the TARGET tag to all those <A> tags? Happily, no, you don't. It's possible to specify a default target, and the browser will send every linked page to whatever frame you specify.

To set the default target, add the following tag to the head section (that is, between the <HEAD> and </HEAD> tags) of the page that contains all the links:

```
<BASE TARGET="FrameName">
```

Here, *FrameName* is the name of the frame you want to use as the default target. For example, to load every link into a frame named "content," you'd use the following tag:

```
<BASE TARGET="content">
```

Frame Frills and Frippery

The frames we've seen so far are serviceable beasts. However, the <FRAME> tag comes with a few extra options that you might need to use. Here's a quick summary of these attributes:

- ◆ **NORESIZE.** Stick this attribute inside a <FRAME> tag to prevent surfers from changing the size of the frame. (Otherwise, the frame can be resized by dragging the frame border with the mouse.)

- ◆ **SCROLLING.** This attribute determines whether or not a scroll bar appears with a frame. If you set this to AUTO (that is, SCROLLING="AUTO") and the content page is too big to fit entirely inside the frame, a scroll bar appears on the right side of the frame. Use SCROLLING="NO" to prevent the scroll bar from appearing. If SCROLLING is set to "YES," a scroll bar will appear whether it's needed or not.

- ◆ **FRAMEBORDER.** Set this attribute to "No" to tell the browser not to display the border between frames. Versions of Netscape before 4.5 didn't understand the "No" value, so to support those older versions you must also use FRAMEBORDER="0".

Handling Frame-Feeble Browsers

I mentioned earlier that you can't add regular text or HTML tags to a frame page. (Actually, you could if you put in a <BODY> tag. However, this would nullify the <FRAMESET> tag, so it would defeat the purpose.) So what happens when a browser that doesn't understand frames comes across your frame page? You guessed it, it doesn't display anything!

This isn't a great way to welcome these surfers to your site, to say the least. However, there is a way to handle these nonframe browsers and at least give them something to chew on. It's called the <NOFRAMES> tag. Any text or HTML tags you insert between this tag and its </NOFRAMES> end tag shows up in a frameless browser. For example, here's the HTML for a page (frame5.htm on this book's CD) that includes the <NOFRAMES> tag, and you can see the result in Figure 13.8:

```
<HTML>
<HEAD>
<TITLE>Handling Lame Frame Browsers</TITLE>
</HEAD>

<FRAMESET ROWS="25%,75%">
<FRAME SRC="1.htm" NAME="upper">
<FRAME SRC="2.htm" NAME="lower">

<NOFRAMES>
<H3>Doh! Looks like you have a browser that is frames-challenged.</H3>
<H3>Here's a <A HREF="2.htm">frame-free page</A> that should be more to your
➥browser's liking.</H3>
</NOFRAMES>

</FRAMESET>
</HTML>
```

Figure 13.8

Frame-ignorant browsers ignore the frame-related tags and just display the other text.

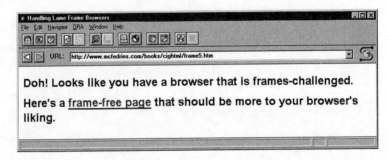

Now wait just a cotton-picking minute! If a browser can't handle frames, how can it know about the <NOFRAMES> tag?

Good question! The answer is that it doesn't. These older browsers are really just bypassing the <FRAMESET> and <FRAME> tags (since they don't understand them) and displaying whatever other text is in the file. The <NOFRAMES> tag actually serves to prevent frame-capable browsers from displaying the text.

Oh.

Fancier Frames

To finish this frames tutorial, let's kick things up a notch and look at a technique that enables you to create some pretty fancy frame effects.

So far, you've learned only how to divide the browser window into horizontal regions or vertical regions. What do you do if you want to combine these types? For example, suppose you define an upper frame and a lower frame and you then want to divide the lower frame into two vertical sections. Well, it turns out that you can use as many <FRAMESET> tags as you like in a single frame page. So you can get your desired layout by defining one <FRAMESET> tag to divide the screen in two horizontally and then insert a second <FRAMESET> tag that divides the lower region vertically. Here's the code for an HTML page (frame6.htm on the CD) that does this:

```
<HTML>
<HEAD>
<TITLE>Nested Frames</TITLE>
</HEAD>

<FRAMESET ROWS="25%,75%">
<FRAME SRC="1.htm" NAME="Upper">
   <FRAMESET COLS="50%,50%">
   <FRAME SRC="2.htm" NAME="Lower">
   <FRAME SRC="3.htm" NAME="Right">
   </FRAMESET>
</FRAMESET>

</HTML>
```

This technique is called *nesting* frames, and you can use it to create whatever layout suits your needs. Figure 13.9 shows how the example looks in the browser.

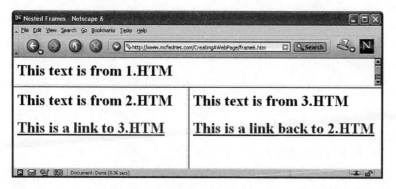

Figure 13.9

You can nest frames to achieve some interesting layouts.

The Least You Need to Know

♦ In your frameset page, you use <FRAMESET> and </FRAMESET> instead of <BODY> and </BODY>.

♦ In the <FRAMESET> tag, use the ROWS attribute to divide the browser into horizontal frames, or use the COLS attribute to divide the browser into vertical frames.

♦ Add the SRC attribute to each <FRAME> tag and set it equal to the address of the regular page that you want loaded into the frame.

♦ If you want a link to display a page in a specific frame, first name all your frames by adding the NAME attribute to each <FRAME> tag. Then plop the TARGET attribute inside the <A HREF> tag and set it equal to the name of the frame in which you want the page to show up.

♦ For the TARGET value, use _self for the current frame (that is, the one containing the link), _top for the entire browser window, and _blank for a new browser window.

Some Web Page Doodads You Should Know About

In This Chapter

- ◆ How to let people search your site
- ◆ Putting up a chat room or bulletin board
- ◆ Getting the hang of server-side includes
- ◆ Making good use of HTML comments
- ◆ A passel of perks for your page-producing pleasure

Over the years, I've discovered that there are basically two types of web page artisans. On the one hand you have those people who are quite happy to cobble together their pages using just the basic HTML tags, with perhaps a style sheet or two (see Part 4) and the odd bit of JavaScript thrown in for good measure (information can be found on the CD). On the other hand, you have those folks whose mantra seems to be, "Okay, but what *else* can I do?" These page hounds are always on the lookout for shiny things they can tack on to their sites to entice visitors or impress their friends.

This chapter is dedicated to the latter group. For those intrepid souls, I've put together a list of extra accessories they can use to adorn their pages.

These include search features, chat rooms, bulletin boards, and server-side includes (a technology I'll tell you about shortly).

The Searchable Site: Adding a Search Feature

If your site contains only a single page, or just a few pages, any visitor with a pulse ought to be able to find what he is looking for. (Assuming, of course, that you've set up the necessary links to your pages.) That may not be the case, however, if your site starts getting a bit big for its britches. Once you start talking about your total number of pages in the dozens or even the hundreds, then finding a specific tidbit may become a real page-needle-in-a-website-haystack exercise.

To keep your visitors happy, there are resources out there in webland that you can use to add a searching component to your site, just like the big-time websites have.

> ### Blog On
>
> If you plan on archiving your old blog entries, a search feature is a must-have addition to your site because it enables your readers to easily find an entry from the past. See Chapter 16 to learn more about archiving blog entries.

> ### Page Pitfalls
>
> Depending on the size of your site, search indexes can get quite large, so be prepared for them to usurp a decent-sized chunk of whatever disk space your web host has set aside for you.

Even better, many of these search services are free. (Although there are some limitations. For example, there might be a maximum number of pages that can be indexed, and you might be required to place an image or ad on your site.)

Before you start checking out specific search services, note that they all return a "results page" after the user runs a search. These results list all the pages on your site that match whatever criteria the user specified for the search. It's important to remember that these results will be useful only if you've done a bit of prep work in advance so that your site is search-ready. This means setting up your pages just like you would if you were preparing for the major search engines to come calling: having descriptive titles on every page, using the "Description" and "Keywords" <META> tags, and so on. (See Chapter 8 for details on setting up your site for search engines.)

In addition to the results page, search features also usually include the following three components:

- **The search engine.** This is the part that does the actual searching of your site. There are many different types of search engines, but there are two main types for you to consider: CGI scripts and search hosting. I discuss these in detail a bit later.

◆ **The search index.** Before the search engine can run searches, it must first "crawl" through your site, reading the text of each page. As it goes along, it compiles a list of the words on each page (usually bypassing common words such as "the" and "and"). The words, along with pointers to the pages in which they appear, are stored in a file called an *index*. When the user searches for a particular word, the search engine looks up the word in the index, grabs a list of the pages in which that word appears, and then displays that list to the user.

◆ **The search form.** This is the form that your visitors use to enter their search criteria. Look for a search service that provides a prebuilt form (ideally, one that can be customized to blend in with your site design).

Your search for a good search feature should begin at home. That is, you should first ask your web hosting provider if it offers a search feature for its customers. If not, then it's time to hit the road. As I mentioned earlier, there are two main types of search features to consider: a CGI script and a search host.

The CGI route involves installing a script on your web host's server, either in your own CGI-BIN (if you have one) or the host's global CGI-BIN. Remember that most hosts will want to inspect a CGI script before they'll let you install it. To find a script, see my list of CGI resources in Chapter 12.

A search host is a separate site that hosts not only the search engine, but also the search index. This type of search is marginally slower because the data has to go to and from the other server. However, it's the only way to go if your web host won't allow you to install a CGI program or Java applet, or if your disk space on the server is running low. Here are some search hosts to check out:

◆ **Atomz.** This site has an "Express Search" product that's free for websites that have fewer than 500 pages. The only requirement is that you place an Atomz logo on the search results page. This is the most popular of the search servers. See www.atomz.com.

◆ **FreeFind.** This service is free for sites that have up to 32 MB of data. You're required to place a banner ad (which will show ads for various products) on the search results page. See www.freefind.com.

◆ **FusionBot.** The "Free Package" offered by this service lets you index up to 250 pages. The results page will have both a banner ad (with ads from FusionBot sponsors) and a FusionBot logo. See www.fusionbot.com.

◆ **Google.** The best search engine for the web also offers a "SiteSearch Companion" for your site. The free version will index an unlimited number of pages, and the results page (on which Google reserves the right to display an ad) looks just like the regular Google page. See www.google.com/intl/en_extra/services/free.html.

Webmaster Wisdom

To help you explore things that are discussed in this chapter, I compiled a page with links to the sites that are mentioned. See doodads.htm on the CD in this book.

♦ **Master.com.** This host has a "Search Your Site" feature, the free version of which is happy to index up to 5,000 pages, or 30 MB of data. You're required to display the Master.com logo on the results page. See www.master.com.

♦ **PicoSearch.** The free version of this service will index up to 1,500 pages, although you're required to place an ad for PicoSearch on the results page. See www.picosearch.com.

Talk Amongst Yourselves: Adding a Chat Room or Bulletin Board

On your site, visitors can "talk" to you if you include a "mailto" link on your pages or if you set up a feedback form. But what if you want your visitors to be able to talk to each other? That may sound strange at first glance, but it's a great way to set up a kind of "community" on your site and to ensure that people keep popping by.

Like search features, chat rooms and bulletin boards come in many different flavors, of which three are the most popular: Java applet, JavaScript (both are hosted on the remote server), and CGI script (which is usually installed on your own host). Here are some chat rooms and bulletin boards to check out:

♦ **BoardServer.** This is a JavaScript-based bulletin board that's hosted on the BoardServer site. It costs (as I write this) U.S. $19.95 per month or U.S. $199 per year. See boardserver.superstats.com.

♦ **Chat-Forum.** This is a free Java-based chat service. You'll see banner ads or pop-up ads. See chat-forum.com/freechat.

♦ **Chat Town.** This is a free chat host service that offers a number of different chat rooms in various categories. See www.chattown.com.

♦ **Infopop.** This site offers the Ultimate Bulletin Board, a CGI script that you install on your web host. It costs (at the time of writing) U.S. $125 for individuals. See www.infopop.com.

♦ **Multicity.** This site offers a free Java chat applet that's hosted on the Multicity site. The chat room displays a Multicity banner ad. See www.multicity.com.

♦ **QuickChat.** This site hosts a chat server and gives you a Java applet to place on your site. See www.planetz.net/quickchat.

Using Server-Side Includes to Insert Files in Your Pages

This section tells you about a clever little technology called server-side includes that enables you to include certain kinds of content automatically in your pages. As you'll see, this can save you *a lot* of time, particularly if you include similar content on all or most of your pages.

The Include Tag

One of the hallmarks of a good site is a consistent layout among your pages. I talk about this in more detail in the next chapter, but part of what this means is having certain elements appear on all or most of your pages. Here are some examples:

♦ Links to the major sections of your site.

♦ A "header" at the top of each page that includes a logo or some other image, the name of your site, and a motto or slogan.

♦ A "footer" at the bottom of each page that includes items such as your name, contact information, and a copyright notice.

Adding snippets such as these to each of your pages isn't really a big deal. You just type it out once, copy it, and then paste the text into your other HTML files. Ah, but what if you make a change to the text or to a link? In that case, you have to open all your files and edit each one accordingly. That's no big thing if you have only a few pages, but what if you have 20 or 120?

To avoid the mind-numbing drudgery of having to edit a ridiculous number of pages each time you make a small change, consider using something called a *server-side include* (SSI). This involves two things:

♦ A small text file that contains any combination of text and tags.

♦ A special SSI tag that you place inside each of your pages. This SSI tag references the text file. What the tag does, essentially, is tell the web server to replace the tag with the entire contents of the text file.

Page Pitfalls

Remember that SSI requires the services of a server to work properly. If you view your page with the include tag on your own computer, you won't see the inserted file.

What's the advantage here? Simply this: It means you need to edit only that lone text file. Since the server always replaces the SSI tag with the latest version of the text file, all your pages display the edited text automatically.

What's the catch? There are two:

◆ Your web host's server must be set up to handle SSI.

◆ You usually need to use the .shtml extension on any files that have the SSI tag. (SSI also works with ASP pages, if your web host supports them.)

To use SSI requires two steps:

1. Create a new text file and use it to insert the tags and text that you want into your pages. When you're done, be sure to upload this file to your web host directory.

> **Words from the Web**
>
> An **SSI include tag** is a special HTML tag that points to a text file and tells the browser to include the text from that file in the page.

2. In each HTML file that you want the text file inserted, add the special SSI tag that I've been blathering on about:

```
<!--#include file="TextFileName"-->
```

This is called the *SSI include tag,* and you need to replace *TextFileName* with the name of the text file from Step 1. Remember, as well, to position this tag *exactly* where you want the text file's contents to appear.

Let's give an example a whirl. Here are the contents of a text file named footer.txt (which you'll find on the CD in this book):

```
<HR>
<ADDRESS>
This page is Copyright &copy; 200?, your-name-here<BR>
company-name-here<BR>
company-address-here<BR>
Phone: (###) ###-####<BR>
Fax: (###) ###-####<BR>
Email: <A HREF="mailto:your-email-address-here">your-email-address-here</A>.
</ADDRESS>
<P>
Last revision: date-goes-here
</P>
<P>
Return to my <A HREF="home-page-URL-goes-here">home page.</A>

</P>
```

Now here's the code for a file named ssi.shtml (also on the CD in this book), which includes an SSI tag that references the footer.txt file:

```
<HTML>
<HEAD>
<TITLE>An SSI Example</TITLE>
</HEAD>

<BODY>
<P>
The regular page text and graphics go here.
</P>
<!--#include file="footer.txt"-->

</BODY>
</HTML>
```

As you can see in Figure 14.1, the server replaces the SSI tag with the contents of footer.txt.

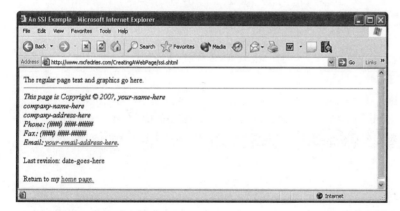

Figure 14.1

When the browser trips over the SSI include tag, it replaces the tag with the entire contents of the file specified by the tag.

The Echo Tag

Most servers that support SSI also support a second SSI tag:

```
<!--#echo var="VariableName"-->
```

This is called the *SSI echo tag*, and you use it to "echo" or write a specific type of data to the page. The data that gets written depends on what you specify for the *VariableName*. For example, you can use the LAST_MODIFIED variable:

```
Last edited on <!--#echo var="LAST_MODIFIED"-->
```

Here, the server replaces the SSI echo tag with the date and time when the file was last modified:

```
Last edited on Friday, August 23 2004 03:02:59
```

Table 14.1 lists some of the more useful echo variable names (as well as a few that are only semi-useful).

Table 14.1   Some SSI Echo Tag Variables

Variable	What It Echoes
DATE_GMT	The current date and time at Greenwich (Greenwich Mean Time)
DATE_LOCAL	The current date and time on the server
DOCUMENT_NAME	The current page's server directory and name
DOCUMENT_URI	The URL of this page (less the host)
LAST_MODIFIED	The date and time this page was last modified
HTTP_REFERER	The address the user came from to get to the current page
REMOTE_ADDR	The IP address of the user

When you're using any of the date and time echo variables, the actual appearance of the output varies depending on the browser and the computer used by the surfer. Thankfully, you can control the appearance of the date and time by using the SSI config tag:

```
<!--#config timefmt="TimeFormat"-->
```

You place this tag immediately before your SSI echo tag, and you replace *TimeFormat* with any of the formats listed in Table 14.2.

Table 14.2   Some SSI Config Tag Formats

Format	What You Get
%a	The abbreviated weekday name
%A	The full weekday name
%b	The abbreviated month name
%B	The full month name
%c	The date and time format that's appropriate for the user's locale

Format	What You Get
%C	The default date and time format
%d	The day of month (from 01 to 31)
%H	The hour in 24-hour format (00 to 23)
%I	The hour in 12-hour format (01 to 12)
%j	The day of the year (001 to 366)
%m	The month of the year (01 to 12)
%M	The minute (00 to 59)
%p	A.M. or P.M.
%S	The second (00 to 59)
%U	The week of the year, where Sunday is the first day of the week (00 to 51)
%w	The day of the week (Sunday = 0)
%W	The week number of year, where Monday is the first day of the week (00 to 51)
%x	The date format for the user's current locale
%X	The time format for the user's current locale
%y	The year without the century (00 to 99)
%Y	The year with the century (for example, 2002)

Here's the code from a page that puts the SSI echo tag through its paces (see ssi2.shtml on the CD in this book):

```
<HTML>
<HEAD>
<TITLE>The SSI Echo Tag</TITLE>
</HEAD>

<BODY>
<B>Some useful (and semi-useful) echo variables:</B>
<TABLE BORDER="1">
<TR><TH>VARIABLE</TH><TH>What Gets Echoed</TH><TH>Description</TH></TR>
<TR><TD>DATE_GMT</TD>
<TD><!--#echo var="DATE_GMT"--></TD>
<TD>Current date and time at Greenwich (Greenwich Mean Time).</TD></TR>
<TR><TD>DATE_LOCAL</TD>
<TD><!--#echo var="DATE_LOCAL"--></TD>
<TD>Current date and time on the server.</TD></TR>
<TR><TD>DOCUMENT_NAME</TD>
<TD><!--#echo var="DOCUMENT_NAME"--></TD>
```

```
<TD>This page's server directory and name.</TD></TR>
<TR><TD>DOCUMENT_URI</TD>
<TD><!--#echo var="DOCUMENT_URI"--></TD>
<TD>URL of this page (less the host).</TD></TR>
<TR><TD>LAST_MODIFIED</TD>
<TD><!--#echo var="LAST_MODIFIED"--></TD>
<TD>Date and time this page was last modified.</TD></TR>
<TR><TD>HTTP_REFERER</TD>
<TD><!--#echo var="HTTP_REFERER"--></TD>
<TD>Address the user came from.</TD></TR>
<TR><TD>REMOTE_ADDR</TD>
<TD><!--#echo var="REMOTE_ADDR"--></TD>
<TD>IP address of the user.</TD></TR>
</TABLE>

<B>Formatting the date and time:</B>
<TABLE BORDER="1">
<TR><TH>TIMEFMT</TH><TH>What the Date and Time Look Like</TH></TR>
<TR><TD>%#c</TD>
<TD><!--#config timefmt="%#c"--><!--#echo var="LAST_MODIFIED"--></TD></TR>
<TR><TD>%c</TD>
<TD><!--#config timefmt="%c"--><!--#echo var="LAST_MODIFIED"--></TD></TR>
<TR><TD>%x</TD>
<TD><!--#config timefmt="%x"--><!--#echo var="LAST_MODIFIED"--></TD></TR>
<TR><TD>%#x</TD>
<TD><!--#config timefmt="%#x"--><!--#echo var="LAST_MODIFIED"--></TD></TR>
<TR><TD>%X</TD>
<TD><!--#config timefmt="%X"--><!--#echo var="LAST_MODIFIED"--></TD></TR>
<TR><TD>%a, %b %d, %Y</TD>
<TD><!--#config timefmt="%a, %b %d, %Y"--><!--#echo var="LAST_MODIFIED"--></TD>
</TR>
</TABLE>
</BODY>
</HTML>
```

Figure 14.2 shows how things look in the browser.

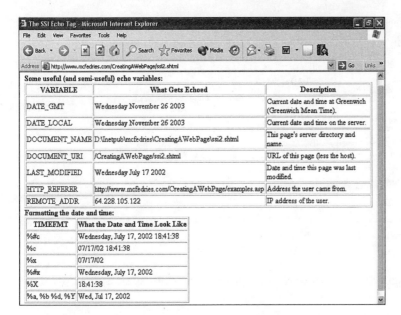

Figure 14.2

Some SSI echo tags.

Sneakily Hiding Text with HTML Comment Tags

In the lingo of HTML, a *comment* is a chunk of text that gets completely ignored by the browser. Yes, you read that right: When the browser comes upon a comment, it averts its electronic eyes and pretends that the comment doesn't even exist. What possible uses could there be for such a thing? Here are a few:

♦ You can add notes to yourself in specific places of the page. For example, you can add a comment such as *Here's where I'll put my logo when I've finished it.*

♦ You can add explanatory text that describes parts of the page. For example, if you have a table that comprises the header of your page, you can add a comment before the <TABLE> tag such as *This is the start of the header.*

♦ You can skip problematic sections of your page. If you have a section that isn't working properly, or a link that isn't set up yet, you can convert the text and tags into a comment so as not to cause problems for the browser or the user.

♦ You can add a copyright notice or other info for people who view your HTML source code.

To turn any bit of text into a comment, you surround it with the HTML comment tags. Specifically, you precede it with <!-- and follow it with -->, like this:

```
<!--This text is a comment-->
```

To prove that this actually works, here's a simple page that includes a comment (see comment.htm on the CD in this book).

```
<HTML>
<HEAD>
<TITLE>A Comment Example</TITLE>
</HEAD>

<BODY>
This text isn't a comment.<BR>

<!--This text is a comment-->

This text isn't a comment, either.
</BODY>
</HTML>
```

> **Page Pitfalls**
>
> Although comment text isn't displayed in the browser, there's no problem seeing it if you simply view the page source code. Therefore, don't put sensitive information inside a comment tag.

As you can see in Figure 14.3, the text inside the comment tags isn't displayed by the browser.

Figure 14.3

Text that resides between the HTML comment tags is totally shunned by the browser.

The Least You Need to Know

♦ There are two main types of search component that you should consider: a CGI script and a search host.

♦ Most chat rooms and bulletin boards are hosted on remote servers and you place either a Java applet or some JavaScripts on your page. There are also CGI scripts that you install on your web host.

♦ Use this tag to automatically insert the tags and test from a specified text file:

```
<!--#include file="TextFileName"-->
```

♦ Use this tag to insert data into a page, depending on the variable you specify:

```
<!--#echo var="VariableName"-->
```

♦ Use the HTML comment tags to force the browser to ignore a section of text:

```
<!--Hidden text goes here-->
```

The Elements of Web Page Style

In This Chapter

- ♦ Prose prescriptions for web page writing
- ♦ Ideas for organizing your pages
- ♦ Tips on using graphics
- ♦ Things to keep in mind when dealing with links
- ♦ The do's and don'ts of world-class webcraft

With all that you've learned so far, you might be able to dress up your web pages, but can you take them anywhere? That is, you might have a web page for people to read, but is it a readable web page? Will web wanderers take one look at your page, say "Yuck!" and click their browser's Back button to get out of there, or will they stay awhile and check out what you have to say? Is your site a one-night surf, or will people add your page to their list of bookmarks?

My goal in this chapter is to show you there's a fine line between filler and killer—between "Trash it!" and "Smash hit!"—and to show you how to end up on the positive side of that equation. To that end, I give you a few style suggestions that help you put your best web page foot forward.

Content Is King: Notes About Writing

In earlier chapters, I've given you the goods on a number of web page techniques that most folks would shelve under "Eye Candy" in the HTML store. These include fonts, colors, animated images, and image maps. In later chapters you'll learn about things like style sheets, mouseovers, and scrolling status bar messages. And while all of these things can and should be used by even the most sober of web page engineers, you should never forget one thing: It's the content, silly! This is the central fact of web page publishing, and all the glitz often obscures it.

And, unless you're an artist or a musician or some other right-brain type, content means text. The vast majority of web pages are written documents that rely on words and phrases for impact. It makes sense, then, to put most of your page-production efforts into your writing. Sure, you'll spend lots of time fine-tuning your HTML codes to get things laid out just so, or tweaking your images, or scouring the web for "hot links" to put on your page, but you should direct most of your publishing time toward polishing your prose.

That isn't to say, however, that you need to devote your pages to earth-shattering topics composed with a professional writer's savoir faire. Many of the web's self-styled "style gurus" complain that most pages are too trivial and amateurish. Humbug! These ivory tower, hipper-than-thou types are completely missing the point of publishing on the web. They seem to think the web is just a slightly different form of book and magazine publishing, where only a select few deserve to be in print. *Nothing could be further from the truth!* With the web, anybody (that is, anybody with the patience to muddle through this HTML stuff) can get published and say what he wants to the world.

In other words, the web has opened up a whole new world of publishing opportunities, and we're in "anything goes" territory. So when I say, "Content is king," I mean you need to think carefully about what you want to say and make your page a unique experience. If you're putting up a page for a company, the page should reflect the company's philosophies, target audience, and central message. If you're putting up a personal home page, put the emphasis on the personal:

♦ **Write about topics that interest you.** Heck, if *you* are not interested in what you're writing about, I guarantee your readers won't be interested, either.

♦ **Write with passion.** If the topic you're scribbling about turns your crank, let everyone know. Shout from the rooftops that you love this stuff—you think it's the greatest thing since they started putting "Mute" buttons on TV remotes.

♦ **Write in your own voice.** The best home pages act as mirrors that show visitors at least an inkling of the authors' inner workings. And the surefire way to make your page a reflection of yourself is to write the way you talk. If you say "gotta" in conversation, go ahead and write "gotta" in your page. If you use contractions such as "I'll" and "you're" when talking to your friends, don't write "I will" and "you are" to your readers. Everybody—amateurs and professional scribes alike—has a unique writing voice; find yours and use it unabashedly.

Blog On
This writing advice applies doubly—nay *triply*—to the blog world. As you'll see in Part 3, content trumps style every time in all the good blogs. In particular, what readers crave in a blog is a *voice*.

Spelling, Grammar, and Other Text Strangers

Having said all that, however, I'm not proposing web anarchy. It's not enough to just slap up some text willy-nilly, or foist your stream-of-consciousness brain dumps on unsuspecting (and probably uninterested) web surfers. You need to shoot for certain *minimum* levels of quality if you hope to hold people's attention (and get them to come back for more).

For starters, you need to take to heart the old axiom, "The essence of writing is rewriting." Few of us ever say exactly what we want, the way we want, in a first draft. Before putting a page on the web, reread it a few times (at least once out loud, if you don't feel too silly doing it) to see if things flow the way you want. Put yourself in your reader's shoes. Will all this rambling make sense to that person? Is this an enjoyable read, or is it drudgery?

Above all, check and recheck your spelling (better yet, run the text through a spell checker, if you have one). A botched word or two won't ruin a page but, if nothing else, the gaffes will distract your readers. And, in the worst case, if your page is riddled with spelling blunders, your site will remain an eternally unpopular web wallflower.

Webmaster Wisdom

Correct spelling is important, so rather than trust your own sense of what's right, you ought to run your text through a handy spell checker. Most high-end word processing programs (such as Microsoft Word) have one, and lots of HTML editors (such as Netscape Composer) are spell-check equipped. If there's no spell checker in sight, consider downloading a great little program called Spell Checker for Edit Boxes. It's free and it can be found at www.quinion.com/mqa.

Grammar ranks right up there with root canals and tax audits on most people's "Top Ten Most Unpleasant Things" list. And it's no wonder: all those dangling participles, passive voices, and split infinitives. One look at that stuff and the usual reaction is "Yeah, well, split *this!*" Happily, you don't need to be a gung-ho grammarian to put up a successful web page. As long as your sentences make sense and your thoughts proceed in a semi-logical order, you'll be fine. Besides, most people's speech is reasonably grammatical, so if you model your writing after your speech patterns, you'll come pretty close. If you're not sure about things, ask some trusted and smart friends or family members to read your stuff and offer constructive criticism.

I should note, however, that this write-the-way-you-talk school of composition does have a few drawbacks. For one thing, most people get annoyed having to slog through too many words written in a "street" style; for example, writing "cuz" instead of "because," "U" instead of "you," or "dudz" instead of "dudes." Once in a while is okay, but a page full of that stuff will rile even the gentlest soul. Also, don't overuse "train of thought" devices such as "um," "uh," or the three-dot ellipsis thing …

Webmaster Wisdom

Although you should always squash all spelling bugs before a page goes public, try to practice *grammar slack*: maintaining a charitable attitude about other people's howlers. Although the lion's share of pages are written in English, not all the authors have English as their native tongue, so some pages include spelling that's, uh, creative. If an e-mail link is provided on the page, send a gentle note pointing out the slips of the keyboard and offer up the appropriate corrections.

More Tips for Righteous Writing

Thanks to the web's open, inclusive nature and its grass-roots appeal, there are, overall, few prescriptions you need to follow when writing your page. In addition to the ideas we've talked about so far, here are a few other stylistic admonishments to bear in mind:

- **Keep exclamation marks to a minimum!** Although I told you earlier to write with passion, keep an eye out for extraneous exclamation marks! Yeah, you might be excited but, believe me, exclamation marks get old in a hurry! See?! They make you sound so darned perky! Stop!

- **DON'T SHOUT!** Many web spinners add emphasis to their epistles by using UPPERCASE LETTERS. This isn't bad in itself, but please use uppercase sparingly. An entire page written in capital letters is tough to read and it feels like you're shouting, WHICH IS OKAY FOR A USED-CAR SALESMAN ON LATE-NIGHT TV, but it's inappropriate in just about any other context (including the world of web-page prose). Instead, use *italics* to emphasize important words or phrases.

- **Avoid excessive font formatting.** Speaking of italics, it's a good idea to go easy on those HTML tags that let you play around with the formatting of your text (as described in Chapter 3). **Bold**, *italic*, and `typewriter text` have their uses, but overusing them diminishes their impact and can make a page tough to read.

- **Be good, be brief, be gone.** These are the "three Bs" of any successful presentation. Being good means writing in clear, understandable prose that isn't marred by sloppy spelling or flagrant grammar violations. Also, if you use facts or statistics, cite the appropriate references to placate the doubting Thomases who want to check things for themselves. Being brief means getting right to the point without indulging in a rambling preamble. Always assume your reader is impatiently surfing through a stack of sites and has no time or patience for verbosity. State your business and then practice the third "B": Be gone!

The Overall Organization of Your Web Pages

Let's now turn our attention to some ideas for getting (and keeping) your web page affairs in order. You need to bear in mind, at all times, that the World Wide Web is all about navigation. Heck, half the fun comes from just surfing page-to-page via links. Because you've probably been having so much fun with this HTML stuff that you've created multiple pages for yourself, you can give the same navigational thrill to your readers. All you need to do is organize your pages appropriately and give visitors some way of getting from one page to the next.

What do I mean by organizing your pages "appropriately?" Well, there are two things to look at:

- How you split up the topics you talk about

- How many total documents you have

The One-Track Web Page: Keep Pages to a Single Topic

Although there are no set-in-stone rules about this site organization stuff, there's one principle that most people follow: one topic, one page. That is, cramming a number of disparate topics into a single page is not usually the way to go. For one thing, it's wasteful because a reader might be interested in only one of the topics, but he or she still has to load the entire page. It can also be confusing to read. If you have, say, some insights into metallurgy and some fascinating ideas about Chia Pets, tossing them together in a single page is just silly. (Unless you have a *very* strange hobby!) Make each of your pages stand on its own by dedicating a separate page for each topic. In the long run, your readers will be eternally thankful.

There's an exception to this one page-one topic rule for the terminally verbose: if your topic is a particularly long one, which means you end up with a correspondingly long page. Why is that a problem? Well, lengthy web pages have lots of disadvantages:

♦ Large files can take forever to load, especially for visitors accessing the web from a slow connection. (This becomes even worse if the page is full of images.) If loading the page takes too long, most people aren't likely to wait around for the cobwebs to start forming; they're more likely to abandon your site and head somewhere else.

♦ If you have navigation links at the top and bottom of the page (which I talk about later on), they aren't visible most of the time if the page is long. (Unless, of course, you're using frames on your page. Not sure what "frames" are? You can find out more about them by surfing back to Chapter 13.)

♦ Nobody likes scrolling through endless screens of text. Pages with more than three or four screenfuls of text are hard to navigate and tend to be confusing for the reader.

CAUTION

Page Pitfalls

Some studies show that many web ramblers don't like to scroll at all! They want to see one screenful and then move on. This is extreme behavior, to be sure, and probably not all that common (for now, anyway). My guess is that many folks make a snap judgment about a page based on their initial impression. If they don't like what they see, they catch the nearest wave and keep surfin'.

To avoid these pitfalls, consider dividing large topics into smaller subtopics and assigning each one a separate page. Make sure you include links in each page that make it easy for the reader to follow the topic sequentially (more on this later).

For example, I have an e-mail primer on my site. It's a long article, so I divided it up into eight separate pages and then added navigation links to help the reader move from section to section. Figure 15.1 shows one of those sections.

Figure 15.1

Break down long-winded topics into several pages by putting navigation links on each page.

Blog On

You can basically ignore the usual cautions about excessively long pages if you're putting together a blog. As you'll see in Part 3, a blog is a sequence of reverse-chronological entries, so the page will usually display anywhere from 10 to 20 (or more) entries at a time. Depending on the length of the entries, this can make for a long page. That's okay, because the important thing is to give blog readers who haven't been to your site for a week or two a chance to easily catch up.

Use Your Home Page to Tie Everything Together

Most people begin the tour of your pages at your home page. With this in mind, you should turn your home page into a sort of electronic launch pad that gives the surfer easy access to all your stuff. Generally, that means peppering your home page with links to all your topics. For example, check out my Word Spy site's home page shown in Figure 15.2. Through the various types of links, readers can get to any part of the site with just a click or two.

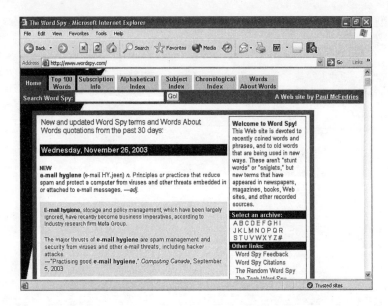

Try to set up your home page so it makes sense to newcomers. For example, most people know that Yahoo! (www.yahoo.com) is a subject catalog of sites, so the subject-related links on its home page make immediate sense. Most people's home pages aren't quite so straightforward. Therefore, include a reasonable description of your major links so visitors know what to expect.

For example, each page on my personal website (www.mcfedries.com) contains a navigation header at the top of the page. On my home page I have a "What's What" section that explains how to use the navigation header, as shown in Figure 15.3.

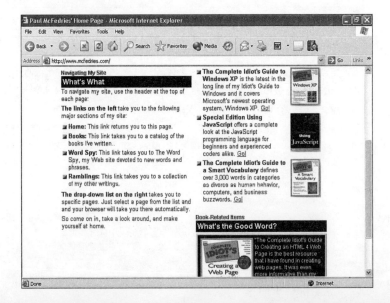

Use a Consistent Layout

Another thing to keep in mind when designing your pages is consistency. When folks are furiously clicking links, they don't often know immediately where they've ended up. If you use a consistent look throughout your pages (or throughout a set of related pages), everyone will know that they're still on your home turf. Here are some ideas you can use to achieve a consistent look:

♦ If you have a logo or other image that identifies your site, plant a copy on each of your pages. Or, if you'd prefer to tailor your graphics to each page, at least put the image in the same place on each page.

♦ Preface your page titles with a consistent phrase. For example, "Jim Bob's Home Page: Why I Love Zima," or "Alphonse's CyberHome: The BeDazzler Page."

♦ Use the same background color or image on all your pages.

♦ If you use links to help people navigate through your pages, put the links in the same place on each page.

♦ Use consistent sizes for your headings. For example, if your home page uses the <H1> tag for the main heading and <H3> tags for subsequent headings, use these tags the same way on all your pages.

Figures 15.4 and 15.5 show you what I mean. The first is the home of my book *The Complete Idiot's Guide to a Smart Vocabulary*, and the second is the home of my book *The Complete Idiot's Guide to Windows XP*. As you can see, the two pages use an almost identical layout. So if you know how to get around in one site, you have no problem figuring out the other.

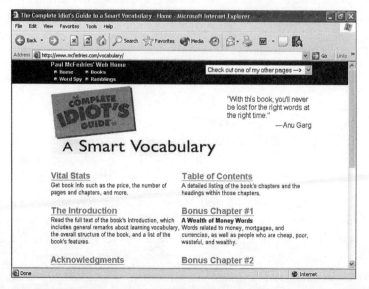

Figure 15.4

The home page of my book The Complete Idiot's Guide to a Smart Vocabulary.

Figure 15.5

The home page of my book
The Complete Idiot's
Guide to Windows XP.
*Note the consistent layout
between the two pages.*

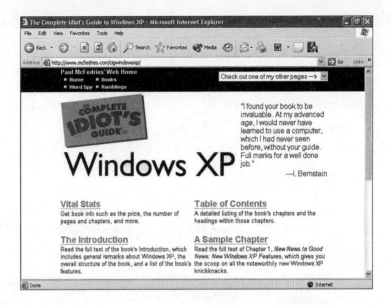

Organization and Layout Hints for Individual Pages

After you get the forest of your web pages in reasonable shape, it's time to start thinking about the trees, or the individual pages. The next few sections give you a few
pointers for putting together perfect pages.

Elements to Include in Each Page

For each of your web pages, the bulk of the content that appears is determined by the
overall subject of the page. If you're talking about Play-Doh, for example, most of
your text and images will be Play-Doh related. But there are a few elements that you
should include in all your pages, no matter what the subject matter:

◆ **A title.** A site without page titles is like a cocktail party without "Hi! My Name
Is …" tags.

◆ **A main heading.** Nobody wants to scour a large chunk of a page to determine
what it's all about. Instead, include a descriptive, large heading (<H1> or <H2>)
at the top of the page to give your readers the instant feedback they need. In some
cases, a short, introductory paragraph below the heading is also a good idea.

◆ **A "signature."** If you're going on the web, there's no point in being shy. People
appreciate knowing who created a page, so you should always "sign" your work. You
don't need anything fancy: Just your name and your e-mail address will do. If the
page is for a business, also include the company name, address, phone number,
and fax number.

♦ **Copyright info.** If the web pages you create are for your company, the company owns the material that appears on the page. Similarly, the contents of personal home pages belong to the person who created them. In both cases, copyright law protects the contents of the pages, and they can't be used by anyone else without permission. To reinforce this, include a copyright notice at the bottom of the page. Here's an example (the © code displays the copyright symbol):

```
The content of this site is Copyright &copy; 2004 Millicent Peeved
```

Page Pitfalls

Many webmeisters include some kind of "Under Construction" icon on pages that aren't finished (a few examples of the species are on this book's CD). This is fine, but don't overdo it. The nature of the web is that most pages are in a state of flux and are constantly being tweaked. (This is, in fact, a sign of a good site.) Scattering cute construction icons everywhere reduces their impact and annoys many readers.

♦ **The current status of the page.** If your page is a preliminary draft, contains unverified data, or is just generally not ready for prime time, let your readers know so they can take that into consideration.

♦ **A feedback mechanism.** Always give your visitors some way to contact you so they can lavish you with compliments or report problems. The usual way to do this is to include a "mailto" link somewhere on the page (as described in Chapter 5).

♦ **A link back to your home page.** As I mentioned earlier, your home page should be the "launch pad" for your site, with links taking the reader to different areas. To make life easier for the surfers who visit, however, each page should include a link back to the home page.

Words from the Web

A web page that hasn't been revised in some time is known derisively as a **cobweb page.**

Most of these suggestions can appear in a separate section at the bottom of each page (this is often called a *footer*). To help differentiate this section from the rest of the page, use an <HR> (horizontal rule) tag and an <ADDRESS> tag. On most browsers, the <ADDRESS> tag formats text in italics. Here's an example footer (look for footer.htm on the CD in this book) you can customize:

```
<HR>
<ADDRESS>
This page is Copyright &copy; 200?, your-name-here<BR>
company-name-here<BR>
company-address-here<BR>
Phone: (###) ###-####<BR>
Fax: (###) ###-####<BR>
Email: <A HREF="mailto:your-email-address-here">your-email-address-here</A>.
</ADDRESS>
<P>
Last revision: date/goes/here
</P>
<P>
Return to my <A HREF="home-page-URL-goes-here.htm">home page</A>.

</P>
```

Simplify Your Readers' Lives

When designing your web pages, always assume your readers are in the middle of a busy surfing session, and therefore won't be in the mood to waste time. It's not that people have short attention spans. (Although I'd bet dollars to doughnuts that the percentage of web surfers with some form of ADD—attention deficit disorder—is higher than that of the general population.) It's just the old mantra of the perpetually busy: "Things to do, places to go."

So how do you accommodate folks who are in "barely-enough-time-to-*see*-the-roses-much-less-stop-and-smell-the-darn-things" mode? Here are a few ideas:

◆ Organize your pages so people can find things quickly. This means breaking up your text into reasonably sized chunks and making judicious use of headers to identify each section.

◆ Put all your eye-catching good stuff at the top of the page where people are more likely to see it.

◆ If you have a long document, place anchors at the beginning of each section and then include a "table of contents" at the top of the document that includes links to each section. (I explain this in more detail in Chapter 5.)

◆ Add new stuff regularly to keep people coming back for more. This is particularly true of blog pages, where frequent updates are standard. You should also mark your new material with some sort of "new" graphic so regular visitors can easily find the recent additions.

Guidance for Using Graphics

As you saw in Chapter 6, graphics are a great way to get people's attention. With images, however, there's a fine line between irresistible and irritating. To help you avoid the latter, this section presents a few ideas for using graphics responsibly.

For starters, don't become a "bandwidth hog" by including too many large images in your page. Remember that when someone accesses your web page, all the page info— the text and graphics—is sent to that person's computer. The text isn't usually a problem (unless you're sending an entire novel, which I don't recommend), but graphics files are much slower. It's not unusual for a large image to take a minute or more to materialize if the surfer has a slow Internet connection. Clearly, your page better be *really* good if someone waits that long. Here are some ideas you can use to show mercy on visitors with slow connections:

- If your graphics are merely accessories, keep them small.

- If you have a large JPEG image, try *compressing* it so that it will download faster. To adjust the compression of a JPEG using Paint Shop Pro, open the image, select the **File, Save As** command, and then click the **Options** button in the Save As dialog box. In the Compression group, move the slider to the right to increase the compression, and then click **OK.** Save the file under a different name and then see how large the new file is. Remember that the higher the compression, the lower the image quality, so you might need to play around with the compression value to find an ideal value.

- If you have a large GIF image, the following sites offer services that will "optimize" the image for faster downloading: www.webreference.com/services/graphics and www.gifworks.com.

- Always use the <IMG> tag's WIDTH and HEIGHT attributes (see Chapter 6).

- Don't populate your home page with a single, massive "Enter My Site Here" image. Few things are as annoying as waiting forever for the image to download, only to find out that you're *still* not at the actual site. Grrr.

- It's acceptable to use graphics to get spiffy fonts because you can't be sure that surfers have the same font installed on their computers. However, don't rely on this too heavily, or your page could end up as nothing but a giant image!

Always bear in mind that a certain percentage of your readership is viewing your pages either from a text-only browser or from a graphical browser in which they've turned off image loading. If you're using an image as a link, be sure to provide a text alternative (by using the <IMG> tag's ALT attribute, as described in Chapter 6). For nonlink graphics, you can use ALT to describe the picture or even to display a blank. If you must use lots of images, offer people a choice of a text-only version of the page.

Finally, be careful if you decide to use a background image on your page. The Internet has lots of sites that offer various textures for background images. Many of these textures are "cool," to be sure, but they're too "busy" to display text properly and end up *flooding* the page. For example, check out the page shown in Figure 15.6. Now *that* is the mother of all ugly backgrounds—or should I say *wrackground!* (Lucky for you, the figure doesn't show the background in color; the actual texture incorporates various shades of sickly green.) For maximum readability, your best bet is to combine solid, light backgrounds with dark text.

> **Words from the Web**
>
> A page rendered unreadable because of a poorly chosen background image is said to be **flooded**. This kind of graphic is sometimes called a **wrackground image** because it "wrecks" the page.

Figure 15.6

Some background textures just aren't worth it!

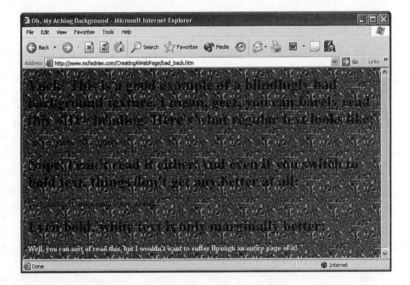

Link Lessons: Keeping Your Links in the Pink

To finish our look at web page style, here are a few ideas to keep in mind when using links in your pages:

♦ Make your link text descriptive. Link text really stands out on a page because browsers usually display it underlined and in a different color. This means the reader's eye is drawn naturally toward the link text, so you need to make the text descriptive. That way, it's easy for the reader to know exactly what they're linking to. Always avoid the "here" syndrome, where your link text is just "here" or "click here." The snippet below shows you the right and wrong way to set up your link text. Figure 15.7 shows how each one looks in a browser.

```
<H3>Wrong:</H3>
<P>
The Beet Poets page contains various odes celebrating our favorite edible
root, and you can get to it by clicking <A HREF="beetpoet.htm">here</A>.
</P>
<H3>Right:</H3>
<P>
The <A HREF="beetpoet.htm">Beet Poets page</A> contains various odes
celebrating our favorite edible root.
</P>
```

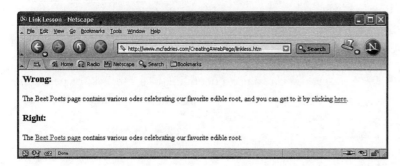

Figure 15.7

The reader's eye gravitates toward the link text, so make sure your text is descriptive.

◆ If you're presenting material sequentially in multiple pages, create "navigational links" to help the reader move forward and backward through the pages. For example, each page could have a **Previous** link that takes readers to the previous page, a **Next** link that takes them to the next page, and a **Top** link that returns them to the first page. (See Chapter 9 for a bit more detail on this.)

Webmaster Wisdom

You might be wondering why the heck you'd want to bother with *Previous* and *Next* buttons when most browsers have similar buttons built in (usually called *Back* and *Forward*). Well, they're not really the same things. For example, suppose you surf to a site and end up on a page that's in the middle of a series of pages. If you select the browser's *Back* button, you find yourself tossed back to the site you just bailed out of. If you select the page's *Previous* button, however, you head to the previous page in the series.

◆ For maximum readability, don't include spaces or punctuation marks either immediately after the <A> tag or immediately before the </A> tag.

- If you're planning a link to a particular page, but you haven't created that page yet, leave the link text as plain text (for example, don't surround it with the <A> and </A> tags). Links that point to a nonexistent page generate an error, which can be frustrating for surfers.

- If you move your page to a new site, leave behind a page that includes a link to the new location. Even better, set up the page to automatically redirect people to your new site. I showed you how to do this in Chapter 11.

- Try to keep all your links (both the internal and external variety) up-to-date. This means trying out each link periodically to make sure it goes where it's supposed to go and hasn't turned into a *vaporlink*. If you have a lot of links, try Xenu's Link Sleuth: home.snafu.de/tilman/xenulink.html.

- A *deep link* is a link to a page other than the site's home page. Many sites frown upon this because their home pages have banner ads or other material that they want all visitors to see. Some sites have been known to sue people who set up deep links to their pages. So if you want to use a deep link to a site, ask for permission first. If you don't get an answer, just link to the site's home page, to be safe.

> **Words from the Web**
>
> A link to a nonexistent page is called a **vaporlink**.

The Least You Need to Know

- Spend the most of your site construction time working on the text, and remember to write passionately and in your own voice about topics that interest you.

- The easy road to acceptably grammatical pages is to write the way you speak and to double-check your prose for sense and sensibility. Also, be sure to eliminate all spelling errors (which may mean running the text through a spell checker).

- Keep your pages short and confined to a single topic wherever possible, use your home page as your site's home base, and use a more-or-less consistent layout on all your pages.

- This means setting up each page so that things are easy to find, putting good stuff at the top of the page, creating a table of contents for long pages, and adding new things regularly.

- Keep nonessential images small, compress large JPEG and GIF images, include the <IMG> tag's WIDTH, HEIGHT, and ALT attributes, and be *very* careful about the image you use as your page background.

- Make your link text descriptive (don't use "here" or "click here"), set up navigation links for a series of pages, don't link to nonexistent pages, keep your external links up-to-date, and ask for permission before setting up a deep link to another site.

Part 3

Building Your Best Blog

Fads and manias erupt in every sphere of human life, and technology is no exception. Technological crazes most often appear in computing circles, and for the longest time they resulted in relatively harmless distractions such as flying-toaster screen savers and Solitaire addictions. The Internet has generated its own share of rages, which have included everything from push media to portals, disintermediation to reintermediation, e-books to eBay. Of this list, perhaps only eBay is still faddish, but that's the nature of Internet manias: They tend to leave almost as fast as they come. Of all things that have remained "in," perhaps the most surprising is the humble blog. This is a variation on the web page that has become enormously popular. Part 3 introduces you to the blog world and shows you how to build a blog that you'll be proud to show off.

Chapter 16

Blog Design Considerations

In This Chapter

- ◆ What on Earth *is* a blog, anyway?
- ◆ How to design your blog entries
- ◆ How to design your blog page
- ◆ Setting up an archive for your blog
- ◆ Tips and techniques for getting your blog feet wet

No one knows how many blogs exist, but a search of Internet domain names returns over 20,000 that include the word "blog." A recent survey by Perseus Development Corporation estimated that there are over 4.1 million blogs just on blog hosting sites such as LiveJournal and Blog-City. It's likely that there are at least as many *standalone blogs*. The Perseus survey also showed that approximately two thirds of the blogs hadn't been updated in over two months, so the total number of active *bloggers* is probably in the neighborhood of three million.

That so few blogs remain active highlights an undeniable fact of *blogging* life: It's difficult and time-consuming to keep a blog fresh with constant new entries. Yet blogs of all stripes still spring up every day like so many mushrooms after a spring rain. So most blogs may be transitory, but the community of blogs—called *blogistan*, the *blogiverse*, or, most often, the *blogosphere*—remains vibrant.

This chapter shows you how to get a foothold in the blogosphere by giving you the basics of good blog design. Your blog home might be a humble one at first, but by practicing the techniques and tips in this and the following few chapters, you might someday become a top-dog blogger and join the so-called *bloggerati*—also known as the *blognoscenti*, or the *A-list bloggers*.

What Is a Blog?

Anyone who has been involved in the blog world over the past few years knows that the apparently straightforward question, "What is a blog?" is really a battlefield where the blog community's hopes and desires vie for supremacy. That's because answering that question is the same as defining what a blog is or should be, and bloggers have widely different notions about this. So perhaps it's better to call a blog a kind of online Rorschach test where answering the question provides a glimpse into the mind and soul of the respondent. There is, in short, no simple answer to this simplest of questions.

It wasn't always this way. In the late 1990s, when the dot-com boom was in full roar and the web had become mainstream, a few people started maintaining sites that were nothing more than links to interesting, wacky, or controversial essays and articles from around the web. These "logs" of the web's greatest hits became known as *weblogs*, and by mid-1999, hundreds of them had sprung up.

The format proved to be immensely popular and, before long there were thousands and then tens of thousands of web logs going strong. With all these new web loggers grabbing a seat on the bandwagon, the format itself began to change, with web log "editors" now often introducing each link with a pithy comment or caution. Some sites began to eschew the links altogether and focus only on this personal commentary, which eventually morphed into posting short pieces on one's beliefs, activities, or emotional state.

This short history explains why you now see two types of blogs:

- **The "filter" blog.** Sometimes called a link-based blog, this type of blog consists primarily of links to other sites that have been *pre-surfed* and usually includes commentary about each link.

Words from the Web

Finding interesting links for other people to check out is often called **pre-surfing** the web.

- **The "journal" blog.** Sometimes called a *freestyle blog*, this kind of blog is composed primarily of personal observations and diarylike entries. One blogger summarized this format perfectly with the following equation:

ego + voice + time = blog

The journal blog is the more common of the two formats today, although there are still a number of pure filter blogs around. Overall, however, most blogs combine the two formats.

This mixing and matching of formats can make the blog world seem confusing, particularly when strident proponents of each format insist that theirs is the One True Way. The real answer here is that there is *no* set-in-stone blog format, and each blog is (or should be) a reflection of the blogger who maintains it. My own definition ignores the different formats:

> A blog is a web page consisting of frequently updated, reverse-chronological entries on a particular topic.

Let's take a closer look at the four key phrases from this definition:

♦ **Web page.** A blog is a web page, plain and simple. The content of the page defines it as a blog, but the page itself uses good old HTML. This is excellent news for you because it means you don't have to learn any new web page tricks to build a blog. You can use the know-how from the first 15 chapters of this book—not to mention the style sheet and JavaScript tidbits you'll be learning about in Part 4 and Chapters 24 and 25 found on the CD—to cobble together a blog that's as good as any out there.

♦ **Frequently updated.** Bloggers often take great glee in dissing sites that remain static for long periods—they call them "brochures" or "cobweb" pages. This is because the essence of blogging is frequent or, at least, regular updating of the page, so pages that remain static are seen as lifeless and dull. Many bloggers add new items several times a day, but you don't have to be that ambitious. Adding to your blog daily, or even every two or three days, is fine, and some of the best bloggers can go a week without posting anything.

♦ **Reverse-chronological entries.** All blog pages organize their items reverse-chronologically, with the most recent item appearing at the top of the page.

♦ **Particular topic.** It's important for a blog to have some kind of focus. This means that your items should all be related in some way to a certain topic, although it's also not unusual for bloggers to cover several different themes. The most common topic, by far, is the blogger him- or herself. Not surprisingly, these mostly use the journal blog format, and each item covers the blogger's activities, thoughts, feelings, and interests.

As you can see, this definition is very broad and therefore encompasses a wide variety of people, styles, and topics. The rest of this chapter delves into the details of building a blog, but always remember that the best blogs are unique and compelling reflections of the bloggers themselves. Above all else, make sure that your blog has *you* written all over it.

Designing Your Blog Entries

The heart of any blog is the collection of entries—sometimes called *posts*—that you publish. People might be initially attracted to a blog's name or its site design, but in the blogiverse, content is both king and queen. So you need to make sure that you present your entries in their best light. The design of each entry is up to you, and it will depend in large part on the type of entry and on the overall format of your blog (filter versus journal). In any case, your entries will consist of some combination of the following elements: headline, date and time, commentary, pull quote, link, credit, permanent link, and "Add a Comment" link. I discuss each element in detail in the sections that follow. Figure 16.1 shows an example of a blog entry that includes all of these elements.

> **Webmaster Wisdom**
>
> No matter which of these elements you incorporate into your post design, the most important thing is to be consistent. If you keep more or less the same design throughout all your entries, it will give your visitors an easier and more enjoyable reading experience, which will go a long way toward making them come back for more.

Figure 16.1

The elements of a typical blog entry.

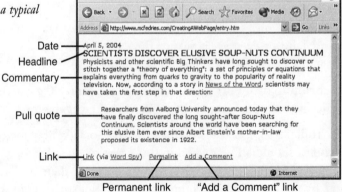

The Headline

The entry headline is pretty much what you'd expect: a short title that describes the entry. The headline almost always appears on a separate line above the entry, and most bloggers format it with bold text. Using a type size that's slightly larger than the regular entry text will also help the headline stand out.

The headline isn't a necessary element, but a funny or intriguing title that will often convince an otherwise reluctant visitor to read the entry.

The Date and Time

A blog's reverse-chronological nature dictates that all entries include the date of their posting. As you'll see in the section "Designing Your Blog Pages," you can either put all of a day's entries under a single date heading, or you can date entries individually. If you post a number of entries every day, it's traditional to also include the time of the post.

The Commentary

For a link entry (that is, an entry that provides a link to an item on another site), use the commentary element to give visitors your opinions about the linked article: why you think it's worth reading, what you think about the person who wrote it, how it changed your life, and so on.

For a journal entry, the commentary element is the entry itself; it is a mini-essay on whatever subject is currently turning your crank. Chapter 17 discusses tips for good commentary. For now, simply let the words flow. The biggest hurdle that most beginning bloggers face is the challenge of writing every (or almost every) day. You may not believe it, but writing *does* get easier the more you do it. So if you have a bee in your bonnet, a bug in your ear, or ants in your pants, go ahead and tell us about it.

The Pull Quote

In the lingo of journalism, a *pull quote* is an excerpt from a story—usually just a sentence or two—that is set off in a separate box in larger type. It's meant to be a kind of teaser that makes the reader want to either start or continue reading the article.

In a link entry for a blog, a pull quote is an excerpt from the linked story. It is often the opening sentence or paragraph of the story, but it can also be a particularly interesting tidbit from the body of the story. Again, the idea here is to use the quote to show the reader why the story is interesting or worth checking out.

The Link

The link is the key element in a link entry: It is the link to the story, web page, blog post, or whatever it is that you want to share with your readership. Some blogs have the link at the bottom of the entry and a consistent link text—such as "Link" or "Go!"

Other blogs incorporate the link in the commentary. It doesn't matter how you do it, as long as it's easy for the reader to recognize and click the link. (In Figure 16.1, the link appears twice—once in the commentary, and once using the "Link" text at the bottom of the entry.)

The Credit

When you're reading other people's blogs, you may come across a link entry that you find fascinating or funny enough to share with your own readers. You could simply point them to the blog containing the link entry, but that means your readers have to first go to that blog, find the link entry, and then go to the interesting item. Most surfers don't want or need those extra steps. Instead, they'd prefer it if you created your own link entry that takes them directly to the interesting item.

This is fine, but good blog etiquette dictates that you give credit to the blog in which you discovered the link. This doesn't have to be anything elaborate—just a simple "Props to X" or "via X," where X is the name of and a link to the original blog.

The Permanent Link

As you'll see a bit later, your blog won't be complete until you set up a separate "archive" page that stores your old posts. The permanent link is a link to the entry's permanent home in your blog's archives, and it usually appears at the bottom of each entry. The "Archiving Blog Entries" section of this chapter covers more about setting this up.

The "Add a Comment" Link

This is a link that enables a visitor to post a comment about the entry. Chapter 18 discusses this type of link in more detail.

Designing Your Blog Pages

Once you've settled on the layout of each blog entry, it's time to step back and consider the design of the blog page as a whole. The overall design—the colors, graphics, fonts, and so on—is, as on any of your pages, entirely up to you. The only caution I'll give you at this early stage is that your design shouldn't get in the way of the reading experience. A blog is almost always a medium for writing, so no busy backgrounds, no faint font colors, no teensy type sizes. It should be easy and comfortable for a visitor to peruse your blog text, and the design of the blog should not detract from your words. This is why you see many blog pages that are purposely under-designed with a simple, almost stark layout.

Beyond that, designing your blog is really a question of designing the page layout. Most blog pages have four distinct sections: the header, the blog entries, the side-blogs, and the footer. As with the blog entries, there's no rule that says you have to use all of these elements. The only required element is the section containing the blog entries (duh); use the rest of the page elements as you see fit.

The Blog Header

The header (not to be confused with an HTML header—that is, the tags that appear between the <HEAD> and </HEAD> tags—or with the headline—the title of a blog post) is the blog's introductory material, which always appears at the top of the page. It usually includes the blog name, its logo, or motto (if you have either one), and perhaps a link or two to the nonblog sections of your site. Mikal Belicove's blog, shown in Figure 16.2, has a substantial header section.

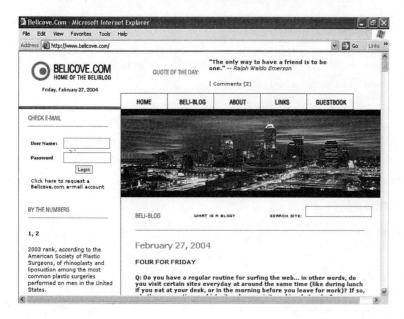

Figure 16.2

Mikal Belicove's Beli-Blog offers visitors a large and useful header section.

The Sideblogs

In the blogosphere, *sideblogs* (sometimes called *modules*) are separate sections of the page containing information that doesn't fit within the blog itself but is related to the blog or blogger. These sideblogs almost always appear in a column to the right or left (or both) of the blog. Figure 16.3 shows an example.

Figure 16.3

A blog layout with sideblogs on the left and right.

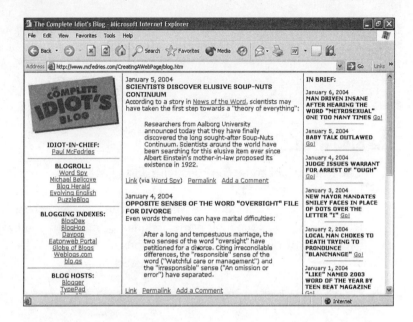

What goes in a sideblog? There are as many answers to that question as there are bloggers. Here's a list of some of the most common items:

- ◆ Short (one or two sentences) blog entries

- ◆ Links and forms related to your blog—for example, a link to the archive of your blog entries and a form for searching your blog

- ◆ Links to other pages on your site

- ◆ Links to other blogs (a *blogroll*)

- ◆ Links to other sites

- ◆ Information about the blogger

- ◆ Trivia and other tidbits of information

- ◆ A list that details the blogger's current reading list, favorite CDs, recent movies, and so on

- ◆ An Amazon.com "wish list"

Words from the Web

A list of links to other blogs is called a **blogroll**; linking to other blogs is called **blogrolling**.

The Blog Entries

The entries provide the meat of the blog, so they should be the most prominent and easily accessed feature. In most blogs, the entries appear in a column beside or between the sideblog column(s). Note that, as befits their prominence in the blog layout, the entries column should be substantially wider than the sideblog columns. For example, if the sideblog columns are 100 to 150 pixels wide, the entries column should be 300 to 400 pixels wide (or more).

Other than that, the look of the entries column is basically determined by the layout of the entries themselves. The only other decision you have to make is how to separate each day's entries, if you want to separate them at all. In most blogs, the date appears prominently (in a large, bold font, for example), and the entries for that date appear below the date text until a new date is started.

The Blog Footer

A blog's footer is usually similar to the typical web page footers described in Chapter 14. That is, it appears at the bottom of the page and contains items such as a copyright notice, contact information (usually an e-mail link), the blogging software or hosting site used (if any), and so on.

Archiving Blog Entries

As you work with your new blog, the page will get longer as you add new entries on the top and the old entries get pushed down the page. This won't be a problem at first, but after a while your page will start to get quite long with all the entries adding up. Before you know it, your page will take forever to load (particularly for those on slower modem connections) and people will stop coming to your site.

How can you avoid this problem? The easiest way is to drop the oldest entry each time you add a new entry. Before you can do that, however, you need to make a decision about the maximum number of entries you want to display on your main blog page:

◆ **Set a specific number of entries.** With this method, you choose a set number of entries to show. Ten to twenty entries is a typical range.

◆ **Set a specific number of days.** With this method, you choose a time frame—such as a week or two—and display all the entries you posted within that time.

◆ **Show only one entry at a time.** With this method, you only show your latest entry on your blog page. This isn't the typical way of doing things in the blogosphere, but many bloggers swear by it because it highlights each blog entry.

Whichever method you choose, when you reach the display limit you must remove the oldest entry to make room for the newest one. What happens to the removed

Blog On

Setting up and maintaining an archive can be a lot of work, particularly if you post frequently. Fortunately, there are blogging tools and services that can help you perform these chores, or even handle them for you automatically. See Chapter 20 for more information.

entry? Some bloggers let these old entries drift off into the ether, but all good blogs use a separate archive to give these entries a permanent home.

The archive doesn't have to be anything fancy. In most cases, it's simply a collection of pages that store the old entries chronologically. For example, each page might represent a month's worth of blog entries. Ideally, the archive pages should look more or less like your main blog page, but with links to the other archive pages.

One of the big advantages to having an archive is that it enables your readers to find your old blog entries. To help them do this easily, you need to give them a direct way to get to an individual entry. In other words, if they like an entry, they may want to create a link to it on their own sites, or even include it in their list of favorites or bookmarks. You can accommodate this by creating a permanent archive address for each entry. After you have done this, you can then inform people by including a *permanent link*—often shortened to *permalink*—as part of the entry.

Creating a permanent link requires that you do two things when setting up your archives:

♦ Give each archive a unique file name based on the date of the archived entries. For example, if an archive includes the entries for the month of August 2004, the name of the archive file could be 2004-08.html.

♦ Use an anchor tag to assign a unique name to each entry. The usual way to do this is to number each entry, where the first entry in the archive is 1, the second is 2, and so on. Here's an example:

```
<A NAME="1">Judge Announces Letter Vendetta</A>
```

Webmaster Wisdom

To ensure that your permanent links always work, archive each entry at the same time that you add it to your blog.

Setting up a permanent link to an archived entry then becomes a simple matter of using the archive file name followed by the entry name, as in this example:

```
<A HREF="2004-08.html#1">Permanent Link</A>
```

The Least You Need to Know

- A blog is a web page consisting of frequently updated, reverse-chronological entries on a particular topic.

- There are two kinds of blogs battling it out for supremacy in the blogiverse: the "filter" blog that consists mostly of links to other sites, usually with commentary related to each link; and the "journal" blog, which is composed mostly of personal observations and diarylike entries.

- The structure of a blog entry depends on the type of blog, but it always includes some or all of the following: headline, date and time, commentary, pull quote, link, credit, permanent link, and "Add a Comment" link.

- Most blog pages have four distinct sections: the header, the blog entries, the sideblogs, and the footer.

- Don't let your web words go to waste. Instead, maintain an archive to hold your old entries and be sure to create permalinks for each entry so readers can link directly to specific items in the archive.

Chapter 17

The Elements of Blog Style

In This Chapter

- ◆ Blog style versus blog substance
- ◆ Choosing your blog topic and satisfying your readers
- ◆ How to build a quality blog that people will clamor to read
- ◆ Tips and techniques to help you make a big splash when you dive into the blog waters

The blogosphere is a vibrant, exciting place because it's populated by a motley collection of interesting and verbose people. These intrepid bloggers have produced a body of blog work that is both jaw-droppingly big and eyebrow-raisingly diverse. Yes, there are the inevitable *kittyblogs* (boring journal blogs, so-named because many of them seem to spend inordinate amounts of space describing what the blogger's cat has done that day) and many *bloggerel* (blog doggerel). However, there are also a surprising number of blogs that say worthwhile things about some interesting topics. Following is a sampling of some blog types that inhabit the blogiverse:

- ◆ **Advocacy blog.** Supports a political cause
- ◆ **Blawg.** Deals with legal matters or is written by a lawyer
- ◆ **Edublog.** Discusses education issues

- **Linguablog.** Covers language and linguistics

- **Moblog.** A blog maintained and updated using a mobile device such as a notebook, palmtop computer, or cell phone

- **News blog** (also called a **pundit blog**). Examines mainstream news media and punditry. (Don't confuse this with a blog that breaks its own news, or *blews*.)

- **Photoblog or photo log.** Posts pictures, particularly candid shots of people in public places. (Many of these are moblogs updated with camera phones.)

- **Tech blog.** Focuses on technology.

- **Warblog.** Tackles war themes, especially the war on terrorism.

In other words, blogging is a "big tent" activity where there's always room to welcome someone new with a unique or unusual viewpoint or style. This chapter helps you find and hone your own style so you can step proudly into your new vocation as a blogger.

Notes About Blog Style

One of the unique things about the blog world is that content and style are practically synonyms. In other media, *content* is the stuff you read or see or hear, while *style* is the way that stuff is presented. Content is the meat and potatoes, while style is the sauce and sprig of parsley.

This distinction is nearly meaningless in the blogosphere, where, for the most part, content *is* style. This is obviously true for link-based blogs, in which the format and content are tightly linked. But it's also true for journal blogs and those that combine the journal and filter formats. In any good blog, what the blogger finds (the links) or says (the commentary) defines the style of that blog.

Style, Schmyle: It's the Content, Silly

When planning your blog, your watchword (watch*phrase*, really) should be, "It's the content, silly." In other words, your blog style is largely determined by your blog theme and what you write about that theme. You may think you have the content angle figured out because you already have a topic for your blog, but not so fast:

Many a promising blog has floundered because the would-be blogger has rushed in with a half-baked idea. To fully bake your blog, you must apply some heat to your basic idea by asking yourself (and, of course, answering) three apparently simple questions:

♦ What turns your crank?

♦ Who is (or who do you want to be) your audience?

♦ Who are you?

What Turns Your Crank?

This may seem like a trivial question. After all, you *know* what you're passionate about, and that's what you want to blog, right? Well, sure, of course. But the successful blog is, to borrow an apt phrase from the inventor Thomas Edison, 1 percent inspiration and 99 percent perspiration. This metaphorical perspiration (few people actually work up a sweat while blogging) comes from the pressure to produce. A blog is, by definition, something that's updated constantly. Even the best blog withers on the vine if it's not infused with a fresh supply of material. Most blogs fail because beginning bloggers don't understand that it's difficult to come up with new content day in and day out. Sure, it's easy enough to post a "Didn't do anything today" lament or a "Don't feel like writing today" sigh. You'd be surprised how often that is done even by some of the bloggerati. But post too much of this content-free *blogorrhea*—or, sin of sins in the blogging community, don't post at all for long periods—and your blog is as good as dead.

To avoid this fate, choose your blog theme wisely. Yes, it should be something that fascinates you. That is the most important criterion for choosing what your blog will be about. But don't make the common beginning blogger mistake of tackling a topic that's too big for one person to handle. "The latest developments in Internet technology" or "What's happening around the world" are laudable topics, to be sure, but they're impossibly broad for one person (or even a hundred people) to manage successfully. You need to narrow things down to a subset (or two) that particularly interests you and that will still generate enough content to keep your blog alive. Something like "The latest developments in Internet headgear" or "What's happening in French Lick, Indiana" are much more manageable topics for a one-man blog operation.

Words from the Web

Trivial or pointless material posted just for the sake of making a blog look like it's being updated regularly is call **blogorrhea**.

Who Is Your Audience?

Although *you* must be interested in your blog topic, other people won't necessarily be interested, too. Your Internet headgear passion might only be shared by a handful of fellow fetishists, or perhaps only the good people of French Lick give a darn about what's happening there. Before putting a lot of work into your blog, you need to give some thought to your potential audience. Who are they, and will they want to read what your write?

One way to gauge the audience potential for your blog is to examine the existing web landscape. Are there nonblog sites related to your topic? If so, then perhaps there's an opportunity to capture some eyeballs by presenting the topic in the fresh and accessible blog format. Of course, you also need to see if there are any existing (and successful) blogs on the same or a similar topic. If so, is the market big enough to support another blog that plows the same land?

It's worth mentioning that you might not be interested in building a big-time blog with hundreds or even thousands of readers. There's nothing wrong with that. A lot of really good blogs have a limited audience, such as a journal blogger's friends and family or a work-related blogger's colleagues and peers.

If a well-read blog is what you seek, then you need to know your audience. Millions of people regularly read at least one blog, and many of those people keep up with the posts of 10 or 20 (or more) blogs. Why do people read blogs? The answers to that question are nearly as varied as the readers themselves:

- **They want to learn.** Some people see a blog as a waste of virtual space if it doesn't at least occasionally teach them something new—even if it's just an obscure factoid that they can pass along to their spouse over dinner.

- **They want an expert's view.** Blogs are a goldmine of unbiased opinion and reviews written by people who know what they're talking about. Whether it's a network engineer deconstructing the hype surrounding the latest wireless networking gadgetry or a nutritionist debunking the latest fad diet, expert opinion is the gold standard of blogging. Of course, you really do have to be an expert to pull this off. Blog readers can spot blusterers and blowhards in seconds flat, so don't dive into these waters unless you're a strong swimmer.

- **They want journalism they can trust.** A growing number of people are turning off TV news and bypassing big-time newspapers because they believe these major media are tainted by their ties to the multinational conglomerates that own them. Instead, people are turning to individuals who have either researched a story on their own or who have experienced an event firsthand. This so-called *peer-to-peer journalism* is perfectly suited to the blog format, and people appreciate getting what appears to be the "real" story in a timely, uncensored way.

♦ **They want to be entertained.** Blogging shouldn't be drudgery, either for you (see the section entitled "Have Fun" later in this chapter) or your readers. Not all visitors are looking for nonstop laughs, but most people enjoy a bit of entertainment. This doesn't mean they want original songs or poems or artwork (although good for you if you have any to share). Rather, they want a well-turned sentence, the thrust-and-parry of a good argument, or a unique opinion.

♦ **They want to get some "cool" links.** The web is unfathomably big, and most surfers spend their online time with the barely-conscious feeling that they're almost certainly missing something that would set their tails wagging, if they had tails. A good filter blog that "pre-surfs" the web's niches is a treasure to metaphorically clutch to one's bosom.

♦ **They want to experience something "real."** I don't have to tell you the impact that "reality" shows such as *The Real World* and *Survivor* have had on our collective television viewing habits. People just seem to crave unscripted reactions to events, no matter how absurd or contrived those events might be. Surfers flock to web logs for a similar reason: because blogs—particularly journal blogs—offer raw access to a person's mental and emotional life.

♦ **They want to watch your life unfold online.** Pure journal blogs can be compelling, but not if most of the posts are of the what-I-had-for-breakfast-and-why-my-life-sucks variety. Not that the minutiae of one's personal life should never be seen as blog fodder, but the audience for such a blog will likely consist only of one's family and closest friends.

Using these ideas as a starting point, you must give a lot of thought to why people will want to spend time reading *your* blog. If you don't satisfy at least one of these desires (and preferably two or three of them), few people will come to your blog, and most of those people won't stick around.

Who Are You?

Finally, don't even think about putting your blog online unless you've thoughtfully and critically examined your own motivations for getting into all this. That doesn't mean you need to go through some kind of soul-searching exercise to determine your life's purpose or to come up with a nobler-than-thou blogging goal such as eradicating child poverty. After all, this is just a blog. Instead, just be honest about your motivations and goals for becoming a blogger:

♦ **You want to share something unique or interesting.** One of the best reasons to get into blogging is the desire to take something—a story, an expert opinion, an intelligent comment, a new perspective, or just a quirky way of looking at the world—and share it with other people. Being unique or interesting won't guarantee a successful blog, but you'll be miles ahead of the bland and the boring.

♦ **You want to be a better writer.** It's a truism among writing gurus and coaches that the more you write, the better your writing becomes. The simple act of putting your thoughts on paper each day has turned many a mediocre writer into a good writer. (*Great* writers are, arguably, born that way.) The web log, with its imposed discipline of daily jottings is an excellent vehicle for taking your writing up a notch or two. And a blog is always better than a paper diary because it has a "real" audience; nothing concentrates a writer's mind better than knowing someone is (or a lot of someones are) going to be reading his or her work. This is particularly true for blogs that solicit reader feedback because you're bound to hear about your writing gaffes (and hopefully get some praise, too).

♦ **You want to tell the world you're here.** I suppose I'm not telling any great secrets when I say that many blogs act as nothing more than "Hey, look at me!" affirmations of the blogger's existence on this earth. That may sound like pure egoism, but there's more to it than that. Humans have *always* affirmed that they exist by creating something, particularly things that contain some kind of stamp of the person's individuality and things that can be seen and appreciated by other people. This is a perfect recipe for a blog, which is (or should be) a unique product of the blogger and a place that other people can visit. The philosophy is a simple one: *blogito ergo sum*—I blog, therefore I am.

♦ **You want to interact with like-minded people.** Save for a few curmudgeons and misanthropes, we humans are relentlessly social creatures. Most of us get our social jollies from our circle of friends, family, and co-workers. However, we've all had the experience of having a passion for something and not having anyone around to share it with. Our spouses and childhood pals will indulge our ravings for a while, but what we really need is to talk to someone who truly understands how we feel. A blog can slake this thirst because it enables you to create a community of like-minded souls centered on a topic that you all feel passionate about. Many bloggers say that the most satisfying (and often the most surprising) thing about building their blog was connecting with others who feel the same way.

♦ **You want to keep your colleagues informed.** This book focuses on personal blogs, but it's not surprising that the blog format lends itself to the business world, too. Whether it's news about an ongoing project, the latest happenings in a department, or staying abreast of the company softball team, blogs are a useful business communications tool.

◆ **You want to connect with your family and friends.** One of the characteristic features of life in the twenty-first century is the ease with which many individuals and families pick up their stakes, pack up their belongings, and haul themselves off to some far-flung locale. It's the human form of the migratory instinct. However, it's a truism that increased distance leads to decreased connection between family and friends. Phone calls, letters, and e-mails can help repair damaged or neglected social ties, and these channels of communication aren't going away (with the possible exception of the letter, which may be all but extinct in a few years). However, many people are turning to the blog format to keep in touch. A journal-style blog is a great way to let people know what's going on in your life and what's important to you. It's cheaper than a phone call, easier than a letter, and comes without an e-mail message's inherent pressure to respond.

Whether your motivation to blog falls within these broad categories or you have your own unique reason to blog, the important thing is that blogging should be something *meaningful to you*. If you're doing it just to be part of the scene, because your best friend is doing it, or because you think it will make you "cool" or rich, then your blogging career will most likely be short-lived. On the other hand, if you're doing it because it has some meaning for you, then you're already well on your way.

Blog Style Tips

The main theme of this chapter is a simple one: In blogland, content and style are synonymous. That's not to say that you should ignore the look of your site—far from it. As I mentioned in Chapter 16, you have several options when it comes to laying out both your blog entries and your blog page as a whole. Mixing and matching the various elements gives you endless possibilities for setting up the blog to suit your personal taste and your topic. Also, of course, you have the gamut of HTML tags at your disposal (as well as the powerful style sheet properties I discuss in Part 4). The important thing to remember when working on the look of your blog is that nothing—I repeat *nothing*—should get in the way of the reading experience. Your choices for fonts, background, and colors should be pleasing to the eye, but they should serve to enhance the reader's pleasure first. This brings us squarely back to the content. The remainder of this chapter gives you a few pointers on how to adapt your style to best present your words to the reading public.

Decide on Your Posting Frequency

No beginning blogger ever felt that posting was a burden. Indeed, the raw excitement of not only getting your words online, but actually having other people—even (gasp!)

strangers—read your words can induce giddiness in even the soberest of souls. The temptation is to post again and again for the sheer joy of it. I don't want to rain on anyone's parade—far from it. But if you find yourself caught up in this blogging exuberance, let me caution you not so much to curb your enthusiasm, but to channel it. Rather than posting a bunch of entries higgledy-piggledy, pick the best of them and use your excitement to hone your prose, deepen your research, or otherwise improve the quality of the entry. Only post it when you're convinced it's the best you can do.

Why the wet blanket routine? Three reasons:

♦ **You're creating great expectations.** If people see you posting ten times a day, they'll figure that's your standard output and will be disappointed if you start posting less frequently.

♦ **You may be labeled as a quantity-over-quality blogger.** You want to avoid the bloggorhea label—someone who posts just for the sake of posting—at all costs.

♦ **You'll burn out.** A few bloggers with the energy of 10 people and access to 48-hour days can post with amazing frequency over the long haul. The rest of us can't; if we try, we burn out.

Posting one entry a day is an ideal frequency for most new bloggers. It doesn't consume your life, but it's often enough to keep interested readers coming back to your site to see the latest entry. Of course, you're the best judge of your own energy level and time commitments. Take these into account and decide how often you want to post new entries (perhaps taking a little off the top to allow for your initial enthusiasm).

After you've decided on your posting frequency, it's important to be consistent about it. Try to post at the same time each day (such as first thing in the morning or in the evening) so people know when to come looking for your latest entry. Also, try to keep the posting frequency consistent. If you normally post only once per day, it's no crime to post two or three items on a particular day if you have something timely or interesting to impart. But do try to avoid the all-too-common scenario of sending out a barrage of posts one day followed by three days off to recover. Keeping a steady pace will help ensure that you maintain your blogging enthusiasm and your readership for a long time.

Create a Catchy Name

The majority of blogs have dull names such as "Biff's Web Log" or "Tammy's Blog World." A surprising number of A-list bloggers have pasted prosaic names on their blogs. Perhaps this implies that the blog's name is meaningless, but I don't think so.

The big-time bloggers with boring names became big-time in the early days of blogging, when there were just a few dozen blogs on the entire web and they couldn't be missed. Now, with blogs everywhere you turn, standing out in the crowd is much more difficult. You can help yourself in that department by coming up with a good moniker for your blog. Here are some tips:

- **Short names are best.** If you want other people to remember your blog, keep the name short and pithy for easier memorization and recall.

- **A good pun is a good thing.** Many people complain about puns, but they usually laugh at the good ones (or groan at the bad ones, which is the same thing to a punster). If you can think of an apt pun, it will help your name stand out from the crowd.

- **Make it descriptive.** As far as possible (particularly considering my injunction to keep the name short), your name should in some way reflect the overall topic or theme of your blog.

- **Incorporate "blog," if possible.** Blog readers like to read blogs (obviously), so they tend to be on the lookout for other blogs to peruse. A link to your blog may simply use your blog name as the link text, so incorporating "blog" somewhere in the title will help people to recognize your page as a member of the blog species. That doesn't mean you should name your page "So and So's Blog." That's boring. Find some clever or natural way to add the word to your name. Coining a compound or blended word is a good way to go. For example, when Mikal Belicove (blogger and acquisitions editors for this book) was looking for a good name, he created a fun blend using part of his last name: the Beli-Blog.

When you've decided on a name, you should immediately carve out a slice of web real estate that has your name on it. You have four choices:

- **Set up a domain name.** This will give you a name like www.YourBlog.com. See Chapter 7 to learn more about domain names.

- **Sign up with a web hosting provider.** This will give you a name like YourBlog.HostingProvider.com. Again, see Chapter 7 for details.

- **Create a directory in your existing domain.** If you already have a domain name that you use for other purposes, create a new directory to hold the blog page and archives. (See Chapter 8 to learn how to use FTP to create a directory on your server.) This will give you a name like www.YourDomain.com/YourBlog.

◆ **Sign up with a blog hosting provider.** This will give you a name such as YourBlog.BlogHost.com. See Chapter 20 to learn about some of the available blog hosting providers.

Link Off the Beaten Track

Including a link to the latest *New York Times* scoop may suit your blog, but rest assured that a few thousand other bloggers will probably do the same thing. Not that there's anything wrong with that. However, you won't gain any new readers (and you'll lose your existing readership awfully quickly) if *all* your links are to obvious Big Media stories. Either try to ferret out the obscure Big Media stories buried deep inside their websites or, even better, try to find links to interesting things in the Small Media universe: the alternative press, e-zines, personal pages, and so on. Developing a reputation as someone who regularly finds interesting stories from the web's nooks and crannies will drive a lot of people to your blog.

Tell a Story

The enjoyment of a good story is hard-wired into the human brain. There's something about an engaging, well-told narrative that captures the imagination of readers and leaves them looking for more.

Telling a tale doesn't mean crafting a Nabokovian short story or a Homeric ode. Rather, it just means narrating a story with some attention to detail, color, and pacing. Even a trip to the Department of Motor Vehicles for a license renewal can turn into a compelling yarn if you take your time and flesh out the characters you saw, the hurdles you had to overcome, the success you finally achieved. Telling individual tales is wonderful, but you can also take advantage of the blog format to spin out longer narratives that develop over the course of a week, a month, or even longer. For example, on the Beli-Blog, Mikal Belicove announced his intention to lose 40 pounds by his 40th birthday, two years hence (see Figure 17.1). Subsequent entries told of his diet struggles, his new exercise regimen, and, of course, regular updates on how much weight he'd lost.

There's really no limit to the creative ways to build blog-based stories. Moreover, you have the full box of storytelling tools at your disposal: using foreshadowing to suggest or hint at future events; introducing other characters (real or imagined) and fleshing them out as either protagonists or antagonists; weaving multiple themes together into a larger, related story; employing suspense and mood to keep readers on the edge of their computer chairs; and, of course, providing an exciting denouement to bring everything to a satisfying close.

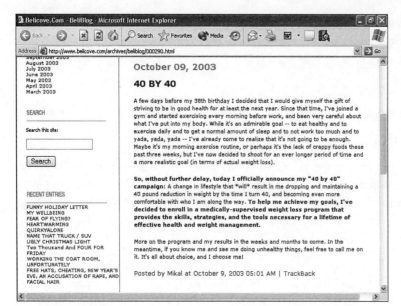

Figure 17.1

The entry from the Beli-Blog stating the author's intention to lose 40 pounds by age 40.

Keep It Short

Throughout their short history, web logs have been characterized by short entries. This is in keeping with the early web log format, which was a log of links with a bit of commentary on each link. The commentaries were short, providing just enough text to enable the reader to decide whether to click the link.

This pithy-post ethos carried over to the journal format, and now most blogs consist of short, easily digested entries. More important, blog readers *expect* entries to be short. In other words, if a blogger consistently posts long-winded entries, his readers will often either complain or take their eyeballs elsewhere.

Therefore, make sure that most of your entries are relatively short. If an entry seems too long, cut out any unnecessary words or sentences. Look for redundant words or multiple sentences that essentially say the same thing. This isn't as easy as it sounds. The philosopher Blaise Pascal once apologized to a correspondent about the length of a letter he'd written, saying "I would have made it shorter, but I did not have the time." Writing good, tight prose is difficult, but your readers will appreciate the effort.

Keep It Relevant

A good way to keep your posts short is to stick to your blog's main theme, or themes. Few things are as frustrating for a reader as an undisciplined blog writer who constantly goes off on tangents and digressions about whatever flits into his or her head.

You may like the sound of your own voice, but chances are that's not why people are reading your blog. Stay on topic and your readers will stay with you.

Be Yourself

As the (by now) old joke goes, in cyberspace, no one knows you're a dog. So it may be tempting to use the relative anonymity of the web to try on different personalities and do a little role-playing. There's nothing wrong with that per se, but your blog is a lousy place to do it. For one thing, your blog is supposed to be a unique expression of who you are, so by definition you should strive for personal honesty. Plus, your readers are savvier than you think and can spot a phony from a mile away. You might think you're being quite clever, but believe me, unless you're a particularly brilliant actor, the rest of us can see right through you.

Having said that, it's also true that each of us has a diverse inner life that allows for many different expressions and ways of being. If, for example, you spend your days being pleasant and polite, but you secretly harbor passionate or even controversial views about, say, politics, it's fair game to give that secret side an outlet in a blog.

The important thing is: What you write in your blog should be a true reflection of who you are. Otherwise you're just wasting both your time and ours.

Be Interesting

File this tip in the easier-said-than-done category. Of *course* you should strive to be interesting; not many people are looking for an *un*interesting blog to read. But *being* interesting—and, moreover, (since this *is* a blog we're talking about) being interesting *every day*—is hard work.

The good news is that "being interesting" is a flexible concept that you can adapt to your personality and your blog theme.

◆ **Be smart.** Most of the opinions and comments you read on the web in general and in blogs in particular are, well, stupid. The web, like life itself, is full of igno-ramuses who aren't shy about demonstrating their mental shortcomings. That's actually good news for you because it gives you a chance to stand out from the ignorant masses. If you think hard about things, do your research, and really try to understand both sides of an issue, you'll come up with smart, informed pieces that people will be clamoring to read.

◆ **Be argumentative.** Posting a link along with a boring "I agree with this guy" commentary is not the road to blog fame. If you want people to take notice, you may need to pick a fight or two. If you find something on the web that you utterly disagree with, post the link and tell us not only that the author is an idiot, but *why* he's an idiot. Rebut his arguments, expose his fallacies, and slice and dice his reasoning. People love a heartfelt, intelligent argument and will happily tune in to any new developments. Remember, though, that they'll eventually tune out once the insults start flying, so keep to the high ground (even if your opponent doesn't).

◆ **Be controversial.** Several bloggers have achieved notoriety in the blog community by stating in no uncertain terms that most blogs and bloggers "suck" (the usual verb that was tossed out). The blog world usually has a good-natured, hurray-for-us vibe, so attacking that world was controversial indeed. I'm not suggesting that you set up an anti-blogging blog (that, having been done, would elicit nothing but yawns today), but a little controversy can go a long way toward getting a blog on the map. Expressing some heartfelt but outrageous opinions in sensitive areas such as politics, religion, and war might be the way to get your blogging career off to a rousing start.

CAUTION **Page Pitfalls** _____

Being controversial is fine, if it's genuine, but I don't counsel an anything-goes attitude. There are still some taboos that should remain unbroken, and of course you should avoid anything that's racist, homophobic, misogynistic, or that elicits hate or advocates illegal activities. Be careful, too, of criticizing your fellow employees, your organization or school, or your family members. These things have been known to come back and haunt bloggers who have ended up losing jobs, getting tossed out of school, and alienating friends and family.

◆ **Be unique.** There are millions of bloggers toiling away out there, so you'll never separate yourself from the crowd by following it. If your blog looks like a thousand others, chances are people will visit one of those other sites instead of yours. As a human, you are automatically a unique being, so try and channel some of that uniqueness into your blog. This can be as simple as expressing your own opinion or as creative as coming up with a concept or two for your entries that you've never seen anywhere else. Above all, cultivate your unique writing voice. If you're not an experienced writer, don't worry about it too much in the beginning. Just keep writing, and eventually you'll find a writing style that naturally enables you to say what you want to say and how you want to say it. That's your writing voice; it will come through loud and clear the more you use it.

◆ **Be bold.** Being shy can be cute or endearing in person, but it's the kiss of death online. A namby-pamby blog is almost a contradiction in terms because blogs are meant to have a certain attitude. More often than not, a good blogger is a bold blogger who doesn't shy away from being opinionated and forceful. Even if you're uncomfortable being in people's faces, you can still give your blog a bold feel through your writing. Use the active voice to give your writing strength; deploy good, sturdy verbs to give your writing momentum; and avoid weasel words such as "perhaps" and "might" to appear more decisive.

Be Consistent

In Chapter 16, I discussed being consistent with respect to the layout of your entries and your pages, and earlier in this chapter with respect to your posting frequency. Consistency is a big virtue in the blog world, and it applies to your blog style, too. A blog that is inconsistent in tone, writing voice, and subject matter won't win any awards, much less attract a following.

I'm not saying that you have to stick with your initial blog formula for all time. Few new bloggers hit the right combination of topic, tone, and voice right off the bat, so in the early stages of your blog, you should feel free to experiment and fix things that aren't working, either for you or for your readers. (Luckily, you probably won't have very many readers at first, so you aren't likely to annoy too many people with your constant tinkering.)

Have Fun

Finally, always remember that blogging is not meant to be a deadly serious activity. It's true that a certain air of triumph and self-congratulations pervades the blogosphere, with its boosters boasting that blogging is superior to the "ancient media." This is mere hype and should not be believed. Blogging is nothing more or less that a wonderful new medium for the likes of you and me to express ourselves, stretch our writing wings a bit, and commune with people who share our warped view of the world. In my mind, that's a recipe not for frown-causing seriousness or yawn-inducing earnestness, but for the smile-cracking joy and brain-stimulating excitement that are a natural byproduct of sharing bits of ourselves within a caring and supportive community. That's a long-winded way of saying a simple thing: Have fun out there!

The Least You Need to Know

◆ You'll enjoy blogging, put more effort into doing quality work, and stay in the game longer if you blog about something you care passionately about.

◆ Don't take on a broad subject that's beyond the scope of one person's ability to do justice. Find a niche and mine it for all it's worth.

◆ Understand the reasons why people read blogs and try to adapt your site to fit in with one or more of those criteria.

◆ Keep your hands away from the keyboard until you've asked yourself why you want to get on the blogging bandwagon and until you've satisfied yourself that you're doing it for the right reasons.

◆ "A man's gotta know his limitations," Clint Eastwood once said, and that's true for the men and women who blog. Consider how much time and energy you have under normal circumstances (not now, when you're cranked about being a blogger) and decide on a reasonable posting frequency. Remember that a quality post once a day is perfectly acceptable in the blog world.

◆ Put most of your efforts into researching and writing your posts in order to make them worth reading. Tell interesting stories, keep them short and to the point, and above all, be true to yourself.

Chapter 18

Building an Audience for Your Blog

In This Chapter

- How to measure the size of your readership

- Easy (and free) techniques for marketing your blog

- Making your blog interactive

- Creating a comment system to enable readers to post feedback

- Syndicating your site content

- A fistful of useful techniques and proven strategies for getting people to notice your blog

Unlike certain baseball diamonds in Iowa cornfields, in the blogging field, if you build it they won't necessarily come. That may not matter much to you if you're blogging only for a select group of family, friends, or colleagues. But if you're like most bloggers, you want (okay, you *crave*) an audience. What's the point of slaving over your entries if no one else reads them? You may as well be scribbling away in a *paper* diary, for gosh sakes.

So how does a budding blogger convince a bunch of perfect strangers to stop by for a visit? It's a tough chore in this busy blog world, but it *can* be done, and that's the topic of this chapter. You'll learn all kinds of tips and techniques that will have them packing the aisles and have you putting out the "Standing Room Only" sign.

Measuring the Size of Your Audience

Before implementing any of the nifty techniques in this chapter, you must have some way of knowing whether they're working for you. That is, you need to know if your blog is attracting hordes or merely collecting dust. You need to know if you've hit the big time, or just hit the skids. In other words, you need to know the number of people who've accessed your blog. There are two ways to go:

◆ **Ask your hosting provider.** Many companies can supply you with statistics that tell you the number of "hits" your site has taken.

◆ **Include a counter in your blog pages.** A counter is a little program that increments each time a surfer requests the page.

CAUTION **Page Pitfalls** _____

Counters are fun, and they're certainly a handy way to keep track of the amount of activity your blog is generating. There are, however, two counter-related caveats you should know about:

◆ The counter program sits on another computer, so it takes time for the program to receive and send its information. This means your page loads a little more slowly than usual.

◆ If the computer that stores the counter program goes "down for the count" (pun intended), the count won't appear on your page.

Creating a counter program is well beyond the scope of this humble book (insert sigh of relief here). However, a few community-minded programmers have made counter programs available on the web. Happily, you don't even have to copy or install these programs. All you have to do is insert a link to the program in your page, and the counter updates automatically whenever someone checks out the page. Here are some counter programs to try:

◆ **Site Meter.** This is a blog-friendly and free counter that gives a lot of juicy site stats, including the number of unique visitors and the total page views they generate. You also get a list of "referring URLs," which are addresses of pages that are linking to your blog. See www.sitemeter.com.

- **eXTReMe Tracker.** This service offers a wide range of tracking options, including referrer tracking. See www.extreme-dm.com/tracking.

- **FastCounter.** This is a basic counter that's easy to set up (several different styles are available) and that sends reports to you via e-mail. See www.bcentral.com/services/fc.

Webmaster Wisdom

This chapter contains many web addresses. To save you from having to type them in by hand, I have links to each site on this book's example blog page: www.mcfedries.com/CreatingAWebPage/blog.htm.

- **Nedstat Basic.** This a reliable counter that's free for noncommercial sites and gives you all the basic stat stuff in a nice, neat package. See www.nedstatbasic.net.

- **The WebCounter.** This is a nicely implemented, no-frills counter. Note that busy sites (those getting more than 1,000 hits a day) have to pay a subscription fee to use it. See www.digits.com.

- **Yahoo!'s Access Counter Index.** As usual, Yahoo! has a long list of sites that supply counters. See dir.yahoo.com/Computers_and_Internet/Internet/World_Wide_Web/Programming/Access_Counters.

Basic Strategies for Drawing a Crowd

Let's get the bitter truth on the table right upfront: A bad blog simply will *not* pack in the crowds. Because there are enough blogs out there no one will take a second look at any effort that's poorly executed. In Chapter 17, I discussed some of the techniques you can use to build a better blog: finding a niche topic you're passionate about; knowing your audience; not posting too often (or, of course, too infrequently); creating a catchy, memorable name; using storytelling techniques; keeping your posts short and on-topic; being your own unique, controversial, interesting, and smart self; and having fun, because people who see that you're having a good time will want to hang around you.

Beyond supplying good content, you can also rely on search engines to drive people your way. Techniques that work just as well with blogs as they do with regular web pages are: using <META> tags; setting up your blog (particularly your archives) so that search engine

Webmaster Wisdom

Google is a particularly pro-blog search engine because it has recognized the chief feature of blogs: They're updated much more frequently than static pages. So instead of crawling for an updated version of a site every few weeks (as it does for static pages), blogs are crawled every day to ensure that searches return the most relevant results.

crawlers can find and navigate your site; and submitting your blog to the most popular search engines. Chapter 8 covers these techniques.

Get the Word Out

To help your blog stand out, you need to blow your own horn by doing a little advertising and promotion. This doesn't mean paying for a 30-second ad in next year's Super Bowl (although feel free if you have a few million lying around that you don't know what to do with). By far the best marketing tool in existence is a little thing called word-of-mouth, so you can get things off to a good start by spreading the word about your blog to friends, family, co-workers, and cocktail-party conversationalists. Tell them not only to visit your site, but also to tell their friends about it.

There are many other things you can do to spread the gospel of you even further. Here are some ideas for online promotion:

- ◆ **Include a brief "ad" about your blog at the bottom of all your e-mail messages.** Even just the URL of the blog page would suffice. (Remember, too, that most e-mail programs can be set up to automatically tack on a "signature" to the bottom of each outgoing message.)

> **CAUTION**
>
> **Page Pitfalls**
>
> Please resist the temptation to broadcast an e-mail about your new blog at work. Sending out an announcement to your department or even the entire company is in poor taste, and is probably not a good career move.

- ◆ **Join mailing lists and participate in newsgroups and discussion lists related to your blog topic.** Also, look out for online communities that discuss themes related to your blog. Establishing a track record of thoughtful, helpful, and on-topic commentary (*not* useless and annoying "Check out my blog!" posts) will do wonders to encourage other participants to visit your site. Note, too, that many community sites have a "member profiles" section that you can use to talk up your blog.

- ◆ **Volunteer to help out at any site that has content related to your blog or participants whom you think might be interested in your blog.** Write articles, create programs, suggest new features, design a logo, or do anything that helps the site with its day-to-day chores. People who work at larger online community sites tend to be well connected; impressing these people might lead them to share your blog information with their long list of friends.

- ◆ **Get all your friends and relatives to link to your site.** The more links that point to you, the greater your ranking will be in some search engines—particularly Google.

Get in the Blog-Specific Indexes

Submitting your blog to general search engines (particularly Google) is a must, but there are also several blog-specific indexes and searching tools you should know about (and that need to know about you). Blog fans use these resources all the time to find specific blog content or blogs that cover a particular subject area. Here are the ones to check out:

♦ **Blogdex.** This is a research project hosted by the Media Laboratory of the Massachusetts Institute of Technology. Its goal is to track the "fastest spreading ideas" in the blogging community, which it does by crawling all the blogs in its database and picking out the links to other sites. Then it compares these links to the ones it found in the previous crawl, and displays the entries and articles with the biggest increase at the top of its list. You can get your blog into the Blogdex database here: blogdex.net/add.asp.

> **Blog On**
>
> You'll find a large list of blog indexes and search engines at www.aripaparo.com/archive/000632.html.

♦ **BlogHop.** This is a directory of blogs that also enables visitors to rate each blog. Submit your blog here: bloghop.com/addblog.htm.

♦ **Daypop.** This is a search engine for frequently updated sites, including news media pages and, yes, blogs. Submit your site to the search engine here: www.daypop.com/info/submit.htm.

♦ **Eatonweb Portal.** This is a blog directory that seems like it has been around forever (it was one of the first to attempt to impose some order on the early blog chaos). It organizes blogs by category, language, country, and alphabetically, and it also includes visitor ratings for each blog. Add your blog here: portal.eatonweb.com/add.php

♦ **Globe of Blogs.** This basic site lists thousands of blogs by title, topic, location, and even date of birth! To register, see www.globeofblogs.com/register.php.

♦ **Weblogs.com.** This site displays a continuously changing list of blogs that have been recently updated. The idea is that when you make changes to your site, you "ping" the Weblogs.comserver. Pinging is a kind of digital tap on the shoulder that says, in effect, "My blog has new stuff on it." The Weblogs.com server goes to your blog, verifies that it has changed, and adds it to the list of

> **Blog On**
>
> A site that's similar to Weblogs is blo.gs. It not only displays a constantly updated list of recently changed blogs, but it can also send you an e-mail notifying you that your favorite blog has new content. The address is its name: blo.gs.

updated blogs. You can ping Weblogs.com manually by filling in the form on the following page: newhome.weblogs.com/pingSiteForm.

Join a Blogring

A *webring* is a collection of related websites that use special links to create a kind of chain that connects one site to another. For example, Site A would have a link to Site B; Site B would have links to Site A (usually labeled "Previous") and Site C (usually labeled "Next"); Site C would have links to Site B and Site D, and so on. Site Z would have links to Site Y and Site A, thus completing the ring. The advantage to this kind of setup is that enables users to easily surf through a group of sites that are all focused on a particular topic.

Although webrings exist for all kinds of sites, they're popular in the blogosphere and a lot of readers use them to access many blogs that relate to a favorite theme. So you can drive a nice chunk of traffic to your site by joining an appropriate blog webring, or *blogring*.

To find a webring or blogring, use your favorite search engine to search for *topic* blogring or *topic* webring, where *topic* is a word or phrase that describes the topic of your blog. You can also try RingSurf, a directory of webrings (see www.ringsurf.com). When you find one you want to join, the main site will give you instructions (note that you may need to be approved) and the code for the "Previous" and "Next" links.

> **Words from the Web**
>
> A webring that consists of a collection of related blogs is often called a **blogring**.

Join a Geographic Index

Vacationers on cruise ships and in resorts often exhibit a strange behavior: If they meet people who hail from the same town, region, or country, they'll strike up a friendship and hang out with those people for the rest of their stay. It seems weird to travel thousands of miles only to end up vacationing with your own kind, but that's human nature for you.

This bonding instinct also shows up among blogizens in the form of the *geographic index*, a collection of blogs from people who live in a particular city, state, region, or country. Sometimes these indexes consist of blogs that discuss the common geographical area, so they're a great resource for people interested in learning more about that area. But these indexes increasingly serve a larger social function, with the bloggers exchanging e-mails and sometimes even getting together offline.

Whether your blog deals with a geographic area or you just want to strike up a friendship with neighboring bloggers, joining a geographic index can be a great way to drum up a bunch of new visitors. To find one, visit a search engine and look for *area* blog, where *area* is the geographic location you're interested in.

Send a Note to an A-List Blogger

If you've been hanging around blogdom for a while, there are probably a few A-List Bloggers (A-LBs) that you like and admire. You probably also know that the mention of a site by a big-time blogger can generate a *ton* of traffic to that site. Your goal is obvious: Get one of your favorite A-LBs to talk up your site. Of course, getting the blogger to do this isn't easy. A slightly easier goal is to get the A-LB to visit your site; occasionally you can make that happen just by dropping a line to the blogger's e-mail address.

Tell the A-LB not only that you like and admire his or her blog, but *why* you like it. Don't flatter just for the sake of it; instead, be sincere and focus on those things you truly do enjoy about the site. Writing with humor or wit will certainly help get you noticed, too. Finally, be sure to include the address of your own blog and cross your fingers that the A-LB deigns to take a look. You could, of course, come right out and *ask* the A-LB to visit your site, but the subtlety and mystery of an otherwise unmentioned address would very likely be too much for the A-LB to resist. (Remember that most bloggers *love* links and find it hard to resist clicking a new address.)

Link to Other Blogs

Earlier on, I mentioned referrer URLs, which are the addresses of pages that link to your page. For example, if Site X has a link to your blog and a user clicks that link, Site X becomes a *referrer* and its address is recorded in the "Referrer" field of your website statistics.

Of course, it works the other way, too. That is, if you link to another site and someone clicks that link, your blog address will show up as a referrer URL for the other site. Many bloggers keep track of their referrers so they know who's linking to them. If they're curious about your referrer address, they may check out your page to see what you're all about. If the blogger likes what he or she sees, you might get a reciprocal link on his or her blogroll, or even a mention in a blog entry. And if that other site happens to be a well-read blog, that could send a lot of new readers your way.

So when you're constructing your own blogroll, be sure to include a few links to some high-traffic blogs. (I hope it goes without saying that these should be blogs that you're comfortable recommending to other people; you should never link to a big-time blog that you dislike because that level of naked ambition and dishonesty will certainly come back to haunt you in this life or the next one.)

Creating a Crowd-Pleasingly Interactive Site

Some bloggers are unabashed "page view monsters" who care only about jacking up the number of times their blog pages get viewed each day. That's fine, but to me it's like counting the number of stars you can see in the night sky: The number itself might be interesting, but it doesn't tell you much else. Wouldn't it be better to be able to recognize constellations and pick out planets and major stars? This would enable you to find your way around the night sky and delve into the stories and science that underlie what you're seeing.

The blog equivalent to this metaphor is recognizing the regular visitors to your site and, of course, encouraging others to become regular visitors. The best way to do this is to make your site *interactive*, by soliciting and encouraging feedback from your visitors. This enables you to go beyond the basic "one-to-many" model of blog communication (one person writing for an audience of many people) and create a new scheme that provides something closer to a "many-to-many" model (many people writing for many people). In other words, your blog monologue turns into a blog conversation and, if you're lucky, even a small blog community.

Simple Interactive Strategies

Blogs with bells and whistles that encourage reader interaction are fun to hang around in; naturally, this leads to other people joining in the reindeer games. Fortunately, the interaction doesn't have to be anything incredibly fancy. Here are a few simple ideas that enable visitors to feel like they are participating in the life of your blog:

♦ **Set up an e-mail link.** At the very least, your blog should have an e-mail link that visitors can use to pass along compliments, corrections, or general chit-chat. (See Chapter 5 to learn how to set up an e-mail link.) Ideally, you should have a separate e-mail account for your blog-related correspondence.

♦ **Create a feedback form.** Forms are a great way to encourage people to interact with you. This can range from a simple "Tell me what you think of the site" to a "Question of the day (or week, or whatever)." Why not set up a regular contest to see who can submit the best suggestion, idea, or response to a challenge? The "prize" needs only be the person's name posted on your site as the winner. Another crowd-pleaser is the online poll where you pose a question and use radio buttons to offer four or five possible responses. (See Chapter 12 for details on setting up a form.)

◆ **Set up a mailing list.** Many bloggers use newsletter-style mailing lists to announce new features or give regular site updates. These are "one-way" lists, which means that each message is sent out once to each subscriber, but the subscribers can't respond to the list. Often a better choice when you're just starting out is a discussion group: a "two-way" list (all subscribers can respond) that centers on the topic of your blog, rather than the blog itself. Several services offer free mailing lists, including Yahoo! Groups (groups.yahoo.com) and Topica (www.topica.com).

> **Blog On**
>
> The pMachine blogging program comes with built-in mailing list capabilities. Chapter 20 describes this program.

◆ **Set up a chat room or bulletin board.** A great way to foster a sense of community on your site is to offer visitors a place to hang out. Chat rooms and bulletin boards are perfect for this. See Chapter 14 for details.

◆ **Use guest bloggers.** The ultimate blogger goal (at least as far as readership goes) is to foster a sense of loyalty among visitors that makes them not only want to return to your site often, but also tell other people about it. You can do that with first-rate content, but an even better route is to give people a sense that they've had a hand in making that content. Asking for—and implementing—site suggestions is a good start, but the royal road to loyalty lies in allowing other people to post blog entries. There are many ways to use "guest" bloggers. For example, you could designate a few visitors you trust to post regularly; you could ask people to submit entries and pledge to post the best one each day; you can make someone the Guest Blogger of the Week as the prize in a weekly contest.

Page Pitfalls _____

Guest bloggers are common in blogistan, but they're not without pitfalls. For example, what do you do if someone wants to post something that is poorly written, inaccurate, or just plain wacko? You need to decide in advance how you're going to handle such situations. Another problem is that having a number of different guest bloggers can give your site an uneven feel and may obscure your own writing voice that you've worked so hard to develop. Finally, using too many guest bloggers can cause your own entries to get lost in the storm; before you know it, your blog doesn't feel like your own creation anymore.

Setting Up a Comment System

The most common and successful interaction strategy is a simple one: Allow your readers to post comments about your entries (and, of course, about other peoples' comments). Implementing such a strategy usually begins with a simple form that asks for the user's name and the text of his or her comment. It's also traditional in the blogiverse to ask for the user's own blog address, assuming that he or she has one. Figure 18.1 shows a basic comment form.

Figure 18.1

Use a form similar to this to elicit comments from your readers.

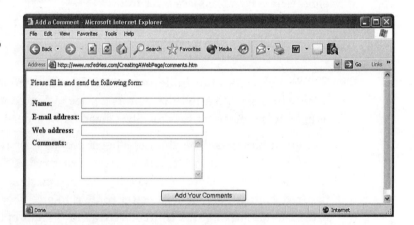

Two problems with this "simple" system rear their ugly heads right off the bat: getting the form data and knowing which entry is the subject of the comment.

Webmaster Wisdom

As you make your way through this section, you can be forgiven for thinking that setting up and maintaining a blog comment system sure sounds like a lot of work. This stuff *can* be tedious and repetitive if you do it by hand. Fortunately, you don't have to do all this manually if you're just not up for it. There are lots of blogging tools and services that can help you perform these chores, or even handle them for you automatically. See Chapter 20 for more information.

Getting the form data is a standard problem with *all* forms. Chapter 12 discusses a few solutions.

By far the nastier problem is figuring out which entry the user is commenting on. You may be able to deduce which entry is involved from the text of the comment, but you can't count on this. (Generic comments such as "Nice entry!" or "This post saved my life!" don't give you much to go on.) Instead, you need a trick to ensure foolproof operation.

This trick begins with the design of each entry's "Add a Comment" link, as discussed in Chapter 16. This link usually calls up a form, but it's also possible to add something called a *query string* to the form address. A query string is a method for passing data from one page to another by using a link. Here's the general structure to use for a query string:

```
FileName?Name=Value
```

Here, *FileName* is the file name of a web page; in this case, it's the file name of your comment form page. *Name* is a short (no spaces) name you make up for the data, and *Value* is the value of that data. An example should help clear things up:

```
comment.html?EntryID=2004-08-1
```

Here, comment.html is the name of the form page, and EntryID is the name assigned to the data. The value of the data is 2004-08-1. The key here is that this value can be interpreted as a blog entry: that is, the first entry in the blog archive of August, 2004. When you know that, you know exactly which entry the user is commenting on.

Here is an example of an "Add a Comment" link that uses this system:

```
<A HREF="comment.html?EntryID=2004-08-1">Add a Comment </A>
```

Unfortunately, you're not out of the woods just yet. You now need some way of capturing the "EntryID" value and passing that along with the rest of the form data. You can do this by setting up a "hidden" form field that uses a bit of JavaScript magic to capture and store the "EntryID" value. Place the following code anywhere inside your form code (that is, between the <FORM> and </FORM> tags):

```
<SCRIPT LANGUAGE="JavaScript" TYPE="text/javascript">
<!--
var query_value = location.search.substring(1).split("=")
document.write('<INPUT TYPE="HIDDEN" NAME="EntryID" VALUE="' +
query_value[1] + '">')
//-->
</SCRIPT>
```

This, I'm sure, gives new meaning to the word "gobbledygook." It may make more sense to you after you read the JavaScript stuff found on the CD. For now, however, it's enough to know that it works. That is, when you get the data from the comment form, it will include a field named "EntryID" that tells you the code for the blog entry.

Your next hurdle involves posting the comments to your site. The comments don't do much good sitting in your e-mail inbox or your computer's hard drive. Instead, you need to post them to your site so that others can read them. The easiest route is to add the comments to your archives, just below the appropriate entry.

Finally, once an entry has one or more comments, you need to give your readers some way of reading those comments. This usually takes the form of adding a "View Comments" link to the blog entry, which is similar to setting up a permanent link. That is, you begin by creating an anchor for the comment section of each entry. The name of the anchor could be the entry number followed by the letter "C" (for comments). For example, if the entry were the third one in the archive, the comment anchor would use the name "3C":

```
<A NAME="3C">Comments</A>
```

Your "View Comments" link then looks like this (assuming you're linking to the August, 2004 archive):

```
<A HREF="2004-08.html#3C>View Comments</A>
```

Syndicating Your Site

You can steer perfect strangers to your blog by allowing other sites to publish bits of your content along with a link back to your page. If people like what they read, they'll probably click the link so they can see what else you have up your online sleeve.

Sharing content seems easy as pie at first glance. The other site just views your page source code, copies the material they want, and pastes it somewhere on their site along with a link back to you. (I'm assuming that you've given this person permission to do this.) That *is* relatively easy for a static page, but it can become mind-numbingly tedious for a frequently updated page such as a blog. For example, if someone wants to display the most recent headlines from your blog and you post daily, that person has to visit your site every day to get your headlines. That's bad enough, but they might be a news *aggregator* that lists headlines from a number of different blogs. Imagine the hassle it would be to grab headlines from 10 or 20 different blogs.

The solution to this is something called *syndication*, which enables the automation of grabbing headlines (or whatever) from a site. The rest of this chapter shows you how to set this up on your blog.

What Is Syndication?

You're probably familiar with the term "syndication" from the world of television. When a show is starting out, it appears at a scheduled time each week. When the show has been around for a while, the producers can make big bucks by selling to television stations the right to broadcast the older shows. Those stations can then broadcast the shows whenever they want.

Web page syndication is similar, although unfortunately there are never any big bucks involved. By syndicating your site, you're giving implicit permission for other people to "rebroadcast" portions of your content on their sites.

This sounds the same as giving people permission to copy bits of your site source code, but there's a big difference: With syndication, the gathering and broadcasting of your content is done automatically—there's no cutting and pasting involved.

The secret to this is something called *Rich Site Summary* (or possibly *Real Simple Syndication* or *RDF Site Syntax*; nobody really knows). RSS is based on the eXtensible Markup Language, or XML. XML uses tags, like HTML, but they serve a different purpose: HTML tags tell a web browser *how* text is supposed to appear to the user (bold, as a link, and so on); XML tags tell the browser *what* the text represents. For example, in HTML you might surround headline text with the <FONT> and <B> tags to distinguish the headline from the other elements of the page. In an XML document, you might surround the headline text with a <headline> tag.

What XML means and how it's implemented are beyond the scope of this book. However, figuring out RSS is well within our purview.

The important point you need to bear in mind is that RSS automates the syndication of blog content. It does that by enabling you to specify exactly which elements of the blog are to be syndicated—usually, one or more headlines and all or part of their corresponding entries. It also provides for links back to your blog, so people who like your syndicated material will drop by your site for more. To perform this magic, you need to create an RSS file.

Building an RSS File

If you read about RSS on the web or in other books, the authors make it seem like some snarling junkyard dog that should be approached with extreme caution. RSS is actually very simple to learn and is, in fact, no more difficult than any of the HTML tags you've mastered elsewhere in this book. As usual, we tackle this from the ground up and build your knowledge slowly.

Like an HTML file, an RSS file is a simple text document. So go ahead and launch your favorite text editor, create a new file, and save it. Give the file a name that ends with the .xml or .rss extension.

Always begin this text file with the following tag:

```
<?xml version="1.0" encoding="UTF-8" ?>
```

This isn't necessary, but it's good to include because it declares to the world that this file conforms to the XML standard.

You're building an RSS document, so the next thing you do is declare the RSS version. Version 0.92 is the standard as of this writing:

```
<rss version="0.92">
```

You also need the closing </rss> tag, so now your file looks like this:

```
<?xml version="1.0" encoding="UTF-8" ?>
<rss version="0.92">
</rss>
```

In RSS, a *channel* is just the data feed provided by a site. You declare the beginning and end of your channel by using, appropriately enough, the <channel> tag and its </channel> end tag. Here's where we stand:

```
<?xml version="1.0" encoding="UTF-8" ?>
<rss version="0.92">
    <channel>
    </channel>
</rss>
```

Notice that I've indented the <channel> and </channel> tags a few spaces. This is purely to make the file easier to read and has absolutely no effect on how it's interpreted.

Your next task is to describe the channel, which you do with four tags:

- ◆ <title>   Use this tag to provide a name for the channel.
- ◆ <link>   Use this tag to provide the address of your blog.
- ◆ <description>   Use this tag to provide a short summary of your blog.
- ◆ <language>   Use this tag to declare the language of your blog. Use **en-us** for U.S. English.

Here's the channel information I use on my Word Spy RSS feed:

```
<title>The Word Spy</title>
<link>http://www.wordspy.com/</link>
<description>The Word Spy - The Latest Entries</description>
<language>en-us</language>
```

Here's how the skeleton RSS file looks now:

```
<?xml version="1.0" encoding="UTF-8" ?>
<rss version="0.92">
    <channel>
        <title>Your Blog Title</title>
        <link>Your Blog Address</link>
        <description>Your Blog Description</description>
        <language>en-us</language>
    </channel>
</rss>
```

Finally, you need to add some tags that represent each of the blog entries that you want to include in the RSS feed. These are called *items* and you begin and end them with the <item> and </item> tags. In between, you define the item using the <title>, <link>, and <description> tags:

- ◆ <title>   The headline of the blog entry.

- ◆ <link>   The permanent address of the blog entry in your archives.

- ◆ <description>   The blog entry, or perhaps just a sentence or two if the entry is a long one.

Page Pitfalls _____

Don't put any regular HTML tags in your RSS file; otherwise, the file will become invalid.

Webmaster Wisdom _____

I've put together a skeleton RSS file that you can use as a starting point. See the file rss.xml on this book's CD.

Here's an example item from Word Spy:

```
<item>
    <title>Chrismukkah</title>
    <link>http://www.wordspy.com/words/Chrismukkah.asp</link>
    <description>(KRIS.muh.kuh) n. A holiday celebration that
➡combines elements of both Christmas and Hanukkah, particularly in
➡households that have both Christian and Jewish members.</description>
</item>
```

Figure 18.2 shows an example RSS file as it appears in a browser.

Figure 18.2

A completed RSS file that is ready for syndication.

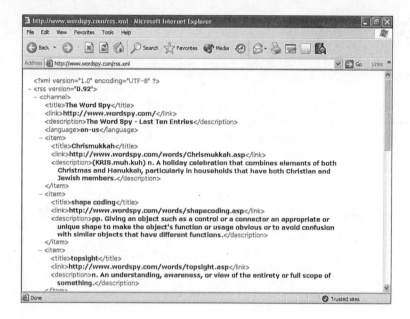

Putting Your Feed Online

After you've completed your RSS file, you must give other people access to the feed. The first thing you need to do is upload the RSS file to your website. When that's finished, check to make sure your RSS code is valid. There are numerous RSS code validators on the web, and you can find one by entering "RSS validator" into any search engine. Here are a couple of validators to get you started:

- ◆ **Feed Validator.** feedvalidator.org
- ◆ **Userland.** aggregator.userland.com/validator

Next, you should load your RSS file into an RSS reader to make sure the feed text and links look and behave the way you want. Again, search for "RSS reader" in any search engine, or use the following page as a starting point:

```
blogspace.com/rss/readers
```

Figure 18.3 shows how the feed from Figure 18.2 looks when it is loaded into the RssReader program.

When your RSS files are checked out and ready for public consumption, you need to let people know you have an RSS feed by setting up a link to the RSS file. For example, if your RSS file is named rss.xml and you stored it in your site's main directory, you'd set up a link like this one:

```
<A HREF="rss.xml">RSS Feed</A>
```

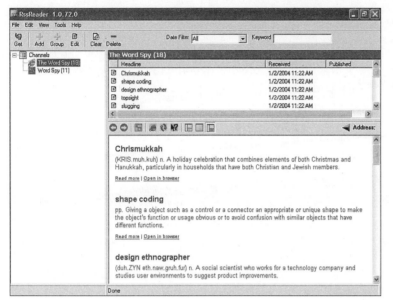

Figure 18.3

The same RSS file displayed within the RssReader program.

Note, too, that many bloggers flag their RSS feed link by placing a standard "XML" image beside the link. Figure 18.4 shows an example.

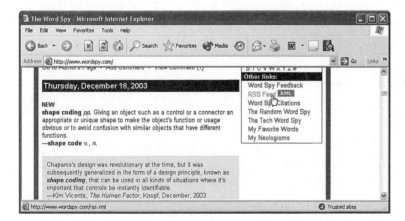

Figure 18.4

Create a link to enable visitors to find your RSS feed.

Finally, you also want to make it easy for news aggregators that crawl sites automatically to find your feed. You do that by adding a special <LINK> tag inside your page header (that is, between the <HEAD> and </HEAD> tags):

```
<LINK REL="alternate" TYPE="application/rss+xml" TITLE="RSS"
HREF="RSS File">
```

Webmaster Wisdom

This book's CD contains a sample "XML" image. Look for the file named xml.jpg.

Here, replace *RSS File* with the full URL of your RSS file. Note, too, that you are not required to wait for an aggregator to come crawling. You can submit the URL of your RSS file to an aggregator yourself. Following are a couple of aggregators for you to check out:

- **NewsIsFree.** www.newsisfree.com

- **Syndic8.** www.syndic8.com

Blog On

Setting up an RSS feed is not difficult, but if you post frequently, you'll begin to wonder if there's an easier way to generate the RSS file. Yup, there is. Many blogging tools come with automatic RSS generators built right in (see Chapter 20). You can also use the RSS Channel Editor, which is available from www.webreference.com/cgi-bin/perl/rssedit.pl.

The Least You Need to Know

- Before trying to attract new visitors, use a site statistics tool or service to measure how many people are visiting your site. Count your audience regularly to gauge the progress of your promotion.

- Encourage friends, relatives, and willing co-workers to tell two friends about your blog; they will then tell two of their friends, who will tell two of their friends, who will … well, you get the idea.

- The more involved you become with other bloggers, the more those bloggers will drive people to your site. Get your blog in every blog index; join an appropriate blogring or geographical index; drop a line to one of the bloggerati that you admire; and link to major blogs that you enjoy reading.

- Create a sense of shared experience among your readers by adding interactive elements to your blog, including an e-mail link, contests, polls, mailing lists, a chat room, and inviting guest bloggers.

- Create a sense of community on your site by adding a comments form that users can fill in and submit to give you their two or three cents' worth.

- Give the gift of you by creating an RSS feed that enables other sites to post summaries of your recent entries.

Getting Along in the Blog World

In This Chapter

◆ How to avoid blunders that are common to blogging newcomers

◆ Basic manners for blog readers

◆ Etiquette tips for blog writers

◆ A miscellany of blogging do's and don'ts to help keep you on the straight and narrow

The blogosphere is a wild and woolly frontier populated with free spirits, hackers, libertarians, and nonconformists of every stripe and hue. There is not a central organization that ties the whole thing together, so you'd think the prevailing ethos would be an anything-goes, dog-eat-dog, free-for-all. It is true that there are a few random pockets of anarchy scattered about, but the overwhelming majority of bloggish interactions are governed by courtesy and civility.

How can this be? The answer is contained in a set of conventions known collectively as *netiquette* (a blend of *network etiquette*). These prescriptions for politeness apply to the Internet as a whole, but a few of them are readily applied to the blog world. Most bloggers learn them early in their careers; they are enforced by pointing out to scofflaws the error of their ways and reminding them of the proper behavior. These remonstrances are usually gentle, but they can often be blunt, caustic, and venomously sarcastic. In other words, you'll want to stay on the good side of the blog community, and this chapter helps you do just that. Think of this as a finishing school for correct netiquette that will prepare you for your blog debut.

Netiquette for Blog Readers

For many people, the word "etiquette" conjures up horrifying visions of forks and spoons multiplying beyond control and arcane social rituals that require a curtsy or two. Fortunately, blog etiquette involves no such terrors. As you'll see in the next couple of sections, it's really just a collection of common sense suggestions and practices designed to grease the wheels of blog social discourse. Let's begin with a few pointers related to reading blogs.

Lurk Before You Leap

If a blog has a comment feature or forum, you may sorely be tempted to dive right into the deep end and post comments left, right, and center. However, first you should get the lay of the blog land by reading a bunch of the entries and any comments that other people have posted. This gives you a chance to gauge the overall tone of the blog, the intellectual level of the entries, and the interests of the blogger and his or her readership. After you feel comfortable with the blog, start posting some comments.

One caveat, however: Introverted types, or those who are uncomfortable with their writing skills, may decide to become full-time *lurkers* who never post their own comments. That's their decision, of course, but it's considered slightly bad form in some blog circles. Why? Well, the more community-minded blogs thrive on participation and the constant thrust and parry of post and comment. Mere rubbernecking adds no value whatsoever to a group, so posting comments or participating in chat room or bulletin board discussions is encouraged.

> **Words from the Web**
>
> Reading entries without commenting on them is known as **lurking,** and a person who does this is a **lurker.**

Read the FAQ

In your travels through the blog universe, you'll come across many sites that deal with specific topics. For example, you might find a blog dedicated to Buddhism. So you check it out for a while and, when you decide to comment or send a note to the blogger, the first question that comes to mind is, "Who the heck was the Buddha, anyway?" That's a good question, but the problem is that most of the other readers of this blog probably asked the same question when they were newcomers. You can imagine how thrilled the blogger is to answer this question for the thousandth time.

To avoid these kinds of annoyingly repetitive queries, many blogs have a Frequently Asked Questions list, or FAQ. Before you even think about commenting on something or writing to the blogger for the first time, give the blog's FAQ a thorough going over to see if your question has come up in the past.

Stay on Topic

When commenting on an entry, keep your text confined to the substance of that entry. Don't go rambling on about something totally unrelated just because you know it will be posted for others to read. If that's your goal, start your own blog.

Similarly, when participating in a chat room or discussion board, respond appropriately to existing messages and keep any new messages focused on the topic or topics that the blog covers.

Don't Get Personal

Everyone—even the calmest and most level-headed among us—has a particular bugaboo or béte noire that gets under their skin and makes their blood boil. In the real world, it could be people who drive too slowly in the fast lane, discourteous types who butt in ahead of you in line, or those annoying, late-night infomercials. In the online world, it could be a thoughtless remark, a misunderstood attempt at irony, or, all too often, an attack or rebuttal that uses personal criticism instead of rational argument.

Whatever the reason, the immediate reaction is usually to pull out the electronic version of your poison pen and compose an emotionally charged, scathing reply that is dripping with sarcasm and venomous abuse. Such messages are called *flames*, and they're an unfortunate fact of life on the Net. Firing off a particularly inventive flame may make *you* feel better, but it will likely make the recipient madder than a hoot owl. They will, almost certainly, flame your flame, and before you know it, a full-blown *flame war* will have broken out.

Flame wars have all but ruined many Usenet newsgroups, and they happen all the time in e-mail exchanges. Thankfully, the blogging world is usually a welcome haven from these kinds of hostilities. Oh, sure, e-fights break out from time to time, but more blog-based exchanges are remarkably civil. Therefore, don't poison the blogging well by responding to someone with insults and imprecations. If you can't respond with a well-articulated argument, consider not responding at all.

Webmaster Wisdom

When the urge to flame hits, give yourself some time to cool off by going for a walk, taking a shower, or just yelling at the top of your lungs for a few minutes.

Leave Your Address

If you're a blogger, it's considered polite in the blogiverse to always include the address of your blog in a comment, post, or e-mail. Most blog forms will offer a field for the address, but the absence of such a field doesn't mean you should leave out your address.

Having said that, don't use the comments feature purely as an excuse to scatter your blog address all over the web. Nobody likes their comments section being used as an advertising service.

Netiquette for Bloggers

As a blogger, your netiquette considerations have a dual edge: You have responsibilities both to your readers and to other bloggers. This makes sense when you consider blogging's unique communal makeup. That is, the blog community isn't divided into separate "blogger" and "reader" camps. Most blogs actually encourage reader interaction, the sharing of links, and inter-blog conversations, so it's easy to treat the blogosphere as a single community.

You'll get along better in that community and will therefore be accepted more readily if you follow a few basic netiquette guidelines—none of which, as you'll see, will in any serious way crimp your unique style and voice.

Take Your Headlines Seriously

As discussed in Chapter 16, busy blog readers often use the headline's contents to make a snap judgment about whether to read an entry. (This is especially true if the reader is new to your blog.) The majority of blog perusers *hate* headlines that are either ridiculously vague or general (for example, "Today's Entry" or "An Interesting

Link"), and they'll just move on to another site without giving the entry a second thought. Give your headlines some thought and make them descriptive enough so the reader can tell at a glance what your dispatch is about.

> **Webmaster Wisdom** _____
>
> Much blog netiquette is similar to the prescriptions and proscriptions for web page writing that I've outlined elsewhere in this book. In particular, in your blog prose you should use a minimum of exclamation marks, AVOID ALL-UPPERCASE WORDS BECAUSE IT LOOKS LIKE SHOUTING, keep font formatting tasteful, and edit for brevity. For more details, see the section in Chapter 15 entitled, "More Tips for Righteous Writing."

Give Credit Where Credit Is Due

In a filter-style blog, the blogger is expected to sniff out his website truffles. However, that doesn't mean that you must dig up *every* link with your own hands. It's perfectly acceptable to include a link on your site that some other blogger has unearthed. However, if you do that, it's considered good form to credit—and link to—the original blog. Just a simple "Thanks to *blogger*"—where *blogger* is the name of the blog (or blogger) set up as a link—will suffice. Note that the link should be to the permalink of the blog entry, not to the blog's main page.

What if the blog where you saw the link isn't the original source? Should you still credit that blog, or should you track down the original source and give it credit? That's a tough call. Following are some guidelines:

◆ If the blog where you found the link offers substantial commentary about the link—particularly if the blogger *does* credit the original source—then you're probably okay to link to that blog.

◆ If the blog where you found the link has only a trivial entry about it, then you're better off trying to find and credit the original source.

If you're in doubt, find the original source anyway, and then credit both:

```
Source: Blog A via Blog B
```

Note, too, that these ideas apply just as much to third-party blog entries that have in some way inspired you or given you a great idea. People won't think you're any less brilliant (and will think you're a pretty nice person) if you mention (and, of course, link to) the inspirational blog.

Reference Earlier Entries

It's common in the blogging world to mention an entry you wrote last week, last month, or last year in today's post. That's fine, but not every reader will have been reading your blog for the last week, month, or year. To help them out, include a link to the earlier entry so the reader can read it and feel part of the conversation.

Preserve Visitor Privacy

Many bloggers are in a position to gather private data about the people who visit their sites. From an e-mail message sent to you, for example, you can gather at least a person's name and e-mail address, and possibly items such as the person's phone number and real address, depending on how much info the writer puts into his or her signature. From a form, you can gather similar information. You can even ask visitors their ages and interests as part of a reader survey.

Any such personal information that you collect should be considered private and treated as such:

> **Webmaster Wisdom**
>
> It's a good idea to include a privacy statement somewhere on your site. The privacy statement is a document that spells out exactly what your policies are regarding the gathering, storing, and using of a reader's private data.

- ◆ Don't expose any user's private data on your blog or on any other page.

- ◆ Don't use private data to spam your visitors.

- ◆ Don't sell, rent, or give visitors' private data to any third party, even a fellow blogger.

If you really, really want to do any of these things, well, shame on you. However, you *must* ask your readers for their permission in advance, and you *must* be clear about what you intend to do with the data.

Don't Quote Without Permission

If a person sends you an e-mail message, that person automatically holds a copyright on the portions of the message that he or she wrote. Therefore, that message isn't yours to do with as you see fit. In other words, you can't just take all or part of the message and post it to your blog. Instead, you need to ask the writer for his or her permission to use the message on your blog. No permission, no quote.

Respect Intellectual Property

Speaking of copyright, things posted to the web—whether it's text, images, or music—also have implicit copyright protection, even if the site doesn't display a copyright notice. The exception to this is material that is in the public domain, such as certain old books and certain media files that are designated as being for public use.

You can't go around copying willy-nilly the work of others for use on your website. Obviously, you can't try to pass it off as your own work (that is plagiarism, and you can't sink much lower than that); however, it's almost as bad to use someone else's work without permission, even if you cite that person as the source. Always ask for permission if another person has written something that you want to use on your blog, otherwise you risk being ostracized as an *IP thief.*

The copyright laws do give some leeway by taking into account something called *fair use.* This simply means that it's okay to use excerpts from a work for purposes of education, criticism, or citation. If your usage of the work falls into one of these categories, then you'll usually be within your rights to quote from the work. However, note that this leeway extends only so far. You can never use the entire work, and you have to be sure to quote only the passages that are directly relevant to your purpose. And, of course, you must credit the original author of the piece and the original publication. The ideal situation is a link to the original article.

Words from the Web

A person who steals another's intellectual property is known as an **IP thief.**

Don't Steal Bandwidth

If you come across an image on another site that you'd love to use in your blog, you must ask permission. If the permission isn't granted, an alternative is to link to the image from your blog. However, you should *never* set up the picture with an <IMG> tag that points to the original on the other site. Each time a person loads your blog, they'll be loading the picture from the other site, which adds bandwidth costs to that site.

Don't Edit Others

If your blog solicits comments from readers for public posting, you have to be prepared to take what comes your way. Most people will be polite and courteous, but you *will* get feedback from people who are stupid, rude, or both. If a comment is pure abuse, or if it contains an excessive amount of profanity or other lurid content and you have children and other linguistically sensitive visitors to watch out for, it's okay to delete the offending comment. Otherwise, resist the temptation to edit comments either to correct factual information or remove statements with which you disagree. If you have a problem with a comment, post your own comment rebutting the author's arguments.

Respond to a Comment with a Comment

One of the perennial blog etiquette questions is, "When someone posts a comment, do I respond with an e-mail message or a comment?" This is an easy one: Always respond with a comment *unless* the writer has specifically asked for a personal e-mail reply. Posting your own comment as a response is better because it puts the response in context and allows others to see that you've responded to the question or criticism. Sending a response via e-mail often causes confusion because the recipient may not remember what it was that he or she was commenting on (this is particularly true with intrepid commentators who leave their two cents' worth all over the blogosphere).

Practice Courtesy Blogroll Visiting

Some bloggers just slap up any old link in their blogroll, the thinking being (I guess) that an incredibly long blogroll is somehow an impressive thing. Fortunately, most bloggers are more choosy about which sites deserve the honor of being included in their blogrolls. Therefore, if you find out you're on a person's blogroll, be flattered. You don't necessarily have to thank that person directly, but you should at least have the courtesy to visit his or her blog and take a look around. You're under no obligation to link back, of course, but, hey, you might just like what you see.

Announce Blog Interruptions

By definition, a blog is a site that is updated regularly, usually one or more times a day; as previously mentioned, letting things slide for even a couple of days or a week isn't a crime in the blogosphere. However, few things are as frustrating as constantly checking in on a site that remains in limbo for a long time. If you're going to take a leave of absence from your blog for an extended time, do your visitors a favor by letting them know. You don't have to say why you're bailing on your blog (although if it's an interesting story, then please do share it), but letting everyone know when you might resume operations (if you have any idea) would be awfully nice of you.

The Least You Need to Know

♦ Do write headlines that actually explain what your entry is about.

♦ Don't use another person's intellectual property without permission.

♦ Do give credit to the original blog that contains a link you used in your own blog.

♦ Don't link to the main blog page; instead, always link to a post's permalink.

♦ Do respond to posted comments with a comment of your own.

♦ Don't leave your blog untouched for long periods of time without announcing the interruption.

Chapter 20

Choosing and Using Blog Tools

In This Chapter

- ◆ Choosing a blog host that's right for you
- ◆ Detailed descriptions of Blogger and TypePad
- ◆ Capsule reviews of half a dozen other blog hosts
- ◆ Using server-side blog software, with reviews of Movable Type, Greymatter, and pMachine
- ◆ Using a third-party service to handle your blog comments
- ◆ Faster, easier, and more efficient ways to do the blog thing

Building a blog certainly isn't brain surgery or rocket science for that matter. Once you have your basic layout in place, simply find some neat links or craft together some writing, format everything using a few well-placed HTML tags, upload the whole shebang, and you're blogging.

Unfortunately, the giddiness of the early blogging experience almost always gives way to despair, if not exasperation. As you've seen throughout the past four chapters, the essence of the blogging experience—the constant addition of new material—is both its greatest strength and its Achilles' heel. That's because the more you blog, the more you have to maintain your blog. You have to add new material at the top; remove old material from the bottom; update your RSS file; archive each new entry; create new archives as needed (weekly or monthly); process comments; answer e-mail; update your blogroll, and on and on. It's a lot of work, and it's this drudgery more than the constant pressure to post that drives bloggers out of the game.

If you're looking for a more modern (read: easier) way to build and maintain your blog, you've come to the right place. This chapter takes you through a few programs and resources that can ease the drudgery of blog production. You'll learn how to choose a blog host, pick out blog software, set up an automated comment system, and more.

Choosing a Blog Host

One of the paradoxes of the blog world is that building a blog (adding new entries) is at odds with the maintenance (removing old entries, archiving entries, and so on). Building a blog takes time, because it's important to do things right, from the research to the writing to the formatting; maintaining a blog also takes time because it's tedious, but necessary, grunt work. So the more maintenance you have to perform, the less time you can devote to building a quality blog. It's a conundrum, to be sure.

The solution preferred by many people who have a day job (and no unlimited hours to spend on blogging) is to slough off the maintenance chores on someone else. No, I'm not talking about hiring your next-door neighbor's geeky teenage son. Instead, I'm talking about using the services of a *blog host*, a company that enables you to set up a blog and offers tools that not only make it easy to post new entries, but also automate the drudgery of archiving, commenting, creating permalinks, and all that tedious rigmarole.

The good news about all this is that there are several dozen blog hosts out there to choose from. The bad news is that there are several dozen blog hosts out there to choose from. How do you know which one is right for you? The best way to determine this is to ask around. If you have any friends or colleagues who blog, ask them if they use a host and, if so, what they think of the company. Check out your favorite blogs and see which hosts they use. Over and above that, you should check out some hosts yourself and see what features they offer. Here's a short checklist:

◆ **How do you post new entries?** Do you use a web-based form? FTP? Can you use e-mail or a separate program that runs on your own computer?

◆ **Do you have layout choices?** Does the host enable you to customize the structure of the page? Does it offer different templates for things like color schemes and fonts? Can you edit those templates?

◆ **Are comments supported?** Although it's rare on low-cost hosts, some of them do come with the ability to automate the posting and display of visitor comments.

◆ **Does the host offer any other features?** Look for extra goodies such as support for images, spellchecking, community tools (for setting up a community of users, such as a forum), and a member directory.

◆ **How much does it cost?** Many blog hosts offer their service free of charge, often with the proviso that you must display ads on your blog. Others offer a basic service for free and a "premium" or "pro" service for a monthly charge.

Webmaster Wisdom

Don't forget that a blog host is similar to a web host in that you store your files on the host's server and the server sends out your files to browsers that request them. Therefore, you should also check potential blog hosts for two criteria that apply to web hosts: how much storage space you get on the server, and how much bandwidth (that is, the number of megabytes or gigabytes that go to and from your blog) you get.

The next couple of sections take you through the basics of using two popular hosts, Blogger and TypePad, and provide some capsule reviews of a few other hosts.

Blogger: Push-Button Publishing

More than any other tool, Blogger spurred the rapid rise of the blogging phenomenon. It enabled people—particularly nongeeks who just couldn't handle HTML—to focus on researching and writing instead of the nuts and bolts of blogging. Suddenly, *anyone* could join the blog revolution, and thousands of people did just that. In fact, even though Blogger lacks some of the features of other hosts, a number of the biggest names in blogdom *still* use Blogger.

In 2003, Blogger was acquired by Google, which (as of this writing) has muddied the Blogger waters a bit. The good part is that a number of features that you had to pay for in the Blogger Pro product are now free (including spellchecking, daily archiving, and sending a post to an e-mail address). The bad part is that some neat Blogger Pro features have been lost, including creating RSS feeds and posting via e-mail.

Webmaster Wisdom

There are dozens of web addresses in this chapter. To save you from having to type them in by hand, I have links to each site on this book's example blog page: www.mcfedries.com/ CreatingAWebPage/blog.htm.

Getting Started with Blogger

Here are the steps to follow to get started with Blogger:

1. Go to www.blogger.com.

2. Click the **Start Now!** button.

3. Fill in the fields to supply your user name, personal name, e-mail address, and password. Click the **Sign Up** button.

4. Enter the title of your blog, its description, and whether you want a public blog (meaning that it appears in the directory of Blogger-hosted sites). Click **Next**.

5. Now you come to the first fork in the Blogger road. (Click **Next** when you've made your choice.)

◆ **Host it at Blog*Spot.** Select this option to host your blog on Blogger's own server, called Blog*Spot. This gives you a blog with the address *myblog*.blogspot.com, where *myblog* is a name you provide in the next step.

◆ **FTP it to your own server.** Select this option if you prefer to store your blog on your own web host. This means that Blogger will update your site via FTP, so you'll need to have your FTP address and login data handy.

CAUTION

Page Pitfalls

Note that the basic Blog*Spot service requires that an ad be displayed on your blog. You can get an ad-free version by paying a small, yearly fee (U.S. $15 as of this writing).

6. The next screen you see will depend on your choice in step 5. (Click **Next** when you're done.)

◆ **If you chose Blog*Spot.** Enter the name you want to use for your blogspot.com address.

◆ **If you chose your own server.** Enter the address of your FTP server, the name of the directory where you want your blog pages stored (this directory must already exist on the server), the blog file name, and the blog address.

7. Choose the blog layout you want by selecting one of the displayed template thumbnail images. Click **Next**.

That's all there is to it. Your Blogger-hosted blog is ready to go.

Configuring Your Blog

When the Blogger setup is complete, you're dropped off at the Create New Post screen, which you'll see again a bit later when you learn how to post entries. Note, too, that you can get to this screen later on by logging in from the blogger.com home page (using the user name and password you supplied in step 3 in the previous section) and then clicking the blog name in the "Your Blogs" list.

Before going any further, however, you should know how to configure your blog. Clicking the **Settings** link takes you to the Basic page shown in Figure 20.1.

Figure 20.1

Use the pages in the Settings category to configure your blog.

The Settings category contains the following seven pages:

♦ **Basic.** Use this page to change your blog title, description, and public status.

♦ **Publishing.** Use this page to switch between using Blog*Spot and FTP. You can also elect to "ping" the Weblogs.com site, which is a constantly updated list of recently updated blogs. If you choose Yes, Blogger will alert Weblogs.com that your site has been updated whenever you publish.

♦ **Formatting.** Use this page to set some layout and formatting options for your blog. For example, you can choose the number of posts to show on the blog page, or the number of days' worth of posts to show. You can also configure the date formats for the header (the date that appears above a particular day's entries) and the archive index (a set of links to your archive files).

- ◆ **Archiving.** Use this page to set whether your entries are archived daily, weekly, monthly, or not at all.

- ◆ **Site Feed.** This page enables you to configure the RSS feed for your site.

- ◆ **E-mail.** Use this page to specify an e-mail address to which each of your posts will be sent after you publish them.

- ◆ **Members.** Use this page to add "team members," or people who can also post to your blog.

Webmaster Wisdom

When perusing the template tags, you'll come across strange ones such as <$BlogTitle$> and <$BlogItemBody$>. These are placeholders that the Blogger program uses. For example, when you publish your blog, Blogger takes all instances of <$BlogTitle$> and replaces them with the title of your blog. Therefore, do *not* edit or delete these custom tags.

In all cases, click **Save Changes** to save your work before moving on to another page.

You can also make changes to the template you chose when you set up your blog. Clicking the **Template** link gives you the following three choices:

- ◆ **Blog Template.** This page shows you the HTML and style sheet tags that underlie your template. (See Part 4 to learn how style sheets work.)

- ◆ **Archive Index Template.** This page shows you the tags for your archive index.

- ◆ **Choose New Template.** Use this page to select a different template.

Posting with Blogger

With all that malarkey out of the way, you're finally ready to post to your blog. Here are the steps to follow:

1. Click **Posting.** Blogger displays the Create New Post page.

2. Use the Post box to enter your post text. Feel free to add HTML tags as needed.

3. To change the date and time of the post, click **Post Options** and use the **Change Time & Date** controls, as shown in Figure 20.2. (If you activate the **Draft** check box, your post will include **Status: Draft** under the date to indicate that the post is subject to change and will not be published until you deactivate the check box.)

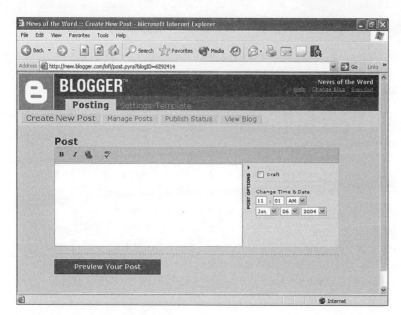

Figure 20.2

Use the Create New Post page to post an entry to your blog.

4. Click **Preview Your Post.** Blogger shows you what your post will look like.

5. If you want to make changes, click **Edit** and repeat steps 2–4. Otherwise, if all looks well, click **Publish Your Post.**

6. If you want to see your handiwork, click the **View Blog** link.

Blog On

Google's acquisition of Blogger had one obvious benefit as I wrote this: The Google toolbar (available for PC users from toolbar.google.com) now sports a Blog This! button with the Blogger logo. Navigate to a page you want to include as a link in your blog and then click the Blog This! button. A small window opens with an <A> tag defining a link for the page. Add your own text, edit the link, if needed, and then click **Post and Publish.**

Note, too, that you can also edit and delete posts at any time by completing the following steps:

1. Click **Manage Posts.**

2. If you don't see the post you want to work with, use the **Show** list to display more posts. You can also use the **From** and **Order** lists to filter the posts, or you can use the **Search** box to find the post by entering one or more keywords.

3. To make changes to the post, click the **Edit** button that appears just below the date.

4. To delete the post, click the **Delete** button.

TypePad: The New Host in Town

The TypePad blog hosting service has only been around since the fall of 2003, but it has already generated more press and won more awards than almost any other host. People seem to be genuinely impressed by its ease-of-use and excellent set of features, all of which are based on the excellent Movable Type blogging software (which I review later in this chapter). It doesn't have a free version, but a 30-day trial is available and the three available plans range from U.S. $4.95 per month to U.S. $14.95 per month. However, even the cheapest plan has a stunningly rich set of features that includes comments, image uploading, searching, daily, weekly, or monthly archives, statistics on page views and referrers, and RSS syndication support.

Getting Started with TypePad

Here are the steps to follow to set up a trial account with TypePad:

1. Go to www.typepad.com.

2. Click the **Sign Up** link.

3. The page that appears requests lots of information, including the following: member name (this will be your login user name), password, password recovery question and answer, first and last name, e-mail address, and subdomain (where sub*domain*.typepad.com will be your blog address). Click **Continue to Next Steps.**

4. Enter your credit card data (your card will not be charged until after the 30-day trial period) and your billing address. Click **Review Your Registration.**

5. Check out your data. If it's correct, click **Begin Your Free Trial.**

Creating a Blog

After creating your account, you end up at your personal TypePad home page. To get there in the future, go to www.typepad.com, log in, and then click **Enter TypePad.**

Follow these steps to create a new blog:

1. Click the **Weblogs** tab.

2. In the **Create a new Weblog** section, enter the **Weblog name.**

3. Edit the name of the **Weblog folder** in which you want your blog files stored.

4. In the **Make this weblog public?** section, select **Yes** to have your blog included in TypePad's blog directories and its list of recently updated blogs; otherwise, select **No.**

5. Click **Create New Weblog.**

Configuring Your Blog

Before getting down to building your blog, you should check out the various configuration options. To see these options, click the **Configure** tab, which displays six links:

◆ **Weblog Basics.** Use this page to change your blog title, description, and folder.

◆ **Archiving.** Use this page to set how your entries are archived: daily, weekly, or monthly. You can also choose the Individual option, which archives each post on its own page. Choose this option for longer entries or if you're going to use the comments feature. Another option is Category, which archives posts according to the category you assign each one (see the next item).

◆ **Categories.** Use this page to select or enter the categories you want to use to organize your posts.

◆ **Publicity & Syndication.** Use this page to set your blog's public status and whether you want TypePad to notify the sites blo.gs or weblogs.com whenever your blog changes. You can also use this page to set up RSS syndication.

◆ **Authors.** Use this page to invite "authors" to contribute to your blog. These are people who can also post to your blog.

◆ **Display.** Use this page to set some layout and formatting options for your blog. For example, you can choose the number of posts or days to show on the blog page, and the order of the posts. You can also configure the date and time formats and the number of words to include in a syndication excerpt. This is also the page where you activate and configure the powerful comments feature that TypePad provides.

In all cases, click **Save Changes** to save your work before moving on to another page.

TypePad also offers a number of options for adjusting the layout and design of your blog. (The available options depend on which TypePad price plan you chose.) To adjust the look of your blog, click the **Design** tab and use the following links:

◆ **Select a Design.** Use this page to choose a *template set*, which is a collection of templates that govern five elements of the blog's design: Layout, Content, Order, Style, and Basics. You can also build your own custom template set.

◆ **Edit Template Sets.** Use this page to make changes to each of the five elements of your chosen template set.

Posting with TypePad

Follow these steps to post to your blog:

1. Click the **Post** tab. As shown in Figure 20.3, the Compose a New Post page appears.

Figure 20.3

Use the Compose a New Post page to post to your blog.

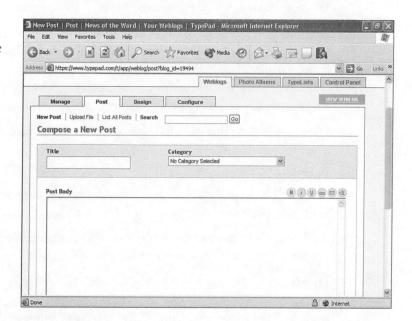

2. Enter the post **Title.**

3. Choose a **Category** for the post.

4. Use the **Post Body** box to enter your post text, including any required HTML tags.

5. Use the **Posting Status** list to set the status of your post: **Draft** (unfinished), **Publish On** (to post at a future date), or **Publish Now.**

6. Use the **Comments** list to choose whether to allow comments: Choose **None** to allow no comments; **Open** to allow comments; or **Closed** to allow no further comments.

7. To activate the TrackBack feature, click **Accept TrackBacks.** (Activating this feature enables other bloggers to automatically alert you when they link to this post.)

8. Click **Preview** to check out the post.

9. If all looks right, click **Save This Post.**

You can also edit and delete posts at any time by following these steps:

1. Click **List All Posts.**

2. If you don't see the post you want to work with, use the list in the lower-right corner to display more posts. You can also use the **Filter Options** list to filter the posts, or the **Search** box to find the post by entering one or more keywords.

3. Click the **Title** link to open the Edit a Post page.

4. To make changes to the post, edit the text or options and then click **Save.**

4. To delete the post, click the **Delete Post** button.

Other Blog Hosts

The blog hosting realm is today where the web hosting world was circa 1998 or so: not quite a dime-a-dozen, but clearly on the way there. Besides Blogger and TypePad, there's a long list of hosts—some are good, but most are not so good. Like web hosts, blog hosts exhibit streetcarlike behavior: They come and they go. To help you keep up with the quick and the dead, here are a couple of directories you can check out to see lists of hosts:

- **Yahoo!** dir.yahoo.com/Computers_and_Internet/Internet/ World_Wide_Web/Weblogs/Hosting

- **Google.** directory.google.com/Top/Computers/Internet/On_the_Web/ Weblogs/Tools/Hosts

The next few sections include some short reviews of a half dozen of the better blog hosts.

Blog-City (blog-city.com)

Blog-City (see Figure 20.4) is known for its user-friendliness, which it accomplishes with a straightforward registration procedure and powerful but easy-to-use blog management tools. With the free service (an ad is automatically placed on your blog), you get a *MyBlog*.blog-city.com address and an impressive set of features: site layout management, comments, calendar-based archive links, RSS feeds, categories, site stats, visitor polls, searching, and more. A premium version (U.S. $2.50 per month) adds the ability to e-mail posts and upload files, among other things.

Figure 20.4

Blog-City is an easy-to-use blog host.

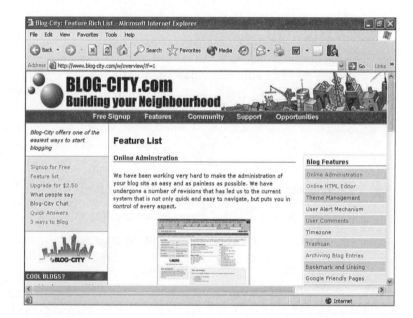

LiveJournal (livejournal.com)

LiveJournal is one of the oldest blog hosts (it was established in 1999, right when blogging began to blossom), and it has always had a strong communal feel to it (it's operated using open-source software and it bills itself as an "interactive community"). You don't get many bells and whistles with the free service, but comments are supported and you get some control over the layout of your blog. More advanced features—detailed customizations, online polls, a subdomain name (*MyBLog*.livejournal.com), RSS feeds, post-by-e-mail, and much more—are available with paid accounts (U.S. $5 for 2 months; U.S. $25 for 12 months).

Pitas (pitas.com)

Pitas.com redefines the phrase "no frills," but it's fine if all you want is a simple and easily updated blog. There is no charge for the service and your blog will be blissfully ad-free. Several design templates are available, and you can tweak the HTML code in those templates to get the exact look you want.

Upsaid (upsaid.com)

Upsaid is a strange name, but it's a good site. The free portion of the service offers a nice list of features, including comments, an extensive choice of templates, control over columns and sideblog layouts, site stats, online polling, and a guest book. For U.S. $2 a month, you can add greater layout control, support for multiple authors, post-by-e-mail, calendar archiving, Weblogs.com pinging, RSS feeds, and much more. The interface is nicely laid out (although I didn't like the light-blue text on a white background), and all the features are easy to use.

Weblogger (weblogger.com)

Weblogger is designed for blogs that are maintained by multiple authors. Although any group of bloggers can use the service, Weblogger's business-oriented approach is betrayed by how it describes its service—*content management*—a phrase that is clearly designed to warm the cockles of an MBA's heart (and one that probably goes over better in the boardroom than "blogging"). The Weblogger service isn't free, unfortunately (plans start at U.S. $9.95 per month), but a 30-day trial is available. However, you certainly get your money's worth because Weblogger offers a truckload of features: editors (people who can contribute to and edit the blog content), comments, trackbacks, memberships (to enable other people to join your blog), discussion groups, e-mail bulletins, searching, RSS feeds, and much more.

Xanga (xanga.com)

Xanga bills itself as "The Weblog Community," and it's easy to see why. The free Xanga Classic service is chock full of features—comments, guest book, customizable layout and formatting—but Xanga goes out of its way to help its users interact and give a community feel. For example, Xanga users can work with "eProps," which enable them to rate particularly good posts; you can also "subscribe" to other Xanga member blogs to get the latest headlines; and Xanga also offers personal member profiles and announcements of upcoming blog events. Another unique Xanga feature is the xTools browser button, which enables you to post to your Xanga blog from anywhere on the web. Note, too, that there's also a Xanga Premium service that starts at U.S. $4 per month and gives you more powerful versions of the basic Xanga tools.

Running a Server-Side Blog Program

A blog host is an attractive idea because it means you never have to open the hood and understand or repair the engine that makes your blog run. You simply get in the interface driver's seat and drive off into the blogospheric sunset.

However, some people *like* getting their hands dirty. These people understand that sometimes it's necessary to tweak the engine yourself to get the kind of performance you want. HTML is an excellent example of this. If you build a web page using an HTML editor or even a word processor such as Microsoft Word, the result will usually look more or less the way you want, but there always seem to be niggling little problems with the layout or presentation of the page. The only way to fix those problems is to get down and dirty with the HTML tags and adjust them by hand.

It's the same with a blog. Sure, the hosting services that I've discussed so far all do a good job, and none will disappoint anyone who just wants a simple, muss-less, fuss-less blog. However, if you want total control over your blog, then you need something with a little more oomph.

In the blog world, so-called *server-side blog programs* supply oomph in spades. These software programs enable you to set up, post to, and maintain your own blog. The "server-side" part means that you must install and run the program on your web hosting provider's server. This leads to several potential problems right off the bat:

◆ Your web hosting provider might not allow you to install programs on their server.

◆ Your web hosting provider's server might not be compatible with the blog software.

◆ Even if these two criteria are met, installing and particular configuring programs on servers tends to be a messy, complex business, so it's not for the faint of heart. Programs vary enormously on this count, so check each program's site to see if they provide you with the installation instructions. Read through the instructions to see what kind of hoops they're going to make you jump through.

Webmaster Wisdom

The easiest way to find out whether a server-side blog program will install and run on your web host is to ask them. Send a note to the customer service or support department, tell them which program you want to run, and give them the address of the program's site so they can check it out for themselves, if need be.

If I haven't scared you off by now, you're probably ready to proceed. The next few sections tell you about three of the most popular server-side blogging programs: Movable Type, Greymatter, and pMachine.

Movable Type (movabletype.org)

Movable Type is the engine behind the excellent TypePad blog hosting service discussed earlier in this chapter. Therefore, if you want to know what features you get with Movable Type, simply look at the feature set behind TypePad. Even better, Movable Type is free for noncommercial use.

Here are the requirements for installing and using Movable Type:

◆ The ability for you to run custom CGI scripts.

◆ Perl version 5.004_04 or later. (Perl is the programming language in which Movable Type was written.)

◆ The ability to FTP files to the server.

◆ Support for the DB_File Perl module (available on almost all servers that support Perl) or the MySQL database & DBD::mysql.

If you're not sure about one or more of these requirements, just drop a note to your web host's customer service department and ask them about it.

Greymatter (noahgrey.com/greysoft)

Greymatter was the first of the server-side blog programs, and it was the most popular until Movable Type usurped that crown. Greymatter still has a large community of users; however, even though the original author (Noah Grey) no longer updates the program, it is now fully open-source, which means that a wide group of programmers is responsible for future developments.

The feature set of Greymatter is impressive: comments (including the capability to ban certain words and web addresses); automatic archiving (including calendars); customizable blog templates; support for multiple bloggers; file and image uploading; the capability to post from anywhere on the web; a search feature; and "karma voting," which enables readers to rate your posts.

You'd expect to pay big bucks for all this, but Greymatter is absolutely free (although donations are accepted). And the requirements for installing Greymatter on your server are about as simple as they come:

◆ Perl 5 or later

◆ The ability to FTP files to the server

pMachine (pmachine.com)

pMachine is the relatively new kid on the server-side blog software block. (In case you're wondering, the "p" in pMachine stands for "publishing.") But even though it hasn't been around as long as Movable Type and Greymatter, pMachine has caught up, and in some respects surpassed, the two older programs. pMachine is stuffed to the rafters with blogging features. All the standard stuff is here, of course: full entry management, comments, categories, templates, searching, image and file uploading, and site statistics. But you also get special features such as allowing visitors to register as members; the capability to produce links to "printer-friendly" versions of a page; a Tell-A-Friend link that e-mails an entry; multiple authors; a simple "post office" that enables you to send out messages to members; trackback; RSS feeds; pinging Weblogs.com; bookmarklets (posting from anywhere on the web); word and web address banning; and members-only content.

And that's all in the *free* version of the program. For just U.S. $45 for noncommercial users, you also get the ability to produce multiple blogs; multiple blog template sets; a more powerful post office; a discussion forum; a "parser" that enables your blog to display RSS feeds from other sites; and a calendar that displays upcoming events and member birthdays.

Here are the pMachine server requirements:

◆ PHP version 4.06 or later (4.1 or later is recommended; PHP is the language in which pMachine is written).

◆ MySQL version 3.23.x or later.

◆ The ability to FTP files to the server.

Blog On

If the idea of installing and configuring a program on your web host makes you think wistfully of getting a root canal, you might want to consider a program called Radio UserLand. This is a blog tool that you install and run within the friendly confines of your own computer. You create your blog locally, and then use Radio UserLand to upload the files to your website. You can even compose posts offline and publish them once you're connected. It's a decent program with many features, but it costs U.S. $39.95 (although a 30-day trial is available). See radio.userland.com.

Blog Comment Systems

You saw earlier that many blog hosting services come with a comments feature, although you most often see this capability only in hosts that charge a fee. (The notable exceptions are LiveJournal, Upsaid, and Xanga.) If you use Blogger or some other host that doesn't support comments, you can use third-party comment systems. Note that most of these systems only work with one or more specific blog hosts (the most common is Blogger), so read the fine print before downloading or signing up for anything. Here's a list of comment systems you can check out:

- **BlogBack.** www.tecknik.net/blogback

- **blogkomm.** www.blogkomm.com

- **Enetation.** www.enetation.co.uk

- **HaloScan.** www.haloscan.com

- **Reblogger.** jsoft.ca/reblogger

- **Tag-Board.** www.tag-board.com

- **YACCS.** rateyourmusic.com/yaccs

- **Google.** directory.google.com/Top/Computers/Internet/On_the_Web/Weblogs/Tools/Commenting/

CAUTION

Page Pitfalls _____

Automatic commenting systems are much easier to set up and maintain, but they do come with a downside: *blog spam*. This is a comment that comes with an innocuous message (such as, "I agree with this") and a link to a site. Unfortunately, that site turns out to be a spam-related site or something more sinister. Ideally, the comment system enables you to block certain addresses from commenting so that you can filter out the spammers.

The Least You Need to Know

◆ When scouting around for a blog host, first ask your blogging friends which company they use (and, of course, if they recommend it). It's also worthwhile seeing which hosts are used by bloggers you admire.

◆ Choose a host with the most. When comparing hosts, be sure to check out how you post entries, what kind of layout choices you have, whether comments are supported, what other features are offered, and by how much it will set you back.

◆ For total control over your blogging experience, turn to a server-side blog program, a bit of software that you install and run from your web host's server.

◆ Before deciding on (or, worse, paying for) a server-side program, check with your web host to make sure they have proper requirements and are willing to let you install the program. Also, read the program's installation instructions to make sure the setup process isn't beyond what you can or want to put yourself through.

◆ Comments are an excellent way to build a community around your blog, and they're not awful to maintain if you only get the occasional one. However, if your blog becomes popular and the comments start pouring in by the dozen, maintaining them by hand is nearly impossible; you'll have to turn to a third-party comment system to relieve the burden.

Part 4

High HTML Style: Working with Style Sheets

After unveiling a new site to friends, family, and colleagues, you might receive constructive criticisms instead of constant kudos. Grrrr. You mutter a few choice epithets under your breath, but then you realize that, hey, they're right. The changes really would make your pages look better. So, conscientious webmeister that you are, you begin the long and laborious process of opening all the pages and editing the dozens of tags that determine the look of each page. Sigh. There's got to be a better way.

If making large-scale changes to your site is getting you down, I have some good news. There's some web technology that will enable you to change fonts, colors, and other features for 2 or 102 pages with only a few keystrokes! This miraculous bit of techno-trickery is called a style sheet, and you learn how it works here in Part 4.

MY HUSBAND'S LOOKING FOR A STYLE SHEET FOR HIS WEBSITE THAT REPRESENTS HIS PERSONALITY, BUT NOTHING QUITE SAYS "SMART AND WITTY."

Chapter 21

A Beginner's Guide to Style Sheets

In This Chapter

♦ Understanding style sheets

♦ Three methods of using style sheets

♦ Applying styles to sections, words, and phrases

♦ Numerous other style sheet shenanigans

This chapter gets your style sheet education off to an easy start by introducing you ever so gently to this brave new web world. You learn just what styles and sheets are, how they affect your pages, and why they're so darned useful. You also learn the basic methods for incorporating style sheets into your pages. Although I run through a few examples in this chapter, the real style sheet goods can be found in the next two chapters where I delve into the style sheet specifics for things like text, paragraphs, positioning, margins, and more.

What's a Style, and What's a Sheet?

If you've ever used a fancy-schmancy word processor such as Microsoft Word or WordPerfect, you've probably stumbled over a style or two in your travels. In a nutshell, a style is a combination of two or more formatting options rolled into one nice, neat package. For example, you might have a "Title" style that combines four formatting options: bold, centered, 24-point type size, and an Arial typeface. You can then "apply" this style to any text and the program dutifully formats the text with all four options. If you change your mind later and decide your titles should use an 18-point font, all you have to do is redefine the Title style. The program then automatically trudges through the entire document and updates each bit of text that uses the Title style.

Styles in the Web Universe

In a web page, a style performs a similar function. That is, it enables you to define a series of formatting options for a given tag, such as <P> or <H1>. Like word processor styles, page styles offer two main advantages:

♦ They save time because you create the definition of the style's formatting once, and the browser applies that formatting each time you use the tag.

♦ They make your pages easier to modify because all you need to do is edit the style definition and all the places where the style is used within the page get updated automatically.

Let's eyeball an example. The following HTML file (see ssbefore.htm on the CD in this book) contains a single <H1> heading, and you can see the result in Figure 21.1:

```
<HTML>
<HEAD>
<TITLE>Style Sheets: Before</TITLE>
</HEAD>
<BODY>
<H1>Style Sheets: What's the Big Whoop?</H1>
</BODY>
</HTML>
```

Figure 21.1

A simple web page, showing a single <H1> heading.

Now suppose that you prefer to use bigger text in your heading. You can't change the size of <H1> headings directly, but you could do it by changing the SIZE attribute of the <FONT> tag, like this:

```
<FONT SIZE="7">
Style Sheets: What's the Big Whoop?
</FONT>
```

That's no big deal if you have only one or two headings, but what if you use dozens of them? Not only is it a pain to add those <FONT> tags, but it also makes your HTML source code more difficult to read.

A better solution is to create a style for the <H1> tag that tells the browser to use a larger font size for the <H1> text. The following HTML file (see ssafter.htm on the CD in this book) shows you one way to do it, and Figure 21.2 displays the results (I explain the specifics of this a bit later; see "Some Style Basics"):

```
<HTML>
<HEAD>
<TITLE>Style Sheets: After</TITLE>

<STYLE>
H1 {font-size: 34pt}
</STYLE>

</HEAD>
<BODY>
<H1>Style Sheets: What's the Big Whoop?</H1>
</BODY>
</HTML>
```

Figure 21.2

Use a style to get a larger heading.

Note the new <STYLE> tag and, in particular, the following line:

```
H1 {font-size: 34pt}
```

What this tells the browser is that, each time it comes across the <H1> tag, it should format the text with a 34-point font size.

And it's easy to make a change if you decide that you want your heading even larger. For example, if you want to use a 72-point font size, you need only make a single change (see ssafter2.htm on the CD in this book):

```
<HTML>
<HEAD>

<STYLE>
H1 {font-size: 72pt}
</STYLE>

</HEAD>
<BODY>
<H1>Style Sheets: What's the Big Whoop?</H1>
</BODY>
</HTML>
```

Figure 21.3 shows how this looks with Internet Explorer.

Figure 21.3

Styles make it easy to change the formatting in your pages.

Combining formats into one easy-to-use bundle is a nifty timesaver, and it's worth the price of admission alone. However, style sheets have a few other tricks up their digital sleeves. These tricks enable you to do things that are either difficult or downright impossible with your garden-variety HTML tags. For example, displaying text at a 72-point type size, as shown in Figure 21.3, is impossible under plain HTML. Here's a tiny sampling of some other style sheet sleight of hand you can do:

◆ You can set a background color or image for paragraphs or even single words.

◆ You can define a margin around your page.

◆ You can indent text precisely.

Sheets: Collections of Styles

So far so good, but what the heck is a sheet? The term *style sheet* harkens back to the days of yore when word processors enabled you to store your styles in a separate document known as a style sheet. This is equivalent to what we today usually call a template. As you'll see later, it's possible to define all your HTML styles in a separate page and then tell the browser where that page is located, so it's a bit like those old style sheets (although *style file* might have been a better—and more fun—name). More generally, an HTML style sheet is any collection of styles, whether it exists in a separate page or within the current page (as in the earlier example with the <H1> tag).

What About Browser Support?

Style sheets have come a long way in the past couple of years. Once considered an obscure section of the HTML 4.0 standard, style sheets are now a much-traveled part of the web design landscape. The reason why style sheets have come into their own is simple: All modern browsers support them.

Technically, style sheet support is built into Internet Explorer versions 3.0 and later and Netscape Navigator versions 4.0 and later. However, that accounts for almost all the browser traffic today (about 98 percent, as of this writing).

Therefore, it's perfectly safe to go ahead and start learning and using style sheets right away. Those few style sheet-ignorant browsers that visit your pages ignore the extra tags (and you can use HTML comment tags to block out other style-related text), so no harm comes to your pages.

CAUTION **Page Pitfalls**

I should warn you, however, that even though most browsers support style sheets, they have a nasty habit of supporting them in different and often unpredictable ways. I'll try to take this into account as we go along, but it's important to check your pages in different browsers to make sure that everyone will see what you want them to see.

Some Style Basics

Before I show you how to implement style sheets, let's take a second to get a grip on just what a style looks like. As an example, let's put the style we used earlier under the microscope. Here it is again:

```
H1 {font-size: 34pt}
```

This is called a *style definition*, and here's a rundown of the various parts:

♦ The definition always begins with the HTML tag that you want the style to modify, without the usual angle brackets (< and >).

♦ The rest of the definition is ensconced inside those curly brackets—{ and }—which are known officially as *braces*.

♦ The first thing inside the braces is the name of the property you want to set, followed by a colon (:). In our example, the property is called `font-size`.

♦ Finally, after the colon, type the value you want to assign to the property (34pt, in the example, where "pt" is short for "points").

As a different example, suppose you want all your <TT> text to appear in a gray font. In style-sheet land, font color is governed by the `color` property, so you'd set this style as follows:

```
TT {color: gray}
```

Finally, you can set multiple properties in a single style by separating each property and value with a semicolon (;). In the following example, <H2> tags are displayed with purple, 20-point text:

```
H2 {color: purple; font-size: 20pt}
```

Three Sheets to the Web: Style Sheets and HTML

One of the most confusing things about style sheets is the sheer number of methods you can use to implement them. To help alleviate the confusion, this section shows you just three methods and explains exactly when you should use each method.

Method #1: The <STYLE> Tag

Probably the most straightforward way to implement a style sheet is to use the <STYLE> tag you saw in the earlier example. The idea is that you plop—or *embed*, as the style sheet geeks say—a <STYLE> tag and a </STYLE> end tag into your document, and then insert all your style definitions in between. The best place to put all this stuff is within the page header, as follows:

```
<HTML>
<HEAD>

<STYLE TYPE="text/css">
<!--
Your style definitions go here
-->
</STYLE>

</HEAD>
<BODY>
The visible web page stuff goes here
</BODY>
</HTML>
```

Words from the Web

Style sheet mavens call the <STYLE></STYLE> method an **embedded style sheet.**

Note, too, that I tossed in the HTML comment tags for good measure. This hides your style definitions from older browsers that don't know a style sheet from a rap sheet.

This method is best when you want to apply only a particular set of style definitions to a single page.

Method #2: Linking to an External Style Sheet

Style sheets get insanely powerful when you use an "external" style sheet, which is a separate file that contains your style definitions. To use these definitions within any web page, you simply add a special <LINK> tag inside the page header. This tag specifies the name of the external style sheet file, and the browser then uses that file to grab the style definitions.

Here are the steps you need to follow to set up an external style sheet:

1. Use your favorite text editor to create a shiny new text file.

2. Add your style definitions to this file. Note that you don't need the <STYLE> tag or any other HTML tags.

3. Save the file in the same directory as your HTML files, and use a "css" extension (for example, "mystyles.css"). This helps you remember down the road that this is a style-sheet file. (The "css" stands for cascading style sheet.)

4. For every page in which you want to use the styles, add a <LINK> tag inside the page header. Here's the general format to use (where *filename.css* is the name of your external style sheet file):

   ```
   <LINK REL="stylesheet" TYPE="text/css" HREF="filename.css">
   ```

For example, suppose you create a style-sheet file named mystyles.css and that file includes the following style definitions:

```
H1 {color: red}
TT {font-size: 16pt}
```

You then refer to that file by using the <LINK> tag shown in the following example (see ssextern.htm on the CD in this book):

```
<HTML>
<HEAD>
<LINK REL="stylesheet" TYPE="text/css" HREF="mystyles.css">
</HEAD>
<BODY>
<H1>This Heading Will Appear Red</H1>
<TT>This text will be displayed in a 16-point font</TT>
</BODY>
</HTML>
```

Why is this so powerful? Well, you can add the same <LINK> tag to any number of web pages and they'll all use the same style definitions. This makes it a breeze to create a consistent look and feel for your site. And if you decide that your <H1> text should be green instead, all you have to do is edit the style-sheet file (mystyles.css). Automatically, every single one of your pages that link to this file will be updated with the new style!

Webmaster Wisdom _____

The HREF part of the <LINK> tag doesn't have to be a simple file name. You can use a full URL, if necessary. This is handy if you've set up your site with multiple directories, or if you want to link to an external style sheet file on another site. (I don't recommend the latter, however; it takes your pages a bit longer to load because the browser has to go fetch the file.)

Method #3: Inline Styles

In the two style sheet methods we've examined so far, the browser applies the style to *every* instance of whatever tag you specify in the definition. This is good because it ensures a consistent look throughout a page. But what do you do if you want a particular instance of a tag to use a different style? For example, suppose you want all your <H1> headings to appear in a 24-point font, but you want the *first* <H1> heading to appear in a 36-point font. You can accomplish this by shoehorning the STYLE attribute inside the tag you want to work with. (Among style sheet wonks, this is known as an *inline* style.) Here's an example (see ssinline.htm on the CD in this book):

```
<HTML>
<HEAD>
<TITLE>Style Sheets: Inline Styles</TITLE>
</HEAD>

<STYLE TYPE="text/css">
<!--
H1 {font-size: 24pt}
-->
</STYLE>

<BODY>
<H1 STYLE="font-size: 36pt">This Heading Uses 36-Point Type</H1>
<H1>This One Uses 24-Point Type</H1>
</BODY>
</HTML>
```

As before, use the <STYLE> tag in the header to define a style for the <H1> tag.
Notice, however, that the first <H1> tag includes a STYLE attribute that specifies a
different font size. (Note, too, that you define the style slightly differently. That is,
you use quotation marks instead of braces.) Figure 21.4 shows the results.

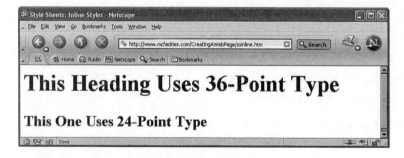

Figure 21.4

*Using inline styles lets you
set a style for individual tags
and thus override the default
style.*

Applying a Style to a Section

The <DIV> tag is used to divide your page into separate sections. It doesn't do much
by itself, although the browser usually inserts a line break (equivalent to a <BR> tag)
before the <DIV> tag and after the </DIV> end tag. However, by including the STYLE
attribute inside the <DIV> tag, you can apply an inline style to everything that falls
inside one of these sections. Here's an example:

```
<DIV STYLE="font-size: 16pt">

<DIV STYLE="font-size: 16pt">
<P>
This is a 16-point paragraph.
</P><P>
```

```
This paragraph also appears in a 16-point font.
</P><P>
So will this one.
</P>
</DIV>
```

In this case, everything between <DIV> and </DIV> gets formatted with the 16-point font size style.

Applying a Style to a Word or Phrase

What if you want to apply a style to only a particular word or phrase? In most cases, you won't want to use <DIV> because it adds line breaks before and after the defined section. The solution is to use the <SPAN> tag. The idea is that you surround your word or phrase with <SPAN> and </SPAN>, and then toss the STYLE attribute inside the <SPAN> tag. Here's an example:

```
Apply the style right <SPAN STYLE="font-size: 20pt">now</SPAN>.
```

Working with Style Classes

Although I promised earlier that I'd show you only three methods for implementing styles in your pages, I must mention a fourth method that can be really handy: the *style class*. The style class was created to solve a common problem: What if you want to apply a specific style to a number of different tags and sections throughout the document? Couldn't you just use inline styles?

Absolutely. However, what if you decide to change the style? You would have to go through the entire page and edit all the inline styles. An easier approach is to set up a style class within your main style sheet (that is, either within the <STYLE> tag or within an external style sheet file). Here's the basic format to use:

```
.ClassName {style definitions go here}
```

Here, *ClassName* is a unique name (without any spaces) that you use for the class. Here are a couple of examples:

```
.TitleText {font-size: 20pt; color: Navy; text-align: center}
.SubtitleText {font-size: 16pt; color: Gray; text-align: center}
```

The TitleText class uses a font size of 20 points, navy text, and a center alignment; the SubtitleText class uses a font size of 16 points, gray text, and a center alignment.

To use these classes, add a CLASS attribute to the tags you want the styles applied to, and set it equal to the class name (without the dot). Here's an example:

```
<DIV CLASS="TitleText">
This is the Title of the Document
</DIV>
```

The advantage here is that if you decide to change this style, you need edit only the style class; after that, every tag that uses the class changes automatically.

Here's a page (see ssclass.htm on the CD in this book) that offers up a complete example:

```
<HTML>
<HEAD>
<TITLE>Style Sheets: Styles Classes</TITLE>
</HEAD>

<STYLE TYPE="text/css">
<!--
.TitleText {font-size: 20pt; color: Navy; text-align: center}
.SubtitleText {font-size: 16pt; color: Gray; text-align: center}
-->
</STYLE>

<BODY>
<DIV CLASS="TitleText">This is the Title of the Document</DIV>
<DIV CLASS="SubtitleText">This is the Subtitle of the Document</DIV>
</BODY>
</HTML>
```

Figure 21.5 shows how Internet Explorer interprets the classes.

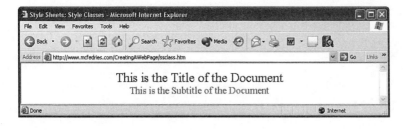

Figure 21.5

Use style classes for even more control over your styles.

The Least You Need to Know

- A style is a collection of formatting instructions for a given tag, and a style sheet is a collection of styles.

- An embedded style sheet is a style sheet that resides inside a document and is defined by the <STYLE> and </STYLE> tags.

- An external style sheet is a collection of styles that sits in a separate file. You let the browser know about the existence of this file by using the <LINK> tag:

  ```
  <LINK REL="stylesheet" TYPE="text/css" HREF="filename.css">
  ```

- An inline style is a style defined by adding the STYLE attribute inside the tag you want to affect.

- Use the <DIV> tag to apply a style to all the tags and text between <DIV> and </DIV>. Use the <SPAN> tag to apply a style to all the text between <SPAN> and </SPAN>.

Sheet Music: Styles for Fonts, Colors, and Backgrounds

In This Chapter

◆ Fiddling with font sizes, families, and weights

◆ Indenting and aligning text

◆ Text formatting such as underlining and strikethrough

◆ Working with style sheet colors

◆ Getting a handle on background styles

◆ Many ways to use styles to gussy up your pages

Okay, now that you know how to sew styles into your HTML creations, it's time to examine the specifics of the various styles available. This chapter examines style definitions for fonts, text, colors, and backgrounds.

Using Styles to Control Fonts

Chapter 3 discussed how to use the <FONT> tag to adjust font properties such as size and typeface. Well, anything the <FONT> tag can do, style sheets can do better. The next few sections show you why.

Font Size Styles

The <FONT> tag's control over the size of the font is limited, at best. Style sheets are vastly superior because they allow you to set the size of your text to just about anything you want.

Just so you know, the *font size* is a measure of the relative height used for each character. Although style sheets give you several ways to specify these heights, it's probably best to stick with *points*. To set the size, use the font-size style and set it to a number that ends with pt, like this:

```
P {font-size: 14pt}
```

You can also plug in half a dozen predefined size values: xx-small, x-small, small, medium, large, and x-large. Finally, you can also use the relative smaller and larger values to get text that's a bit smaller or larger than the regular page text.

Webmaster Wisdom

I cover most of the available style attributes in this chapter, but not all of them. For a complete list, see my Style Sheets Reference on the CD in this book or on my site: www.mcfedries.com/ CreatingAWebPage/css.

Webmaster Wisdom

Following is a list of the various types of units that are used in style sheets:

Unit	What It Represents
em	em dash (the width of the lowercase letter "m" in the current typeface)
ex	x-height (the height of the lowercase "x" in the current typeface)
px	pixels
in	inches
cm	centimeters
mm	millimeters
pt	points (there are 72 points to an inch)
pc	picas (one pica equals 12 points)

The following HTML file (see ss-size.htm on the CD in this book) tries a few different values on for, uh, size, and Figure 22.1 shows how the browser interprets them:

```
<HTML>
<HEAD>
<TITLE>Style Sheets: Font Sizes</TITLE>
</HEAD>
<BODY>

Our t-shirts are available in sizes
<SPAN STYLE="font-size: xx-small">xx-small</SPAN>,
<SPAN STYLE="font-size: x-small">x-small</SPAN>,
<SPAN STYLE="font-size: small">small</SPAN>,
<SPAN STYLE="font-size: medium">medium</SPAN>,
<SPAN STYLE="font-size: large">large</SPAN>,
<SPAN STYLE="font-size: x-large">x-large</SPAN>, and
<SPAN STYLE="font-size: xx-large">xx-large.</SPAN>
<DIV STYLE="font-size: small">
You can also special order t-shirts in
<SPAN STYLE="font-size: smaller">smaller</SPAN> or
<SPAN STYLE="font-size: larger">larger</SPAN> sizes.
</DIV>
Our biggest shirt is <SPAN STYLE="font-size: 24pt">Size 24</SPAN>.

</BODY>
</HTML>
```

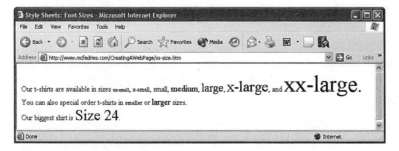

Figure 22.1

Styles enable you to set all kinds of different font sizes.

Font Family (Typeface) Styles

The *font family* represents the overall look associated with each character (it's more commonly known as the *typeface*). Unlike the other styles, there are no set values you can use. Instead, you usually specify several possibilities, and the browser uses the first one that's installed on the user's computer. Here's an example:

```
TT {font-family: Courier, "Courier New"}
```

CAUTION

Page Pitfalls _____

As with the <FONT> tag's FACE attribute (see Chapter 3), the reader sees only a specified typeface if it's installed on the reader's computer. If the typeface is not installed, the reader sees only the browser's default typeface.

Notice that multiple-word family names must be enclosed in quotation marks. If you're using an inline style (the STYLE attribute), enclose multiple-word family names in single quotation marks, like this:

```
<SPAN STYLE="font-family: 'Comic Sans MS'">
```

There are also five so-called *generic* family names you can use:

♦ cursive. Displays text in a cursive font (such as Comic Sans MS), which is a flowing style reminiscent of handwriting.

♦ fantasy. Displays text in a fantasy font (such as Broadway), which is a decorative style.

♦ monospace. Displays text in a monospace font (such as Courier New), which means that each character—from the wide "w" to the skinny "i"—is given the same amount of horizontal space. This is similar to the effect produced by the <TT> tag.

♦ serif. Displays text in a serif font (such as Times New Roman), which means that each character has extra cross strokes (called *feet* in the typographic biz).

♦ sans-serif. Displays text in a sans serif font (such as Arial), which means that each character doesn't have the extra cross strokes. (Although this is a two-word value, it doesn't require quotation marks because it's a built-in value.)

These names are most often used at the end of a list of font families as a "catch all" value that renders the text the way you want if the user doesn't have any of the specific font families installed. For example, if you want to display sans serif text, you might set up your style like this:

CAUTION

Page Pitfalls _____

All version 4 and later browsers render the monospace, serif, and sans serif families reliably. However, support for the cursive and fantasy families is spotty, so you should probably avoid them.

```
.title {font-family: Arial, Helvetica, "MS Sans
Serif", sans-serif}
```

The following HTML file (it's ssfamily.htm on the CD in this book) puts a few families to the test. Figure 22.2 shows how they look with Internet Explorer 6 for Windows, and Figure 22.3 shows the results in Netscape 6 for the Macintosh.

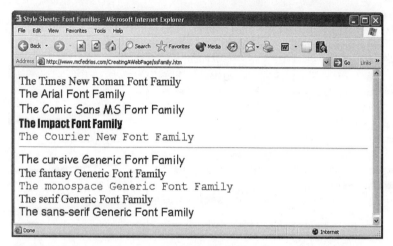

Figure 22.2

A few font families in Internet Explorer 6.

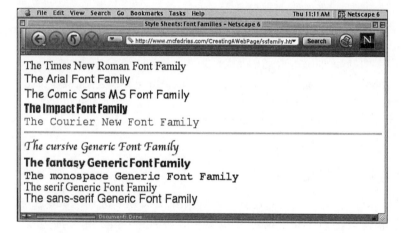

Figure 22.3

The same families in Netscape 6 for the Mac.

```
<HTML>
<HEAD>
<TITLE>Style Sheets: Font Families</TITLE>

<STYLE TYPE="text/css">
<!--
.family1 {font-size: 18pt; font-family: "Times New Roman"}
.family2 {font-size: 18pt; font-family: Arial}
.family3 {font-size: 18pt; font-family: "Comic Sans MS"}
.family4 {font-size: 18pt; font-family: Impact}
.family5 {font-size: 18pt; font-family: "Courier New"}
-->
</STYLE>

</HEAD>
<BODY>
```

```
<DIV CLASS="family1">The Times New Roman Font Family</DIV>
<DIV CLASS="family2">The Arial Font Family</DIV>
<DIV CLASS="family3">The Comic Sans MS Font Family</DIV>
<DIV CLASS="family4">The Impact Font Family</DIV>
<DIV CLASS="family5">The Courier New Font Family</DIV>
<HR>
<DIV STYLE="font-size: 18pt">
<DIV STYLE="font-family: cursive">The cursive Generic Font Family</DIV>
<DIV STYLE="font-family: fantasy">The fantasy Generic Font Family</DIV>
<DIV STYLE="font-family: monospace">The monospace Generic Font Family</DIV>
<DIV STYLE="font-family: serif">The serif Generic Font Family</DIV>
<DIV STYLE="font-family: sans-serif">The sans-serif Generic Font Family</DIV>
</DIV>

</BODY>
</HTML>
```

Font-Weight Styles (Bolding)

The font weight controls the thickness of text. For example, the <B> tag renders text as bold by displaying thicker letters. As usual, however, style sheets give you much greater control. In this case, you use the font-weight style:

font-weight: *value*

Here, *value* can be either of the following:

Page Pitfalls

Unfortunately, most browsers don't do much of anything when confronted with font-weight values from 100 to 500 (as you can see in Figure 22.4). Also, the version 6 and later browsers seem to render the values from 600 to 900 in the same way.

♦ **A predefined weight.** Use one of the following predefined values: normal, bold, bolder, or lighter. The latter two are relative values that make the text appear bolder or lighter than the surrounding text.

♦ **A specific weight.** Use one of the following: 100, 200, 300, 400 (normal), 500, 600, 700 (bold), 800, or 900.

Here's an example file (it's ssweight.htm on the CD in this book) that puts the font-weight style through its paces (Figure 22.4 shows what happens in Netscape 7):

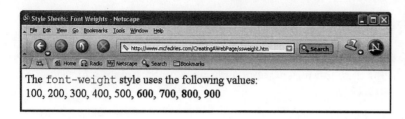

Figure 22.4

The various values for the font-weight style.

```
<HTML>
<HEAD>
<TITLE>Style Sheets: Font Weights</TITLE>
</HEAD>
<BODY>

<DIV STYLE="font-size: 18pt">
The <SPAN STYLE="font-family: 'Courier New', Courier">font-weight</SPAN>
style uses the following values:<BR>
<SPAN STYLE="font-weight: 100">100</SPAN>,
<SPAN STYLE="font-weight: 200">200</SPAN>,
<SPAN STYLE="font-weight: 300">300</SPAN>,
<SPAN STYLE="font-weight: 400">400</SPAN>,
<SPAN STYLE="font-weight: 500">500</SPAN>,
<SPAN STYLE="font-weight: 600">600</SPAN>,
<SPAN STYLE="font-weight: 700">700</SPAN>,
<SPAN STYLE="font-weight: 800">800</SPAN>,
<SPAN STYLE="font-weight: 900">900</SPAN>
</DIV>

</BODY>
</HTML>
```

Font-Style Styles (Italics)

If font-weight is the style sheet equivalent of the <B> tag, you might be wondering if there's an equivalent style for the <I> tag. Indeed there is, but it has the confusing name of font-style. Yeah, that's *really* descriptive. Anyway, it's very simple:

```
font-style: italic
```

Also, some fonts have an *oblique* style that looks sort of like italic, but it's really just the letters slanted to one side. If a particular font has an oblique version, you can use the following style to specify it:

```
font-style: oblique
```

Text Styles: More Ways to Format Text

Besides fiddling with fonts, style sheets offer a few other ways to format your page text. This section looks at four of them: indentation, alignment, underlining, and casing.

Indenting the First Line of a Paragraph

Many professionally typeset pages indent the beginning of each paragraph. The only way to do that in regular HTML is to string together a series of nonbreaking spaces ( ) at the start of each paragraph. With style sheets, however, it's easy because you just use the text-indent style. For example, the following page (see ssindent.htm on the CD in this book) includes a style sheet that tells the browser to indent the first line of every paragraph by half an inch, as shown in Figure 22.5.

```
<HTML>
<HEAD>
<TITLE>Style Sheets: Text Indents</TITLE>

<STYLE TYPE="text/css">
<!--
P {text-indent: 0.5in}
-->
</STYLE>
</HEAD>
<BODY>

<H3>Textstyles: More Ways to Format Text</H3>
<P>
Besides fiddling with fonts, style sheets offer a few other
ways to format your page text. This section looks at four of them:
indentation, alignment, underlining, and casing.
</P>
<H4>Indenting the First Line of a Paragraph</H4>
<P>
Many professionally typeset pages indent the beginning of each
paragraph. The only way to do that in regular HTML is to string
together a series of nonbreaking spaces (<TT>&#38;nbsp;</TT>) at the start of
each paragraph. With style sheets, however, it's easy because
you just use the <TT>text-indent</TT> style. For example, the following
page includes a style sheet that tells the browser to indent the
first line of every paragraph by half an inch.
</P>

</BODY>
</HTML>
```

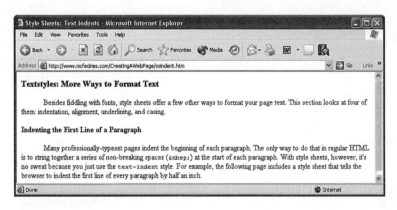

Figure 22.5

Use text-indent to indent the first line of a paragraph.

Aligning Text

To set the alignment of a section of text, use the text-align style:

text-align: *alignment*

Here, *alignment* can be one of the following four values:

- left. Aligns the text with the left side of the browser window.

- center. Centers the text within the browser window.

- right. Aligns the text with the right side of the browser window.

- justify. Aligns the text with both the left and right sides of the browser window.

Webmaster Wisdom

If you want the entire paragraph indented instead of just the first line, work with the various margin styles. I tell you about them in Chapter 23.

The following page (see ssalign.htm on the CD in this book) gives these alignment values a test drive (see Figure 22.6):

```
<HTML>
<HEAD>
<TITLE>Style Sheets: Aligning Text</TITLE>
</HEAD>
<BODY>

<TABLE BORDER="1">
<TR>
<TH WIDTH="25%">
Left-aligned text
</TH>
```

```
<TH WIDTH="25%">
Centered text
</TH>
<TH WIDTH="25%">
Right-aligned text
</TH>
<TH WIDTH="25%">
Justified text
</TH>
</TR>
<TR>
<TD WIDTH="25%" STYLE="text-align: left">
Puns are little plays on words that a certain breed of person
loves to spring on you and then look at you in a certain
</TD>
<TD WIDTH="25%" STYLE="text-align: center">
self-satisfied way to indicate that he thinks that you must
think that he is by far the cleverest person on Earth
</TD>
<TD WIDTH="25%" STYLE="text-align: right">
now that Benjamin Franklin is dead, when in fact what you
are thinking is that if this person ever ends up in a
</TD>
<TD WIDTH="25%" STYLE="text-align: justify">
lifeboat, the other passengers will hurl him overboard by the end of
the first day even if they have plenty of food and water. &#150;Dave Barry
</TD>
</TR>
</TABLE>

</BODY>
</HTML>
```

Figure 22.6

The align values in action.

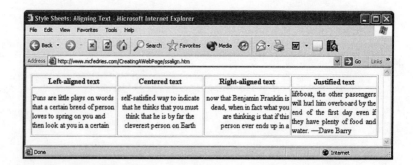

Using the Text Decoration Styles

One of the most common questions that readers ask me is "How can I display my links without an underline?" And my answer is "Use the text-decoration style on the <A> tag and set it to none":

```
A {text-decoration: none}
```

This is a nice trick, but the text-decoration style has a few others up its sleeve. Here's a complete list of the values you can use with this style:

- ◆ blink. This is a Netscape-only (version 4.0 and up) value, and it's the equivalent of the dumb <BLINK> tag.

- ◆ line-through. Formats text with a line through the middle (this is usually called *strikethrough* text). Most people use this style to represent text that's been "deleted" from a document. This is a common technique in the blog world, where it is used to show the evolution of a blog item or simply to give the blog the feel of a physical diary.

- ◆ none. Formats text without any decoration.

- ◆ overline. Formats text with a line over the top. (Note that, in the Netscape universe, only versions 6 and up support this value.)

- ◆ underline. Formats text with an underline.

Here's some sample code that uses a few text-decoration values (see ssdecor.htm on the CD in this book):

```
<HTML>
<HEAD>
<TITLE>Style Sheets: Text Decoration</TITLE>
</HEAD>
<BODY>
<H2 STYLE="text-decoration: none">None</H2>
<H2 STYLE="text-decoration: line-through">Line-through</H2>
<H2 STYLE="text-decoration: overline">Overline</H2>
<H2 STYLE="text-decoration: underline">Underline</H2>
</BODY>
</HTML>
```

Figure 22.7 shows how these styles look in Netscape 7.

Figure 22.7

Some text-decoration style examples.

Working with Uppercase and Lowercase Letters

You can format text as all uppercase, all lowercase, or with only the first letter of each word as uppercase (this is often called title case). The style that accomplishes this goes by the unlikely name of text-transform. (Sheesh. Only a major league geek could come up with such an obscure name.) This style comes equipped with four values for your style pleasure:

◆ capitalize. Converts the first letter of every word to uppercase.

◆ lowercase. Converts every letter to lowercase.

◆ none. Leaves the text as is.

◆ uppercase. Converts every letter to uppercase.

The following code demonstrates the various text-transform values (check out sstrans.htm on the CD in this book), and Figure 22.8 shows how they look with Internet Explorer.

```
<HTML>
<HEAD>
<TITLE>Style Sheets: Text Transform</TITLE>
</HEAD>
<BODY>
<H2 STYLE="text-transform: capitalize">
I left my heart in Truth or Consequences, New Mexico</H2>
<H2 STYLE="text-transform: lowercase">
I left my heart in Truth or Consequences, New Mexico</H2>
<H2 STYLE="text-transform: none">
I left my heart in Truth or Consequences, New Mexico</H2>
<H2 STYLE="text-transform: uppercase">
I left my heart in Truth or Consequences, New Mexico</H2>
</BODY>
</HTML>
```

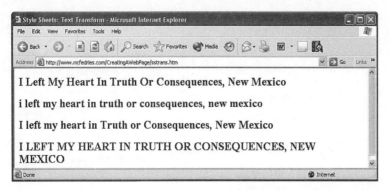

Figure 22.8

Examples of the ill-named
text-transform style.

Coloring Your Web World with Color Styles

Using color within a style sheet is more or less the same as using the <FONT> tag's COLOR attribute (discussed in Chapter 3). In this case, you use the color style and set it to one of the weird six-digit RGB values, as in this example:

```
<SPAN STYLE="color: #FF0000">This text is red</SPAN>
```

The big advantage you get with style sheet colors is that you can finally get those unintuitive RGB values out of your life. That's because color names are part of the style sheet specification. These color names—semiofficially known as the *X11 color set*—enable you to use friendly monikers such as "red" and "yellow" instead of the obscure RGB values. There are 140 names in all and they cover most of the color spectrum, from AliceBlue to WhiteSmoke. In between are all kinds of fun names, such as PapayaWhip, DodgerBlue, and PeachPuff. Here's an example:

```
Try my <SPAN STYLE="color: LemonChiffon">Lemon Chiffon</SPAN> pie!
```

To help you get a handle on this riot of colors, I've put together a table of the various color names (along with the RGB equivalents, so you'll remember how much easier the names are to use). The file is called x11color.htm, and you'll find it on the CD in this book. Figure 3.7, shown in Chapter 3, gives you a peek at this page.

Using Background Styles

As discussed in Chapter 6, you can use the <BODY> tag to set up your page with either a background color (using the BGCOLOR attribute) or a background image (using the BACKGROUND attribute). Either way, the attribute you set applies to the entire page.

With style sheets, however, you can apply a background color or image to sections of your page, or even to individual words. The secret to this lies in two styles: background color and background image.

To set a background color, use either a color name or an RGB value:

```
background-color: blue
background-color: #0000FF
```

To specify a background image, use the following syntax:

```
{background-image: URL(filename)}
```

Here, *filename* is the name of the graphics file you want to use (or an URL that points to the file). The HTML code below shows a few examples of these styles (see ssback.htm on the CD in this book).

```
<HTML>
<HEAD>
<TITLE>Style Sheet Backgrounds</TITLE>
</HEAD>
<BODY>

<DIV STYLE="background-color: black; color: white">
The background style is great for setting off entire sections
of text using a different color. For example, this section
uses a black background with white text.
</DIV>

<DIV STYLE="background-color: skyblue; color: navy">
On the other hand, this section achieves a slightly different
effect by using a pleasant Sky Blue background with Navy text.
</DIV>

<P>You can also use the background style to
<SPAN STYLE="background-color: yellow">highlight individual words</SPAN>.
<P>

<DIV STYLE="background-image: URL(bg03.gif); font-size: 16pt">
<B>One of the most interesting ways to use the background style
is to specify a background image. The browser will tile the
image so that it fills the entire section, like this.</B>
</DIV>

</BODY>
</HTML>
```

Figure 22.9 shows this file displayed in Internet Explorer 6.

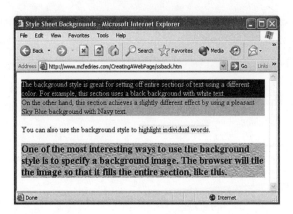

Figure 22.9

Some background styles.

Another background style you might want to check out is `background repeat`, which controls whether (and how) the browser tiles the background image to fill the window. There are four possible values:

- `repeat`. Tiles the background image to cover the entire browser window.

- `repeat-x`. Tiles the background image horizontally, only.

- `repeat-y`. Tiles the background image vertically, only.

- `no-repeat`. Doesn't tile the background image.

Also, Internet Explorer supports the `background attachment` style. If you set this style to `fixed`, the background image remains in place when the user scrolls up and down the page. Set this style to `scroll` to revert to the usual background behavior (that is, the background image scrolls along with the text).

The Least You Need to Know

- To change the font size, use the `font-size` style and set it equal to a value in points (`pt`).

- To change the font typeface, use the `font-family` style and set it to the name of one or more typefaces. Be sure to enclose multiple-word typeface names in quotation marks.

- To align your text with the margins, use the `text-align` style and set it to one of the following: `left`, `center`, `right`, or `justify`.

- To format your links without the traditional underline, use the following:

```
A {text-decoration: none}
```

◆ To create colored text, use the `color` style and set it to a color name or RGB color value.

◆ To change the background of the page or some text, use either `background color` (set it to a color name or RGB color value) or `background image` (set it to `URL(filename)`, where *filename* is the name or address of the image file).

The Box Model: Styles for Dimensions, Borders, Margins, and More

In This Chapter

- ◆ Knocking some sense into the box model
- ◆ Setting the box dimensions
- ◆ Putting extra padding around the content
- ◆ Adding borders to the box and messing with the box margins
- ◆ Positioning the box precisely on the page
- ◆ Wrapping your page boxes in the style sheet equivalent of paper, bows, and ribbons

So far, you've learned what style sheets are and how to implement them (Chapter 21), and you've learned some specific styles for fonts, text, colors, and backgrounds (Chapter 22). Style sheets are pretty useful little beasts, aren't they? They just give you so much more control over what your pages look like than plain old HTML.

This chapter takes this control up a notch by eyeballing quite a few more styles that cover things such as dimensions (the height and width of things), padding and margins (the amount of space around things), borders (lines around things), and position (where things appear on the page).

Thinking Outside the Box: Understanding the Box Model

Everything in this chapter is based on something called the style sheet *box model.* So let's begin by figuring out just what this box model thing is all about and why it's important.

In the geeky world known as Style Sheet Land, stuff inside a page is broken down into separate *elements.* In particular, there's a class of elements called *blocks* that includes those tags which start new sections of text: <P>, <BLOCKQUOTE>, <H1> through <H6>, <DIV>, <TABLE>, and so on.

In this strange world, each of these block elements is considered to have an invisible box around it (okay, it's a *very* strange world). This box has the following components:

- **Content.** The stuff inside the box (the text, the table, and so on).
- **Dimensions.** The height and width of the box.
- **Padding.** The space around the content. It's similar to the <TABLE> tag's CELLPADDING attribute discussed in Chapter 10.
- **Border.** A line that surrounds the box and marks its edges.
- **Margin.** The space outside of the border. It separates the box from other boxes to the left and right, as well as above and below.
- **Position.** The location of the box within the page.

Figure 23.1 illustrates the box's basic structure. The shaded area is the box itself.

Figure 23.1

The style sheet box model.

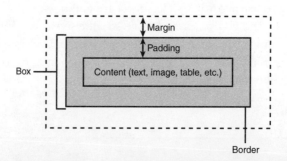

All the styles that you learned about in Chapter 22 dealt with formatting the box content. This chapter covers the five components that comprise the rest of the box: the dimensions, padding, border, margin, and position.

Webmaster Wisdom

Page knickknacks that don't create blocks—things like <B> and <I>—are called *inline elements*. You can use many of the style properties discussed on the inline elements I discussed in Chapter 22, but I don't recommend it. The big problem is that Netscape 4 tends to convert inline elements to block elements if you try to apply block styles (such as a border or margin). Note that Netscape 6 and later do not have this problem.

Box Blueprints: Specifying the Dimensions

The dimensions of the box are straightforward: the width property specifies how wide the box is, and the height property specifies how tall the box is. Note, however, that although Netscape 6 and later get along fine with the height property, Netscape 4 doesn't support it (and will, in fact, crash horribly when confronted by it).

To set these properties, use either an absolute value in pixels (px) or a percentage of the browser's current width and height.

Here's some simple HTML code that tries out these two styles (see ssdimens.htm on the CD in this book). Note that I included a <STYLE> tag that sets the border property for the <P> tag so that you can easily see the dimensions of the resulting paragraphs (I discuss the border property in detail a bit later in the section titled "The Box Revealed: Setting Borders"). Figure 23.2 shows what Internet Explorer 5 makes of the whole thing.

```
<HTML>
<HEAD>
<TITLE>Style Sheet Dimensions</TITLE>

<STYLE TYPE="text/css">
<!--
P {border: thin solid}
-->
</STYLE>

</HEAD>
<BODY>
```

```
<P>This is a regular paragraph.</P>
<P STYLE="height: 50px">This is a paragraph that's 50 pixels high.</P>
<P STYLE="width: 100px">This is a paragraph that's 100 pixels wide.</P>

</BODY>
</HTML>
```

Figure 23.2

Some paragraphs with different dimensions.

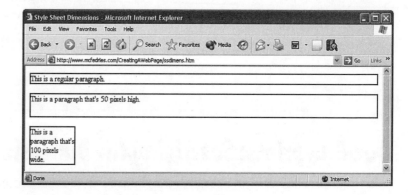

Cushy Content: Adding Padding to the Inside of the Box

If you look at Figure 23.2, you can see that the text tends to cozy right up against the border of the box, particularly on the left and right. If your text feels claustrophobic, you can give it some extra elbow-room by increasing the amount of padding that surrounds the content within the box. Style sheets give you four padding properties to play with:

- ◆ `padding-top`. Adds space on top of the content.

- ◆ `padding-right`. Adds space to the right of the content.

- ◆ `padding-bottom`. Adds space below the content.

- ◆ `padding-left`. Adds space to the left of the content.

It's usually easiest to specify a value in pixels, like this:

```
P {padding-left: 10px}
```

There's also a shorthand property called `padding` that you can use to apply all four padding properties, in this order: `padding-top`, `padding-right`, `padding-bottom`, and `padding-left`. (To remember this order, start at the top and work your way clockwise around the other sides.) Separate each property with a space, like this:

```
DIV {padding: 10px 25px 10px 25px}
```

Note that if you specify only a single value, it applies to all four padding sides.

Page Pitfalls

You have to be concerned with some browser peculiarities when it comes down to the padding properties. In Netscape 4 and Internet Explorer 4 and later, when you use `padding-left` or `padding-right`, the block's width remains the same and the height is increased to fit the text. In Netscape 6 and later, however, the width of the block is increased to make way for the new padding.

Also, it's possible to use a percentage value for the padding, but the value is interpreted differently in different browsers. With Internet Explorer, the percentage is based on the dimensions of the current block; with Netscape, it's based on the current size of the browser window. Therefore, I recommend avoiding percentages altogether and using only absolute values.

Here's some code (see sspaddng.htm on the CD in this book) that tries out each padding property on a few <DIV> sections. Figure 23.3 shows the result in Internet Explorer 6.

```
<HTML>
<HEAD>
<TITLE>Style Sheet Padding</TITLE>

<STYLE TYPE="text/css">
<!--
DIV {border: thin solid;
   width: 100px;
   margin-bottom: 5px}
-->
</STYLE>

</HEAD>
<BODY>

<DIV STYLE="padding-top: 10px; padding-bottom: 10px">
This section has 10 pixels of padding on the top and bottom.</DIV>
<DIV STYLE="padding-left: 15px; padding-right: 15px">
This section has 15 pixels of padding on the left and right.</DIV>
<DIV STYLE="padding: 10px 15px 10px 15px">This section has 10 pixels of padding
on the top and bottom, and 15 pixels of padding on the left and right.</DIV>

</BODY>
</HTML>
```

Figure 23.3

Trying out the padding properties.

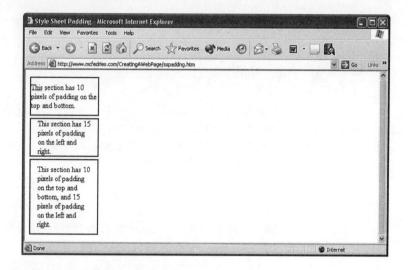

The Box Revealed: Setting Borders

In the last couple of examples, I included borders so you could explicitly see the box in each element. So it's high time we checked out this border stuff to see what kind of fun you can have with it. The various border properties come in three flavors: width, style, and color.

The border width is controlled by the following five properties:

♦ `border-top-width`. Specifies the width of the top border.

♦ `border-right-width`. Specifies the width of the right border.

♦ `border-bottom-width`. Specifies the width of the bottom border.

♦ `border-left-width`. Specifies the width of the left border.

♦ `border-width`. Specifies the width of all the borders, in this order: border-top-width, border-right-width, border-bottom-width, and border-left-width. Separate each property with a space, or use a single value for all four sides.

To set the width, use either an absolute value (such as `5px` for a border that is 5 pixels wide) or one of the following predefined values: `thin`, `medium`, or `thick`.

The border style has five similar properties:

♦ `border-top-style`. Specifies the top border's style.

♦ `border-right-style`. Specifies the right border's style.

♦ `border-bottom-style`. Specifies the style of the bottom border.

♦ `border-left-style`. Specifies the style of the left border.

♦ `border-style`. Specifies the style of all the borders, in this order: border-top-style, border-right-style, border-bottom-style, and border-left-style. As usual, separate each property with a space, or use a single value for all four sides.

Page Pitfalls

For borders to work properly, make sure you set at least the border style. Also, Netscape 4's support of the border properties is flaky, so check your code. (Netscape 6 and later appear to handle borders reasonably well.)

Table 23.1 outlines the various values you can use for each border style property.

Table 23.1   Values for the Various Border Style Properties

Enter ...	To Get a Border That Uses ...
double	A double line
groove	A V-shaped line that appears to be etched into the page
inset	A line that appears to be sunken into the page
none	No line (that is, no border is displayed)
outset	A line that appears to be raised from the page
ridge	A V-shaped line that appears to be coming out of the page
solid	A solid line

For the border color, you can probably guess which five properties you can use:

♦ `border-top-color`. Specifies the color of the top border.

♦ `border-right-color`. Specifies the color of the right border.

♦ `border-bottom-color`. Specifies the color of the bottom border.

♦ `border-left-color`. Specifies the color of the left border.

♦ `border-color`. Specifies the color of all the borders, in this order: border-top-color, border-right-color, border-bottom-color, and border-left-color. Separate each property with a space, or use a single value for all four sides.

You can set each border color property to one of the usual color values.

The following code (it's ssborder.htm on the CD in this book) demonstrates some of the border-width and border-style values. Figure 23.4 shows how they look in Internet Explorer.

```
<HTML>
<HEAD>
<TITLE>Style Sheet Padding</TITLE>

<STYLE TYPE="text/css">
<!--
DIV {margin-bottom: 5px}
-->
</STYLE>

</HEAD>
<BODY>

<DIV STYLE="border-width: thin; border-style: solid">
This &lt;DIV&gt; uses a thin border with a solid style.
</DIV>

<DIV STYLE="border-width: medium; border-style: groove">
This &lt;DIV&gt; uses a medium border with a groove style.
</DIV>

<DIV STYLE="border-width: thick; border-style: outset">
This &lt;DIV&gt; uses a thick border with an outset style.
</DIV>

<DIV STYLE="border-width: 1cm; border-style: inset">
This &lt;DIV&gt; uses a 1-centimeter border with an inset style.
</DIV>

<DIV STYLE="border-width: 10px; border-style: ridge">
This &lt;DIV&gt; uses a 10-pixel border with a ridge style.
</DIV>

</BODY>
</HTML>
```

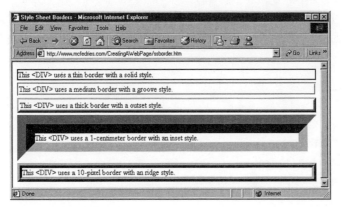

Figure 23.4

Internet Explorer trying some border styles on for size.

Webmaster Wisdom

If you want to format all the borders at once, here's a shorthand notation you can use:

```
{border: border-width border-style border-color}
```

Here, replace *border-width*, *border-style*, and *border-color* with values for each of those properties:

```
{border: thin solid Gray}
```

Room to Breathe: Specifying Margins Around the Box

For our next style sheet trick, I show you how to use styles to specify margins. The default margins used by the browser depend on what element you're dealing with. For example, each new paragraph creates a bit of margin space above itself, and you always get a little bit of space at the top and bottom of the page, and on the left and right sides of the page. On the other hand, <DIV> sections don't use margins.

To control all this, use any of the following margin properties:

- ◆ `margin-top`. Specifies the size of the top margin.

- ◆ `margin-right`. Specifies the size of the right margin.

- ◆ `margin-bottom`. Specifies the size of the bottom margin.

- ◆ `margin-left`. Specifies the size of the left margin.

- ◆ `margin`. Specifies the size of all the margins, in this order: margin-top, margin-right, margin-bottom, and margin-left. Separate each property with a space, or use a single value for all four margins.

In each case, set the width to a specific value (such as 0px for no margin). The following HTML code (ssmargin.htm on the CD in this book) sets two different margins (see Figure 23.5):

♦ A <STYLE> block sets the margins of the <BLOCKQUOTE> tag to be 100 pixels on the left and right.

♦ The <BODY> tag's STYLE attribute sets the overall margins of the page to 0 for the left, top, and right. As you can see in Figure 23.5, Internet Explorer handles this perfectly, but Netscape 7 ignores the margin-top property (and Netscape 4 doesn't support messing with the <BODY> tag's margins at all).

```
<HTML>
<HEAD>
<TITLE>Style Sheet Margins</TITLE>
</HEAD>

<STYLE TYPE="text/css">
<!--
BLOCKQUOTE {margin-left: 100px;
     margin-right: 100px;
     font-size: 14pt;
     font-family: Arial}
-->
</STYLE>

<BODY STYLE="margin-left: 0px;
      margin-top: 0px;
      margin-right: 0px">

<DIV STYLE="background: black;
     color: white;
     text-align: center">
<H1>This Heading Appears at the Top of the Body</H1>
</DIV>

<BLOCKQUOTE>
A pun does not commonly justify a blow in return. But if a blow
were given for such cause, and death ensued, the jury would be
judges both of the facts and of the pun, and might, if the
latter were of an aggravated character, return a verdict of
justifiable homicide.<BR>
&#151;Oliver Wendell Holmes, Sr.
</BLOCKQUOTE>

</BODY>
</HTML>
```

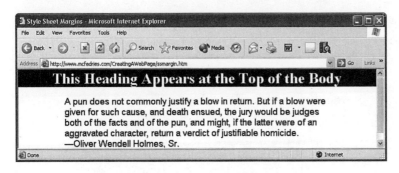

Figure 23.5

Some margin styles in action in both Internet Explorer 6 and Netscape 6.

Where the Box Goes: Working with Position Styles

Now that you've determined the structure and layout of your box, the last thing you have to decide is where to put it on the page. This might seem like a strange thing. After all, don't elements such as paragraphs and headings always go exactly where you put them on the page? They do in regular HTML, but style sheets, as you've seen so often, give you much more flexibility.

Your first chore is to decide how you want your element positioned. This is determined by, appropriately enough, the position property, which can take any of the following three values:

◆ `position: absolute`. When you use this value, you can toss the element anywhere on the page. For example, you could tell the browser to display a heading 100 pixels from the left and 50 pixels from the top.

◆ `position: relative`. This value first positions the element according to where it would normally appear in regular HTML. It then offsets the element horizontally and vertically, according to the values you specify.

◆ `position: static`. This value positions the element according to where it would normally appear in regular HTML.

If you decide to use either `position: absolute` or `position: relative`, you must specify the exact position you want. For this, you need to use some or all of the following four properties:

◆ `top`. The element's position from the top of the browser window (if you're using `position: absolute`) or below the element's natural position in the page (if you're using `position: relative`).

◆ `right`. The element's position from the right side of the browser window, if you're using `position: absolute`. Note that this value has no effect if you're using `position: relative`.

◆ `bottom`. The element's position from the bottom of the browser window if you're using `position: absolute`. This value has no effect if you're using `position: relative`.

◆ `left`. The element's position from the left side of the browser window (if you're using `position: absolute`) or to the left of the element's natural position in the page (if you're using `position: relative`).

The following code (ssposit.htm on the CD in this book) tries out some absolute and relative positioning, and Figure 23.6 shows what happens in Netscape 4.

```
<HTML>
<HEAD>
<TITLE>Style Sheet Positioning</TITLE>
</HEAD>

<STYLE TYPE="text/css">
<!--
DIV {font-family: Arial;
    font-size: 16pt}
-->
</STYLE>

<BODY>

<DIV STYLE="position: absolute; left: 600px; top: 150px">Section 1</DIV>
<DIV STYLE="position: absolute; left: 100px; top: 100px">Section 2</DIV>
<DIV STYLE="position: absolute; left: 500px; top: 50px">Section 3</DIV>
<DIV STYLE="position: absolute; left: 50px; top: 0px">Section 4</DIV>
<P>This is regular text. Even though it comes after all those &lt;DIV&gt;
tags, it still appears at the top of the page. That's because elements
that are positioned absolutely aren't part of the regular document flow.</P>
<P STYLE="position: relative; left: 200px">
This paragraph is shoved left from its normal position by 200 pixels
using relative positioning.</P>

</BODY>
</HTML>
```

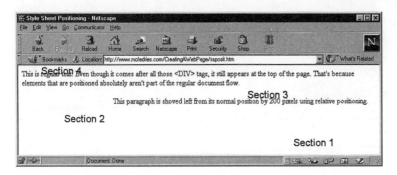

Figure 23.6

Use position styles to toss elements all over your page.

Positioning in the Third Dimension

Style sheets understand not only the usual 2-D positioning, but also positioning in the third dimension. It sounds like science fiction, but all it really means is that you can "stack" elements on top of each other for interesting effects. The style property that controls this is called z-index. An element with a higher z-index value is displayed "on top" of an element with a lower z-index value. Here's an example (see sszindex. htm on the CD in this book):

```
<HTML>
<HEAD>
<TITLE>Style Sheet 3-D Positioning</TITLE>
</HEAD>

<STYLE TYPE="text/css">
<!--
DIV {font-family: Arial;
   font-size: 12pt}
-->
</STYLE>

<BODY>

<IMG SRC="home2.gif" STYLE="z-index: 0; position: absolute; left: 100px; top:
10px">
<DIV STYLE="z-index: 1; position: absolute; left: 10px; top: 30px">
<B>This text appears on top of the image.</B>
</DIV>

</BODY>
</HTML>
```

Figure 23.7 shows how this looks in the browser.

Figure 23.7

Use the z-index *property to place one element "on top" of another.*

The Least You Need to Know

♦ The invisible box around each block element has six components: *content* (what's inside), *dimensions* (the height and width), *padding* (the space around the content), *border* (the line around the box), *margin* (the space outside the box), and *position* (where the box appears in the page).

♦ To set the box dimensions, use the height and width properties.

♦ To change the box padding, use the padding-top, padding-right, padding-bottom, and padding-left properties, or use the padding shortcut property.

♦ To change the border width, use the border-top-width, border-right-width, border-bottom-width, and border-left-width properties, or use the border-width shortcut property. For the border style, use the border-top-style, border-right-style, border-bottom-style, and border-left-style properties, or use the border-style shortcut property.

♦ To set the box margin, use the margin-top, margin-right, margin-bottom, and margin-left properties, or use the margin shortcut property.

♦ To change the box position, use position: absolute to place the element anywhere on the page; use position: relative to offset the element relative to its normal HTML position; use position: static to place the element in its normal HTML position. For the first two, position the element using the top, right, bottom, and left properties.

Frequently Asked Questions About HTML

This appendix presents a list of FAQs (frequently asked questions) about HTML. The questions are listed in the following categories: General HTML, Graphics, Publishing, Multimedia, Forms, Frames, and Page Design. A slightly longer list of FAQs is available on my website: www.mcfedries.com/CreatingAWebPage/faq.asp

General HTML Questions

How can I spell check my web page?

You have two choices for making your spelling letter-perfect:

♦ Compose your pages in a program that has a spell check feature. You can find this feature in word processors (such as Word), HTML editors (such as Netscape Composer), or in text editors (such as UltraEdit: www.ultraedit.com or Notetab: www.notetab.com).

♦ Use a spell check program such as Spell Checker for Edit Boxes (see www.quinion.com/mqa/index.htm).

The browser shows the tags I put into the page. What's wrong?

I explain how to solve this problem in Chapter 2. See the section titled "Help! The Browser Shows My Tags!"

Internet Explorer handles my link/graphic/whatever no problem, but Netscape doesn't. What's wrong?

The usual culprit here is a space that you've included in either a file name or a directory name. Netscape doesn't like spaces, so you need to rename your file or directory to remove the space. If you want to separate words in a file or directory name, a good substitute is the underscore character (_).

What's the difference between the .htm and .html file extensions?

There's no difference whatsoever. Both are legit HTML file extensions, and browsers process them equally. Note, however, that these extensions create separate files. For example, the files index.htm and index.html are distinct files.

How can I open a link in a separate browser window?

The usual method is to set the <A> tag's TARGET attribute equal to _blank:

```
<A HREF="whatever.html" TARGET="_blank">New Window</A>
```

However, if you set the <A> tag's TARGET attribute equal to an undefined name—that is, it's not the name of a frame or one of the prefab names—then the browser opens a new window and assigns the TARGET value as the name of the new window.

For example, consider the following:

```
<A HREF="whatever.html" TARGET="LinkWindow">Click this!</A>
```

This opens a new window and displays the "whatever.html" page within that window. The browser assigns the name "LinkWindow" to that window. This means that you can load anything into that window just by referring to the same window name, like this:

```
<A HREF="another.html" TARGET="LinkWindow">Click this, too!</A>
```

This link displays the "another.html" page in the same window that the previous link opened.

How do I use a custom bullet in a bulleted list?

The solution I use is a two-column table, like this one:

```
<TABLE>

<TR VALIGN="TOP">
<TD><IMG SRC="yourbullet.gif"></TD>
<TD>Bullet point 1 text goes here …</TD>
</TR>

<TR VALIGN="TOP">
<TD><IMG SRC="yourbullet.gif"></TD>
<TD>Bullet point 2 text goes here …</TD>
</TR>

etc.

</TABLE>
```

Is there a way to make table columns have a constant width?

Absolutely! Provided you're putting only text in each cell, you have to do two things:

◆ Specify an exact width for each cell.

◆ Use our old friend spacer.gif, the transparent 1×1 pixel image (see Chapter 6).

For example, if you want a column to always be 100 pixels wide, use this:

```
<TD WIDTH="100">
Cell text goes here
<BR><IMG SRC="spacer.gif" WIDTH="100" HEIGHT="1">
</TD>
```

Instead of displaying the symbol represented by a character code or entity, I want to display the actual character code or entity. Is that possible?

Yes. All character codes and entities begin with an ampersand (&). So the easiest way to display the code is to remove the ampersand and replace it with the character code for the ampersand (&). For example, the character code for the copyright symbol (©) is ©. To display the code, you'd use the following:

```
&#38;#169;
```

How can I let surfers download a file from my site?

In most cases, you set up a regular link and point it to the file you want to be able to download. For example, suppose you have a file named mystuff.zip. To set up a download link, you'd use the following:

```
<A HREF="mystuff.zip">Download my stuff<A>
```

This assumes that you've uploaded mystuff.zip to your server and that the file is in the same directory as your HTML file. When the user clicks the link, the browser will display a dialog box asking whether the user wants to open the file or save it to his or her hard disk.

For files that get displayed in the browser (such as text files), you need to add instructions on your page that tell the user to load the file and then select the browser's **File, Save As** command.

Is there any way to specify a Subject line with a mailto link?

Most (but not all) browsers and e-mail programs let you specify the Subject line by adjusting the <A> tag as follows:

```
<A HREF="mailto:biff@isp.com?Subject=My Subject Line">
```

Replace *My Subject Line* with the actual Subject line you want.

What is ASP?

If you come across a page file name that uses the .asp extension, you've come across a species of page known as an Active Server Page (ASP, for short). Most ASP files contain one or more scripts that are very similar to JavaScripts (information can be found on the CD). However, they're vastly different:

- ◆ JavaScripts run when the browser loads the page or when the user initiates some action (such as submitting a form). In other words, JavaScripts are executed by the browser.

- ◆ An ASP script is executed by the server. That is, when the user requests an ASP file, the server first checks to see if it contains a script. If it does, it runs that script and then sends the file to the user's browser.

The big advantage you get with ASP is that you no longer have to worry about browser compatibility, as you do with JavaScript. Since the script runs on the server, it doesn't matter what browser the user is running. Also, since the script runs on the server, it's fairly easy to do things such as access a database, send an e-mail, and do other fancy tricks.

ASP is a Microsoft technology, so it's designed to run on Microsoft web servers, such as Internet Information Server. If you want to give ASP a whirl, you have to find a web host that supports it.

Note, too, that a similar technology called PHP also exists. However, PHP usually runs on Unix and Linux web servers.

What is XML?

XML (eXtensible Markup Language) is still pretty highfalutin stuff, and it's not really on the radar screens just yet (at least, not for the likes of us). The basic idea is that XML enables the designer to create his or her own tags in such a way that an XML-smart browser knows what to do with those tags. This won't be a big deal for folks who just have straightforward pages. If you deal with databases or specialized fields (such as medicine or mathematics), however, you can create tags that describe database components or elements from your field of expertise. For example, a Math XML is already being proposed, and it'll enable math types to render equations and other elements that HTML just can't do. See www.w3.org/Math.

The problem with XML is that it requires some heavy-duty programming to "teach" the browser what each hand-built tag is supposed to do. For that reason, XML will remain a geeks-only technology for some time to come.

Graphics Questions

Why don't my images appear when I view my page in the browser?

The fact that you're not seeing your images is probably due to one of the following reasons:

♦ If you're viewing your page on your home machine, the HTML file and the image files might be sitting in separate directories on your computer. Try moving your image files into the same directory that holds your HTML file.

♦ If you're viewing your page on the web, make sure you sent the image files to your server.

♦ Make sure you have the correct match for uppercase and lowercase letters. If an image is on your server and it's named "image.gif", and your IMG tag refers to "IMAGE.GIF", your image won't show up. In this case, you'd have to edit your IMG tag so that it refers to "image.gif".

Is it possible to change the color of the border that appears around images used as links?

The image link border color is the same as the regular link color. Therefore, you can change the border color by using the LINK, ALINK, and VLINK attributes in the <BODY> tag. For example, if you want a red border, you use this:

```
<BODY LINK="#FF0000" ALINK="#FF0000" VLINK="#FF0000">
```

When I'm using an image as a link, how do I remove the border around the image?

Add BORDER="0" to your <IMG> tag, as in this example:

```
<A HREF="something.html">
<IMG SRC="jiffy.gif" BORDER="0">
</A>
```

How do I create thumbnail images?

A thumbnail is just a smaller version of an existing image. What you need to do is load the original image into a graphics program and then use the program's **Resize** command to scale down the image to an appropriate size (which depends on the original image). Then use the program's **File, Save As** command to save the smaller image under a different name. I usually just add "-thumbnail" to the name. For example, if the original is mypic.jpg, I name the smaller version mypic-thumbnail.jpg.

Webmaster Wisdom

This book's CD contains the necessary files for the Mapedit image map program.

To use the thumbnail, put it in your page with an <IMG> tag, and then set up that image as a link to the normal size file. Here's an example:

```
<A HREF="mypic.jpg">
<IMG SRC="mypic-thumbnail.jpg">
</A>
```

How do I make an image map with weird shapes, not just the usual rectangle, circle, or polygon?

You need to create a *server-side* image map, which requires a special program. Here are a couple to check out:

◆ **Image Mapper:** www.coffeecup.com/image-mapper

◆ **Mapedit:** www.boutell.com/mapedit

See also the following Yahoo! index:

www.yahoo.com/Computers_and_Internet/Internet/World_Wide_Web/Imagemaps

How do I get those little banners to pop up when the user puts the mouse over an image?

Add ALT text to your <IMG> tag:

```
<IMG
SRC="vacation12.gif"
ALT="This is a picture of me getting mugged in Marrakesh">
```

Most modern browsers display that text as a banner when the mouse pointer sits over an image for a second or two.

I'm an AOL user, and my uploaded images are distorted. What's the problem?

AOL compresses uploaded images, which causes problems for some files. There's a full explanation on the AOL Webmaster Info site: webmaster.info.aol.com.

When you get there, click **Graphics** and then **Graphic Compression Info.**

How can I prevent people from stealing my web page images?

This is extremely difficult, if not impossible, to do. However, here are three things that can help:

♦ Put a strongly worded copyright message on all your pages.

♦ Disable the right-click functionality that most image thieves use to grab graphics. I have a script on my site that shows you how to do this: www.mcfedries.com/JavaScript/NoRightClick.asp.

♦ Add a "digital watermark" to your images. See the Digimarc Corporation: www.digimarc.com.

How do I reduce the size (in bytes) of a photo or other high-quality image?

The best way to reduce the size of a photographic image is to convert it to the JPEG format. JPEG enables you to "compress" an image without losing much of the quality. In most cases, you can reduce the image size (in kilobytes) to a tenth of its original girth or less. I usually use Paint Shop Pro for this (it's on this book's CD):

1. Open the GIF image in Paint Shop Pro.

2. Select the **File, Save As** command to open the Save As dialog box.

3. In the **Save as type** list, choose the **JPEG – JFIF Compliant** item.

4. Click the **Options** button.

5. Enter a value (say, **50**) in the **Compression factor** box (or drag the slider below it back and forth).

6. Click **OK** to return to the Save As dialog box.

7. Click **Save.**

You'll probably need to try this whole procedure several times using different values for the compression in step 5. Start with 50 percent and work higher in, say, increments of 10 percent. After each save, check the right-hand side of the status bar to see the size of the image in kilobytes (KB). Also, check the quality of the image in the browser. The idea is that you want to compress the image as much as possible while still maintaining acceptable quality.

How can I slice up a large image to put in a table or use as an image map?

The easiest way I know is to use the Picture Dicer program: www.ziplink.net/ ~shoestring/dicer01.htm.

How do I get text to wrap around an image?

Add one of the following to your <IMG> tag:

♦ **ALIGN="LEFT".** Aligns the image on the left side of the screen. Subsequent text wraps around the right side of the image.

♦ **ALIGN="RIGHT".** Aligns the image on the right side of the screen. Subsequent text wraps around the left side of the image.

Publishing Questions

How can I get my own domain name?

Please see Chapter 7.

Why do I see only a list of my files when I plug my address into the browser?

In your directory, you need to have a file that uses your server's *default name*. I explain how this works in Chapter 7.

How do I register my site with search engines?

Once again, see Chapter 7 for the answer.

How do I copyright my page?

There's no official process you have to go through to copyright your web page text. According to copyright law (see www.copyright.gov), as soon as your text is published in a fixed form (such as being uploaded onto your web server), then your copyright is automatically in place. To be safe, always include a copyright notice at the bottom of all your pages. The usual format is the word "Copyright," followed by the © symbol (use either © or ©), followed by the year of publication, followed by your name: Copyright © 2004 Paul McFedries.

Multimedia Questions

I have a MIDI version of a popular song. Is it okay to use it on my site?

Using MIDI variations of commercial music is definitely a copyright violation. As responsible webmeisters, we should use *licensed* MIDI music wherever possible.

How can I get a MIDI file to play as a background sound in both Internet Explorer and Netscape?

It's okay to use both the <BGSOUND> and <EMBED> tags in the same document:

```
<BGSOUND SRC="earsore.mid" LOOP="INFINITE">
<EMBED SRC="earsore.mid" AUTOSTART="TRUE" HIDDEN="TRUE" LOOP="0">
```

Can I use a sound file with a mouseover instead of an image?

To play a sound in JavaScript, you set the `location.href` property equal to the sound file you want to play, like this:

```
location.href="applause.au"
```

So with a mouseover, you'd tack this on to the end (note the semicolon in between):

```
onMouseover="books.src='books-on.gif'; location.href='applause.au'"
```

How do I create RealAudio or RealVideo files?

RealNetworks has a products page that offers programs for creating streaming media: www.real.com/products/index.html.

Forms Questions

What is this "cgi-bin" thing that I see all over the web?

"cgi-bin" is the name of a directory where CGI scripts and programs are stored.

How do I use a form's Submit button to create a link to another page?

Set up cute little miniforms that consist of just a single **Button** control. You add the JavaScript onClick attribute and use it to set the location property to the address of the web page you want to load:

```
<FORM>
<INPUT
    TYPE="BUTTON"
    VALUE="Paul's Place"
    onClick="location='http://www.mcfedries.com/'">
</FORM>
```

Create a separate miniform for each link. Note, too, that you need to use a table if you want to line up the buttons side by side.

Is it possible to use JavaScript to take form data and record it on another page?

No, JavaScript can't create a page or add text to an existing page. This can be done only by using CGI or ASP.

How can I use an image instead of the usual Submit button?

Use the <INPUT TYPE="IMAGE"> control:

```
<INPUT TYPE=IMAGE SRC="someimage.gif">
```

Replace *someimage.gif* with the name of the image file that you want to use. Two things to note:

- This type of button acts just like a **Submit** button. That is, when the user clicks the image, the form is submitted to the server.

- When the user clicks the image, the browser sends not only the form data, but also the coordinates, in pixels, of the spot on the image where the user clicked. These are sent as "x" (the horizontal coordinate) and "y" (the vertical coordinate).

How do I get the e-mail address of a person who fills in my form?

Include a field in the form and ask the user to enter his or her e-mail address in that field. If you use my MailForm service (see Chapter 12), name this field "Email" or "E-mail." This ensures that when you reply to a MailForm message, your reply gets sent automatically to the address that the user filled in.

Can MailForm get the user's e-mail address automatically?

No, it can't.

I'm using your MailForm service, but it doesn't seem to work. Is it still available?

Yes, MailForm is still available. If you're not getting messages, check the following:

- ◆ The most common MailForm mistake is to misspell one of the hidden field names. For example, lots of people accidentally spell the "MFAddress" field as "MFAdress".

- ◆ Double-check that your e-mail address is correct in the MFAddress field.

- ◆ Make sure you have all your quotation marks in place.

- ◆ Check out the MailForm site for the latest updates and improvements: www.mcfedries.com/MailForm.

Frames Questions

How do I set up my frames without borders?

You need to add both FRAMEBORDER="0" and BORDER="0" to your <FRAME-SET> tag, like this:

```
<FRAMESET COLS="25%,*" FRAMEBORDER="0" BORDER="0">
```

I have a frame with lots of links. Is there an easier way to specify the TARGET than adding it to every single <A> tag?

Yes! You can define a default target by including the <BASE TARGET> tag in the page header:

```
<BASE TARGET="YourFrameName">
```

Here, *YourFrameName* is the name of the frame that you want to use for all your links. It can also be one of the prefab frame names, such as "_top" or "_blank." After you put this in place, you don't need to use TARGET in your links (unless, of course, you want to use a different target for a particular link).

How do I change more than one frame from a single link?

The only way to do this is to have your link point to another frameset page. For example, suppose your original frameset page looks like this:

```
<FRAMESET COLS="100,*">
<FRAME SRC="menu.html" NAME="Left">
```

```
<FRAMESET ROWS="50%,*">
<FRAME SRC="one.html" NAME="TopRight">
<FRAME SRC="two.html" NAME="BottomRight">
</FRAMESET>

</FRAMESET>
```

This page sets up a frame on the left (named, boringly, "Left") and two frames on the right ("TopRight" and "BottomRight"). To change the two right frames in one fell swoop, set up your link to point to an identical frameset page that uses different SRC values in the "TopRight" and "BottomRight" frames:

```
<FRAMESET COLS="100,*">
<FRAME SRC="menu.html" NAME="Left">

    <FRAMESET ROWS="50%,*">
    <FRAME SRC="three.html" NAME="TopRight">
    <FRAME SRC="four.html" NAME="BottomRight">
    </FRAMESET>

</FRAMESET>
```

I don't want my site displayed in someone else's frames. Is it possible to prevent this from happening?

Yes. Assuming your frames page is named "myframes.html," insert the following JavaScript into your page between the </HEAD> and <BODY> tags:

```
<SCRIPT LANGUAGE="JavaScript">
<!--
if (top != self)
    top.location.href="myframes.html"
//-->
</SCRIPT>
```

How do search engines index framed pages?

Here are some pointers about frames and search engines:

♦ Most search engines index only the frameset page (the one with the <FRAMESET> and <FRAME> tags). Therefore, be sure to include <META> tags in this page.

♦ Some search engines don't index <META> tags, so you might consider putting some kind of indexable content between <NOFRAMES> and </NOFRAMES>.

♦ If you want the search engine to index your "inside" pages, then it's also a good idea to include a link to those pages between <NOFRAMES> and </NOFRAMES>. This gives the search engine an entry point into the rest of your site.

◆ The problem with the latter suggestion is that surfers can easily end up in an inside page that lacks your framed navigation controls. However, you can use JavaScript to "reframe" the page. I have a script on my site that does just that: www.mcfedries.com/JavaScript/reframer.asp.

Page Design Questions

Is it possible to determine the resolution of the user's screen?

Yes, using JavaScript's `screen.height` property. In the following example, the script checks this property and then replaces the current page with another page that's optimized (presumably) for the user's screen resolution:

```
<SCRIPT LANGUAGE="JavaScript" TYPE="text/javascript">
<!--

// Check for 640x480
if (screen.height == '480')
    location.replace('480.html')

// Check for 800x600
else if (screen.height == '600')
    location.replace('600.html')

// Check for 1024x768
else if (screen.height == '768')
    location.replace('768.html')

// Check for 1280x1024
else if (screen.height == '1024')
    location.replace('1024.html')

// Everything else
else
    location.replace('else.html')
//-->
</SCRIPT>
```

How do I create a stationary background that doesn't scroll along with the page text?

Add the BGPROPERTIES="FIXED" attribute to your <BODY> tag:

```
<BODY BGPROPERTIES="FIXED">
```

You can also do it with style sheets:

```
<BODY STYLE="background-image: url(http://www.wherever.com/whatever.gif);
             background-attachment: fixed">
```

Note, however, that both methods work only with Internet Explorer.

How do I center page text both vertically and horizontally?

You can use <CENTER> to center text horizontally, but there is no HTML tag for centering vertically. However, you can do it if you create a table for your entire page, and then use the VALIGN="MIDDLE" and ALIGN="CENTER" attributes within the main TD tag. Here's the skeleton:

```
<BODY>

<!--Set up a table for the entire window-->
<TABLE WIDTH="100%" HEIGHT="100%">
<TR>
<TD VALIGN="MIDDLE" ALIGN="CENTER">

<!--The real page text and stuff goes here-->
This text appears smack dab in the middle of the screen.

<!--Close the big table-->
</TD>
</TR>
</TABLE>

</BODY>
```

How do I provide users with an easy way to return to the top of a page?

Right below your <BODY> tag, add the following anchor:

```
<A NAME="top">
```

You can then send the surfer to the top of the page by including a link such as this one:

```
<A HREF="#top">Return to the top of the page</A>
```

HTML Codes for Cool Characters

Symbol	Character Code	Entity Name
Space	 	
!	!	
"	"	"
#	#	
$	$	
%	%	
&	&	&
'	'	
(	(	
)	)	
*	*	
+	+	
,	,	
-	-	
.	.	
/	/	

Symbol	Character Code	Entity Name
0	0	
1	1	
2	2	
3	3	
4	4	
5	5	
6	6	
7	7	
8	8	
9	9	
:	:	
;	;	
<	<	<
=	=	
>	>	>
?	?	
@	@	
A	A	
B	B	
C	C	
D	D	
E	E	
F	F	
G	G	
H	H	
I	I	
J	J	
K	K	
L	L	
M	M	
N	N	
O	O	

Symbol	Character Code	Entity Name
P	P	
Q	Q	
R	R	
S	S	
T	T	
U	U	
V	V	
W	W	
X	X	
Y	Y	
Z	Z	
[	[	
\	\	
]	]	
^	^	ˆ
_	_	
`	`	
a	a	
b	b	
c	c	
d	d	
e	e	
f	f	
g	g	
h	h	
i	i	
j	j	
k	k	
l	l	
m	m	
n	n	
o	o	

Symbol	Character Code	Entity Name
p	p	
q	q	
r	r	
s	s	
t	t	
u	u	
v	v	
w	w	
x	x	
y	y	
z	z	
{	{	
|	|	
}	}	
~	~	
N/A	&#127;	
	€	
N/A		
‚	‚	
f	ƒ	ƒ
„	„	
…	…	…
†	†	†
‡	‡	‡
ˆ	ˆ	
‰	‰	‰
Š	Š	Š
‹	‹	‹
Œ	Œ	Œ
N/A		
Ž	Ž	
N/A		

Symbol	Character Code	Entity Name
N/A	&#144;	
'	&#145;	&lsquo;
'	&#146;	&rsquo;
"	&#147;	&ldquo;
"	&#148;	&rdquo;
•	&#149;	&bull;
– (en dash)	&#150;	&ndash;
— (em dash)	&#151;	&mdash;
~	&#152;	&tilde;
™	&#153;	&trade;
š	&#154;	&scaron;
›	&#155;	&rsaquo;
œ	&#156;	&oelig;
N/A	&#157;	
ž	&#158;	
Ÿ	&#159;	&Yuml;
Nonbreaking space		
¡	&#161;	&iexcl;
¢	&#162;	&cent;
£	&#163;	&pound;
¤	&#164;	&curren;
¥	&#165;	&yen;
¦	&#166;	&brvbar;
§	&#167;	&sect;
¨	&#168;	&uml;
©	&#169;	&copy;
ª	&#170;	&ordf;
¬	&#172;	&not;
Soft hyphen	&#173;	&shy;
®	&#174;	&reg;
¯	&#175;	&macr;
°	&#176;	&deg;

Symbol	Character Code	Entity Name
±	±	±
²	²	²
³	³	³
´	´	´
µ	µ	µ
¶	¶	¶
·	·	·
¸	¸	¸
¹	¹	¹
º	º	º
»	»	»
¼	¼	¼
½	½	½
¾	¾	¾
¿	¿	¿
À	À	À
Á	Á	Á
Â	Â	Â
Ã	Ã	Ã
Ä	Ä	Ä
Å	Å	Å
Æ	Æ	Æ
Ç	Ç	Ç
È	È	È
É	É	É
Ê	Ê	Ê
Ë	Ë	Ë
Ì	Ì	Ì
Í	Í	Í
Î	Î	Î
Ï	Ï	Ï
Ð	Ð	Ð
Ñ	Ñ	Ñ

Symbol	Character Code	Entity Name
Ò	&#210;	&Ograve;
Ó	&#211;	&Oacute;
Ô	&#212;	&Ocirc;
Õ	&#213;	&Otilde;
Ö	&#214;	&Ouml;
×	&#215;	&times;
Ø	&#216;	&Oslash;
Ù	&#217;	&Ugrave;
Ú	&#218;	&Uacute;
Û	&#219;	&Ucirc;
Ü	&#220;	&Uuml;
Ý	&#221;	&Yacute;
þ	&#222;	&THORN;
ß	&#223;	&szlig;
à	&#224;	&agrave;
á	&#225;	&aacute;
â	&#226;	&acirc;
ã	&#227;	&atilde;
ä	&#228;	&auml;
å	&#229;	&aring;
æ	&#230;	&aelig;
ç	&#231;	&ccedil;
è	&#232;	&egrave;
é	&#233;	&eacute;
ê	&#234;	&ecirc;
ë	&#235;	&euml;
ì	&#236;	&igrave;
í	&#237;	&iacute
î	&#238;	&icirc;
ï	&#239;	&iuml;
ð	&#240;	&eth;
ñ	&#241;	&ntilde;

Symbol	Character Code	Entity Name
ò	ò	ò
ó	ó	ó
ô	ô	ô
õ	õ	õ
ö	ö	ö
÷	÷	÷
ø	ø	ø
ù	ù	ù
ú	ú	ú
û	û	û
ü	ü	ü
ý	ý	ý
þ	þ	þ
ÿ	ÿ	ÿ

The CD: The Webmaster's Toolkit

As I've mentioned before, this book's whole purpose is to be a one-stop shop for budding websmiths. To that end, the text is geared toward getting you up to speed with this HTML rigmarole without a lot of fuss and flap-doodle. But fine words butter no parsnips, as they say (no, they really do), so you'll also find a complete Webmaster's Toolkit on the CD that's pasted into the back of this book. This toolkit is jammed to the hilt with handy references, files, and software that should provide everything you need to get your web authorship off to a rousing start. This appendix describes what's on the CD and tells you how to install it.

Accessing the CD's Contents

To get to the goodies on the CD, there are two routes you can take:

- Use your browser to open the file named index.htm in the main folder of the CD. This gives you a nice, clickable interface to everything that's on the CD.

- Open the CD and access the files directly.

Bonus Chapters

If you're looking to add JavaScripts to your pages, the CD contains bonus material—Chapters 24 and 25—that tell you everything you need to know. Chapter 24 gives you some JavaScript background and contains a fistful of examples that you can insert inside your pages right away, even if you know nothing about programming. Chapter 25 takes things up a notch by taking you through lots of example scripts that do all kinds of amazingly useful things.

Webmaster References

With over 100 HTML tags and over 100 style sheet properties in existence, there's a lot to keep track of. To help you out, I've created a few references that give you the full scoop on all the available tags, styles, and more. Here's a summary:

- ◆ **HTML tag reference.** This reference supplies you with the nitty-gritty on all the HTML tags. For each tag, you get a description of the tag, notes on using the tag, a complete list of the tag's attributes, browser support (including links to the appropriate Microsoft and Netscape pages, as well as to the corresponding official W3C page), and an example that shows the tag in action.

- ◆ **Style sheet reference.** This reference runs through a complete list of the available style sheet properties. For each property, you get a description of the property, notes on using it, a list of the property's possible values, browser support, and an example that shows how the property works.

- ◆ **The 216 "safe" web colors.** This page shows you all the 216 so-called "safe" web colors to use on your pages. ("Safe" means that these colors display well on almost all screens.) One table shows you the colors and another table shows you the corresponding RGB values.

- ◆ **The X11 color set.** This page runs through all the colors that have defined names (such as "Red," "Blue," and "Chartreuse").

The HTML Examples from the Book

Many of this book's chapters (especially those in Part 1) are sprinkled with examples showing HTML tags on the go. If you'd like to incorporate some of these examples into your own web work, don't bother typing your poor fingers to the bone. Instead, all the example files are sitting on the CD, ready for you to use. These example files are in the \Examples directory on the CD. Note, too, that everything is organized by chapter. The files for Chapter 1 are in \Examples\Chap01, the files for Chapter 2 are in \Examples\Chap02, and so on.

Web Graphics Sampler

Back in Chapter 6, you saw how a graphic or two can add a nice touch to an otherwise drab web page. There are lots of spots on the web where you can find images to suit any occasion. But before you go traipsing off to one of these sites, you might want to check out what's on the CD. There you'll find hundreds of files that give you everything from simple bullets and lines to useful icons and pictures. There's even a section with some high-quality animated GIFs.

Programs for Web Weavers

The Webmaster's Toolkit is also loaded with a ton of Windows and Mac software that can help you create better pages. The rest of this appendix presents a summary of the programs you'll find.

HTML Editors

Here's a list of the HTML editors that are in the Webmaster's Toolkit:

◆ **Dreamweaver.** This is an excellent, professional-quality HTML editor that's loaded with great features for churning out top-notch pages. It also boasts some impressive site-management features, templates, and much more.

CD site: /Software/Dreamweaver/

Website: www.macromedia.com

◆ **GoLive.** This is an advanced HTML editor that's packed with features to make your webmastering life easier. It uses a "visual design" model for precise control, and also supports esoterica such as style sheets, Dynamic HTML, and XML.

CD site: /Software/GoLive/

Website: www.adobe.com

CAUTION

Page Pitfalls

Please note that most of the programs on the CD are demonstration versions of commercial programs. You can try out any program without charge, but if you want to continue to use a program, you need to purchase it from the vendor.

◆ **HomeSite.** This is one of the best HTML editors on the planet. It has a great interface and more features than you can shake a stick at: a built-in spell checker, the ability to edit multiple documents at once, color-coded HTML tags, the ability to search-and-replace text across multiple files, and much more.

CD site: /Software/Homesite/

Website: www.allaire.com

◆ **HotDog Professional.** This is one of the veterans of the HTML editor wars, and has emerged from the front lines better than ever. If you just want a good editor that doesn't offer a lot of unnecessary accessories, give HotDog a taste.

CD site: /Software/HotDog/

Website: www.sausage.com

◆ **HTML Assistant.** This is a decent HTML editor that gives you a graphical way to build your web pages. It includes a built-in spell checker as well as easy methods for creating forms and tables.

CD site: /Software/HTMLAssistant/

Website: www.brooknorth.com

◆ **NetObjects Fusion.** This is an extremely powerful editor that not only excels at regular HTML, but can also make it a breeze to create truly interactive sites that use JavaScript, Java, style sheets, and even dynamic HTML. It also features some amazing site management tricks (such as automatically updating links if you move or rename a page).

CD site: /Software/Fusion/

Website: www.netobjects.com

Graphics Software

Chapter 6 gave you the basics for adding images to your pages. Here are a few tools that help take some of the drudgery out of graphics work:

◆ **ACDSee.** If you just need to take a quick gander at an image, ACDSee is the program to use because this utility excels in displaying image files. It's extremely fast, so it's perfect for sneak peeks. However, it can also do a bit of image manipulation, and it can convert graphics from one format to another.

CD site: /Software/ACDSee32/

Website: www.acdsystems.com

- **GIF Animator.** This is a great program for creating animated GIFs. It's a snap to use (I gave you the basics in Chapter 11), and it's crammed with cool features such as a banner-creation tool, transitions, and image optimization.

  CD site: /Software/Gifanimator/

  Website: www.webutilities.com

- **Mapedit.** This program gives you an easy, graphical method for defining server-side image maps (as opposed to the client-side image maps that I yammered on about in Chapter 9).

  CD site: /Software/Mapedit/

  Website: www.boutell.com

- **Paint Shop Pro.** This is one of the best graphics programs on the market today. It supports all kinds of formats, offers great tools for creating drawings, makes effects such as drop shadows a breeze, and does much more.

  CD site: /Software/PaintShopPro/

  Website: www.jasc.com

FTP Programs

I discussed using FTP to get your web handiwork onto your web host's server back in Chapter 8. To help out, the CD boasts two of the best FTP programs around:

- **CuteFTP.** CuteFTP has a bizarre name, but it's an easy-to-use FTP program that gives you a no-muss, no-fuss way to fling files around the Net.

  CD site: /Software/CuteFTP/

  Website: www.globalscape.com

- **WS_FTP Pro.** This program's easy interface and long list of features have made it one of the most popular FTP utilities on the Net.

  CD site: /Software/WS_FTPPro/

  Website: www.ipswitch.com

Other Stuff

To wrap things up, the CD also contains the following miscellaneous tools:

- **CommNet.** This is a data communications application that seamlessly integrates Internet Telnet and modem dial-up and capabilities into a single, fast, full-featured, and easy-to-use application. CommNet supports both Zmodem and Telnet Zmodem file transfers and VT100/full-color PC ANSI and SCO ANSI emulations.

  CD site: /Software/Commnet/

  Website: www.radient.com

- **Drag & Zip.** This program is an add-on that gives Windows Explorer the ability to compress and decompress files.

  CD site: /Software/DragandZip/

  Website: www.canyonsw.com

- **Koan Plugin.** This music plug-in supports not only MIDI files, but MP3 files as well.

  CD site: /Software/Koan/

  Website: www.sseyo.com

- **TextPad.** This is a powerful replacement for Windows' Notepad text editor.

  CD site: /Software/Textpad/

  Website: www.textpad.com

- **UltraEdit.** This is a great text editor that understands HTML (for example, it uses color coding to distinguish tags from regular text), enables you to work on multiple files at once, supports macros, and has lots of other powerful features.

  CD site: /Software/Ultraedit/

  Website: www.idmcomp.com

- **WinZip.** For faster service, many of the Net's files and documents are stored in a "compressed" format that makes them smaller. After you download a compressed file to your computer, you need to "uncompress" the file in order to use it. WinZip is a handy little utility that makes it a breeze to uncompress any file. You can also use it to compress your own files if you'll be shipping them out.

  CD site: /Software/WinZip/

  Website: www.winzip.com

Legal Stuff

By opening this package, you are agreeing to be bound by the following agreement:

This software product is copyrighted, and all rights are reserved by the publisher and author. You are licensed to use this software on a single computer. You may copy and/or modify the software as needed to facilitate your use of it on a single computer. Making copies of the software for any other purpose is a violation of the U.S. copyright laws.

This software is sold *as is* without warranty of any kind, either expressed or implied, including but not limited to the implied warranties of merchantability and fitness for a particular purpose. Neither the publisher nor its dealers or distributors assumes any liability for any alleged or actual damages arising from the use of this program. (Some states do not allow for the exclusion of implied warranties, so the exclusion might not apply to you.)

Index

T

X-Y-Z

License Agreement

By opening this package, you are also agreeing to be bound by the following agreement:

You may not copy or redistribute the entire CD-ROM as a whole. Copying and redistribution of individual software programs on the CD-ROM is governed by terms set by individual copyright holders.

The installer and code are copyrighted by the publisher. Individual programs and other items on the CD-ROM are copyrighted or are under an Open Source license by their various authors or other copyright holders.

This software is sold as-is without warranty of any kind, either expressed or implied, including but not limited to the implied warranties of merchantability and fitness for a particular purpose. Neither the publisher nor its dealers or distributors assumes any liability for any alleged or actual damages arising from the use of this program. (Some states do not allow for the exclusion of implied warranties, so the exclusion may not apply to you.)

NOTE: This CD-ROM uses long and mixed-case filenames requiring the use of a protected-mode CD-ROM Driver.

Check Out These
Best-Selling
COMPLETE IDIOT'S GUIDES®

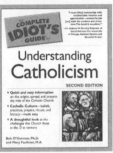

Understanding Catholicism
SECOND EDITION

Bob O'Gorman, Ph.D. and Mary Faulkner, M.A.

1-59257-085-2
$18.95

Learning Spanish
THIRD EDITION

Gail Stein

0-02-864451-4
$18.95

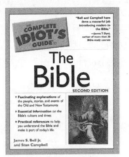

The Bible
SECOND EDITION

James S. Bell Jr. and Stan Campbell

0-02-864382-8
$18.95

Being a Groom
SECOND EDITION

Jennifer Lata Rung and Mark Rung

0-02-864456-5
$9.95

Grammar and Style
SECOND EDITION

Laurie E. Rozakis, Ph.D.

1-59257-115-8
$16.95

Playing the Guitar
SECOND EDITION

Frederick Noad

0-02-864244-9
$21.95 w/CD

Personal Finance in Your 20s & 30s
SECOND EDITION

Sarah Young Fisher and Susan Shelly

0-02-864374-7
$19.95

Knitting and Crocheting
SECOND EDITION
Illustrated

Barbara Breiter and Gail Diven

1-59257-089-5
$16.95

The Perfect Resume
THIRD EDITION

Susan Ireland

0-02-864440-9
$14.95

Buying and Selling a Home
FOURTH EDITION

Shelley O'Hara and Nancy D. Lewis

1-59257-120-4
$18.95

Low-Carb Meals

Lucy Beale and Sandy G. Couvillon, M.S., L.D.N., R.D.

1-59257-180-8
$18.95

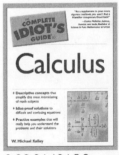

Calculus

W. Michael Kelley

0-02-864365-8
$18.95

More than *450 titles* in *30 different categories*
Available at booksellers everywhere

ALPHA